GLEIM® | Aviation

FIRST EDITION

PRIVATE PILOT
ACS & Oral Exam Guide

Airplane Single-Engine Land

by
Irvin N. Gleim, Ph.D., CFII and Garrett W. Gleim, CFII

Gleim Publications, Inc.
P.O. Box 12848 · University Station
Gainesville, Florida 32604

(352) 375-0772
(800) 87-GLEIM or (800) 874-5346
Fax: (352) 375-6940

Internet: www.GleimAviation.com
Email: admin@gleim.com

For updates to the first printing of the first edition of

Private Pilot ACS & Oral Exam Guide

Go To: www.gleim.com/updates

Or: Email update@gleim.com with **PPACS 1-1** in the subject line. You will receive our current update as a reply.

Updates are available until the next edition is published.

ISSN Pending
ISBN 978-1-61854-064-5

First Printing: August 2016

Environmental Statement -- This book is printed on recyclable, environmentally friendly groundwood paper, sourced from certified sustainable forests and produced either TCF (totally chlorine-free) or ECF (elementally chlorine-free).

This first edition is designed specifically for private pilot students. Please submit any corrections and suggestions for subsequent editions to www.gleim.com/AviationQuestions.

Two other volumes are also available to help you pass the practical exam. **Private Pilot Flight Maneuvers and Practical Test Prep** focuses on your flight training and the maneuvers. **Pilot Handbook** is a complete pilot ground school text in outline format with many diagrams for ease of understanding.

If necessary, we will develop an update for **Private Pilot ACS and Oral Exam Guide**. Visit our website or email update@gleim.com for the latest updates. Updates for this edition will be available until the next edition is published. To continue providing our customers with first-rate service, we request that technical questions about our materials be submitted at www.gleim.com/AviationQuestions. We will give each question thorough consideration and a prompt response. Questions concerning orders, prices, shipments, or payments will be handled via telephone by our competent and courteous customer service staff.

ABOUT THE AUTHORS

Irvin N. Gleim earned his private pilot certificate in 1965 from the Institute of Aviation at the University of Illinois, where he subsequently received his Ph.D. He is a commercial pilot and flight instructor (instrument) with multi-engine and seaplane ratings and is a member of the Aircraft Owners and Pilots Association, American Bonanza Society, Civil Air Patrol, Experimental Aircraft Association, National Association of Flight Instructors, and Seaplane Pilots Association. He is the author of flight maneuvers and practical test prep books for the sport, private, instrument, commercial, and flight instructor certificates/ratings, and study guides for the sport, private/recreational, instrument, commercial, flight/ground instructor, fundamentals of instructing, airline transport pilot, and flight engineer FAA knowledge tests. Three additional pilot training books are *Pilot Handbook*, *Aviation Weather and Weather Services*, and *FAR/AIM*.

Dr. Gleim has also written articles for professional accounting and business law journals and is the author of widely used review manuals for the CIA (Certified Internal Auditor) exam, the CMA (Certified Management Accountant) exam, the CPA (Certified Public Accountant) exam, and the EA (IRS Enrolled Agent) exam. He is Professor Emeritus, Fisher School of Accounting, University of Florida, and is a CFM, CIA, CMA, and CPA.

Garrett W. Gleim earned his private pilot certificate in 1997 in a Piper Super Cub. He is a commercial pilot (single and multi-engine), ground instructor (advanced and instrument), and flight instructor (instrument and multi-engine), and is a member of the Aircraft Owners and Pilots Association and National Association of Flight Instructors. Mr. Gleim is the author of study guides for the sport, private/recreational, instrument, commercial, flight/ground instructor, fundamentals of instructing, and airline transport pilot FAA knowledge tests. He received a Bachelor of Science in Economics from The Wharton School, University of Pennsylvania. Mr. Gleim is also a CPA (not in public practice).

REVIEWERS AND CONTRIBUTORS

Paul Duty, CFII, MEI, AGI, is a graduate of Embry-Riddle Aeronautical University with a Master of Business Administration-Aviation degree. He is one of our aviation editors and an aviation marketing specialist. Mr. Duty researched questions, wrote and edited answer explanations, and incorporated revisions into the text.

Char Marissa Gregg, CFII, LTA, Glider, ASES, ATP, is the Gleim 141 Chief Flight Instructor and one of our aviation editors. Ms. Gregg researched questions, wrote and edited answer explanations, and incorporated revisions into the text.

The CFIs who have worked with us throughout the years to develop and improve our pilot training materials.

The many FAA employees who helped, in person or by telephone, primarily in Gainesville, Orlando, Oklahoma City, and Washington, DC.

The many pilots who have provided comments and suggestions during the past several decades.

A PERSONAL THANKS

This manual would not have been possible without the extraordinary effort and dedication of Julie Cutlip, Blaine Hatton, Kelsey Olson, Breanna Rodriguez, Teresa Soard, Justin Stephenson, Joanne Strong, and Elmer Tucker, who typed the entire manuscript and all revisions and drafted and laid out the diagrams, illustrations, and cover for this book.

The authors also appreciate the production and editorial assistance of Jacob Bennett, Melody Dalton, Jessica Felkins, Jim Harvin, Kristen Hennen, Katie Larson, Diana León, Jake Pettifor, Shane Rapp, and Drew Sheppard.

Finally, we appreciate the encouragement, support, and tolerance of our families throughout this project.

TABLE OF CONTENTS

PREFACE

All aspiring Private Pilots should bring the following resources to refer to during the oral section of their practical test: their personal logbook, the aircraft's logbook, POH/AFM, Chart Supplements, the Airman Certification Standards (ACS), VFR chart, *FAR/AIM*, and *Aviation Weather and Weather Services*. In addition, all students should have an Oral Exam Guide to prep for the assortment of questions they may face. Unlike most publishers, Gleim combines the ACS and the Oral Exam Guide into one convenient, easy-to-use book, the *Private Pilot ACS and Oral Exam Guide*.

The ACS portion comes first and includes a direct reprint of the most current version of the FAA Airman Certification Standards at the time of print (August 2016). Gleim has removed references to multi-engine airplanes and seaplanes because the Gleim *Private Pilot ACS and Oral Exam Guide* is specific to single-engine land airplanes. Accordingly, tasks in this reprint are not always sequentially numbered because tasks that do not apply to single-engine land airplanes have been omitted.

The Oral Exam Guide comes after the ACS portion. Most flight schools and many CFIs recommend that pilots preparing for their practical test study an Oral Exam Guide, and we agree. Your evaluator will ask a wide-ranging series of questions during the oral portion of your practical test. Those questions may pertain to any subject or task included in the ACS for the private pilot certificate. By studying the series of potential questions in this book, you will gain a significant advantage as you prepare for your testing experience.

The convenient table of contents in the Gleim Oral Exam Guide cross-references each question to the appropriate ACS Area of Operation; Appendix A includes abbreviations of sources; and Appendix B includes abbreviations and acronyms used by private pilots.

Think of this book as both an "ACS guide" and an "oral exam guide." It is a thoroughly researched tool that supports the entire Gleim system of oral and practical test preparation, which includes the following manuals: *Private Pilot FAA Knowledge Test*, *Private Pilot Flight Maneuvers and Practical Test Prep*, *Private Pilot Syllabus*, *Aviation Weather and Weather Services*, *FAR/AIM*, and *Pilot Handbook*. These books contain all of the information you need to do well on your practical test.

Enjoy Flying -- Safely!

Irvin N. Gleim
Garrett W. Gleim

August 2016

FAA PRIVATE PILOT
AIRMAN CERTIFICATION STANDARDS REPRINTED
(FAA-S-ACS-6)
SINGLE-ENGINE LAND ONLY

This portion of the book contains a reprint of the FAA's Private Pilot ACS (FAA-S-ACS-6). Note that the FAA publishes the Private Pilot ACS for all airplane classes (single- and multi-engine, land and sea) in a single document. We have removed all references to multi-engine airplanes and seaplanes because the Gleim *Private Pilot ACS and Oral Exam Guide* is specific to single-engine land airplanes. Accordingly, tasks in this reprint are not always sequentially numbered because tasks that do not apply to single-engine land airplanes have been omitted.

Table of Contents

Introduction

Airman Certification Standards Concept

The goal of the airman certification process is to ensure the applicant possesses the knowledge and skill consistent with the privileges of the certificate or rating being exercised, as well as the ability to manage the risks of flight in order to act as pilot in command.

In fulfilling its responsibilities for the airman certification process, the Federal Aviation Administration (FAA) Flight Standards Service (AFS) plans, develops, and maintains materials related to airman certification training and testing. These materials have included several components. The FAA knowledge test measures mastery of the aeronautical knowledge areas listed in Title 14 of the Code of Federal Regulations (14 CFR) part 61. Other materials, such as handbooks in the FAA-H-8083 series, provide guidance to applicants on aeronautical knowledge, risk management, and flight proficiency.

The FAA recognizes that safe operations in today's complex National Airspace System (NAS) require a more systematic integration of aeronautical knowledge, risk management, and flight proficiency standards than those prescribed in the Practical Test Standards (PTS). The FAA further recognizes the need to more clearly calibrate knowledge, risk management, and skills to the level of the certificate or rating, and to align standards with guidance and test questions.

To accomplish these goals, the FAA drew upon the expertise of organizations and individuals across the aviation and training community to develop the Airman Certification Standards (ACS). The ACS integrates the elements of knowledge, risk management, and skill listed in 14 CFR part 61 for each airman certificate or rating. It thus forms a more comprehensive standard for what an applicant must know, consider, and do for the safe conduct and successful completion of each Task to be tested on either the knowledge exam or the practical test.

The ACS significantly improves the knowledge test part of the certification process by enabling the development of test questions, from FAA reference documents, that are meaningful and relevant to safe operation in the NAS. The ACS does not change the tolerances for any skill Task, and it is important for applicants, instructors, and evaluators to understand that the addition of knowledge and risk management elements is not intended to lengthen or expand the scope of the practical test. Rather, the integration of knowledge and risk management elements associated with each Task is intended to enable a more holistic approach to learning, training, and testing. During the ground portion of the practical test, for example, the ACS provides greater context and structure both for retesting items missed on the knowledge test and for sampling the applicant's mastery of knowledge and risk management elements associated with a given skill Task.

Through the ground and flight portion of the practical test, the FAA expects evaluators to assess the applicant's mastery of the topic in accordance with the level of learning most appropriate for the specified Task. The oral questioning will continue throughout the entire practical test. For some topics, the evaluator will ask the applicant to describe or explain. For other items, the evaluator will assess the applicant's understanding by providing a scenario that requires the applicant to appropriately apply and/or correlate knowledge, experience, and information to the circumstances of the given scenario. The flight portion of the practical test requires the applicant to demonstrate knowledge, risk management, flight proficiency, and operational skill in accordance with the ACS.

Note: As used in the ACS, an evaluator is any person authorized to conduct airman testing (e.g., an FAA aviation safety inspector, designated pilot examiner, or other individual authorized to conduct test for a certificate or rating).

Using the ACS

The ACS consists of **Areas of Operation** arranged in a logical sequence, beginning with Preflight Preparation and ending with Postflight Procedures. Each Area of Operation includes **Tasks** appropriate to that Area of Operation. Each Task begins with an **Objective** stating what the applicant should know, consider, and/or do. The ACS then lists the aeronautical knowledge, risk management, and skill elements relevant to the specific Task, along with the conditions and standards for acceptable performance. The ACS uses **Notes** to emphasize special considerations. The ACS uses the terms "will" and "must" to convey directive (mandatory) information. The term "may" denotes items that are recommended but not required. The **References** for each Task indicate the source material for Task elements. For example, in Tasks such as "Current and forecast weather for departure, en route and arrival phases of flight." (PA.I.C.K3), the applicant must be prepared for questions on any weather product presented in the references for that Task.

Each Task in the ACS is coded according to a scheme that includes four elements. For example:

PA.XI.A.K1:

PA = Applicable ACS (Private Pilot – Airplane)
XI = Area of Operation (Night Operation)
A   = Task (Night Preparation)
K1 = Task element Knowledge 1 (Physiological aspects of night flying as it relates to vision)

Knowledge test questions are mapped to the ACS codes, which will soon replace the system of "Learning Statement Codes." After this transition occurs, the airman knowledge test report will list an ACS code that correlates to a specific Task element for a given Area of Operation and Task. Remedial instruction and re-testing will be specific, targeted, and based on specified learning criteria. Similarly, a Notice of Disapproval for the practical test will use the ACS codes to identify the deficient Task element(s).

The current knowledge test management system does not have the capability to print ACS codes. Until a new test management system is in place, the Learning Statement Codes (e.g., "PLT" codes will continue to be displayed on the Airman Knowledge Test Report (AKTR). The PLT codes are linked to references leading to broad subject areas. By contrast, each ACS code is tied to a unique Task element in the ACS itself. Because of this fundamental difference, there is no one-to-one correlation between LSC (PLT) codes and ACS codes.

Because all active knowledge test questions for the private pilot airplane (PAR) certificate knowledge test have been aligned with the corresponding ACS, evaluators can use PLT codes in conjunction with the ACS for a more targeted retesting of missed knowledge. The evaluator should look up the PLT code(s) on the applicant's AKTR in the Learning Statement Reference Guide. After noting the subject area(s), the evaluator can use the corresponding Area(s) of Operation/Task(s) in the ACS to narrow the scope of material for retesting, and to evaluate the applicant's understanding of that material in the context of the appropriate ACS Area(s) of Operation and Task(s).

Applicants for a combined private pilot certificate with instrument rating, in accordance with 14 CFR part 61, section 61.65 (a) and (g), must pass all areas designated in the Private Pilot – Airplane ACS and the Instrument Rating – Airplane ACS. Examiners need not duplicate Tasks. For example, only one preflight demonstration would be required; however, the Preflight Task from the Instrument Rating – Airplane ACS would be more extensive than the Preflight Task from the Private Pilot – Airplane ACS to ensure readiness for Instrument Flight Rules (IFR) flight.

A combined checkride should be treated as one practical test, requiring only one application and resulting in only one temporary certificate, disapproval notice, or letter of discontinuance, as applicable. Failure of any Task will result in a failure of the entire test and application. Therefore, even if the deficient maneuver was instrument related and the performance of all visual flight rules (VFR) Tasks was determined to be satisfactory, the applicant will receive a notice of disapproval.

The applicant must pass the private pilot airplane knowledge test before taking the private pilot practical test. The practical test is conducted in accordance with the ACS that is current as of the date of the test. Further, the applicant must pass the ground portion of the practical test before beginning the flight portion.

The ground portion of the practical test allows the evaluator to determine whether the applicant is sufficiently prepared to advance to the flight portion of the practical test. The oral questioning will continue throughout the entire practical test.

The FAA encourages applicants and instructors to use the ACS to measure progress during training, and as a reference to ensure the applicant is adequately prepared for the knowledge and practical tests. The FAA will revise the ACS as circumstances require.

I. Preflight Preparation

Task	*Task A. Pilot Qualifications*
References	14 CFR parts 61, 91; FAA-H-8083-2, FAA-H-8083-25
Objective	To determine that the applicant exhibits satisfactory knowledge, risk management, and skills associated with airman and medical certificates including privileges, limitations, currency, and operating as Pilot-in-Command (PIC) as a private pilot.
Knowledge	The applicant demonstrates understanding of:
PA.I.A.K1	1. Currency, regulatory compliance, privileges and limitations.
PA.I.A.K2	2. Location of airman documents and identification required when exercising private pilot privileges.
PA.I.A.K3	3. The required documents to provide upon inspection.
PA.I.A.K4	4. Pilot logbook/record keeping.
PA.I.A.K5	5. Compensation.
PA.I.A.K6	6. Towing.
PA.I.A.K7	7. Category and class.
PA.I.A.K8	8. Endorsements.
PA.I.A.K9	9. Medical certificates: class, expiration, privileges, temporary disqualifications.
PA.I.A.K10	10. Drugs, alcohol regulatory restrictions that affect the pilot's ability to operate safely.
Risk Management	The applicant demonstrates the ability to identify, assess and mitigate risks, encompassing:
PA.I.A.R1	1. Distinguishing proficiency versus currency.
PA.I.A.R2	2. Setting personal minimums.
PA.I.A.R3	3. Maintaining fitness to fly.
PA.I.A.R4	4. Flying unfamiliar aircraft.
PA.I.A.R5	5. Operating with unfamiliar flight display systems or unfamiliar avionics.
Skills	The applicant demonstrates the ability to apply requirements to:
PA.I.A.S1	1. Act as PIC under VFR in a scenario given by the evaluator.

I. Preflight Preparation

Task	*Task B. Airworthiness Requirements*
References	14 CFR parts 39, 43, 91; FAA-H-8083-2, FAA-H-8083-25
Objective	To determine that the applicant exhibits satisfactory knowledge, risk management, and skills associated with airworthiness requirements, including aircraft certificates.
Knowledge	The applicant demonstrates understanding of:
PA.I.B.K1	1. General airworthiness requirements and compliance for airplanes.
PA.I.B.K1a	a. Certificate location and expiration dates
PA.I.B.K1b	b. Required inspections
PA.I.B.K1c	c. Inspection requirements
PA.I.B.K2	2. Individuals who can perform maintenance on the aircraft, including A&P and IA roles in aircraft maintenance and inspections.
PA.I.B.K3	3. Pilot-performed preventive maintenance.
PA.I.B.K4	4. Equipment requirements for day and night flight for example: flying with inoperative equipment (approved Minimum Equipment List (MEL), Kinds of Operation Equipment List (KOEL), VFR and placards).
PA.I.B.K5	5. Proving airworthiness (specifics of the aircraft–compliance with Airworthiness Directives or applicability of Safety Bulletins).
PA.I.B.K6	6. Obtaining a special flight permit.
PA.I.B.K7	7. Experimental aircraft airworthiness.
PA.I.B.K6	8. Equipment malfunctions.
Risk Management	The applicant demonstrates the ability to identify, assess and mitigate risks, encompassing:
PA.I.B.R1	1. Inoperative equipment.
PA.I.B.R2	2. Equipment failure during flight.
PA.I.B.R3	3. Discrepancy records or placards.
Skills	The applicant demonstrates the ability to:
PA.I.B.S1	1. Locate aircraft airworthiness and registration information.
PA.I.B.S2	2. Determine the aircraft is airworthy in a scenario given by the evaluator.
PA.I.B.S3	3. Explain conditions where flight can be made with inoperative equipment.
PA.I.B.S4	4. Explain requirements for obtaining and flying with a Special Flight Permit.
PA.I.B.S5	5. Locate and explain operating limitations, placards, instrument markings, POH/AFM, weight and balance data, and equipment list.

I. Preflight Preparation

Task	Task C. Weather Information
References	14 CFR part 91; FAA-H-8083-25; AC 00-6, AC 00-45; AIM
Objective	To determine that the applicant exhibits satisfactory knowledge, risk management, and skills associated with weather information for a flight under VFR.
Knowledge	The applicant demonstrates understanding of:
PA.I.C.K1	1. Acceptable sources of weather data for flight planning purposes.
PA.I.C.K2	2. Weather products required for preflight planning and en route operations.
PA.I.C.K3	3. Current and forecast weather for departure, en route, and arrival phases of flight.
PA.I.C.K4	4. Meteorology applicable to airport, local area, departure, en route, alternate, and destination of a VFR flight in Visual Meteorological Conditions (VMC) to include expected climate and hazardous conditions such as:
PA.I.C.K4a	a. Atmospheric composition and stability
PA.I.C.K4b	b. Wind (e.g., crosswind, tailwind, wind shear, etc.)
PA.I.C.K4c	c. Temperature
PA.I.C.K4d	d. Moisture/precipitation
PA.I.C.K4e	e. Weather system formation, including air masses and fronts
PA.I.C.K4f	f. Clouds
PA.I.C.K4g	g. Turbulence
PA.I.C.K4h	h. Thunderstorms
PA.I.C.K4i	i. Icing and freezing level information
PA.I.C.K4j	j. Fog
PA.I.C.K4k	k. Frost
PA.I.C.K4l	l. METARs and TAFs
PA.I.C.K4m	m. Weather related charts
PA.I.C.K4n	n. Weather advisories
PA.I.C.K4o	o. PIREPs
PA.I.C.K5	5. En route weather resources.
PA.I.C.K6	6. Cockpit displays of digital weather and aeronautical information.
PA.I.C.K7	7. Seasonal weather phenomena.
Risk Management	The applicant demonstrates the ability to identify, assess and mitigate risks, encompassing:
PA.I.C.R1	1. Factors involved in determining a valid go/no-go decision.
PA.I.C.R2	2. Dynamic weather affecting flight.
PA.I.C.R3	3. The limitations of weather equipment.
PA.I.C.R4	4. The limitations of aviation weather reports and forecasts.
PA.I.C.R5	5. The limitations of inflight aviation weather resources.
PA.I.C.R6	6. Identification of alternate airports along the intended route of flight and circumstances that would make diversion prudent.
PA.I.C.R7	7. Identification of weather conditions that may increase or reduce risk for the planned flight.
PA.I.C.R8	8. Establishing personal weather minimums based on the parameters of the flight (e.g., ceilings, visibility, cross-wind component, etc.), and determining when existing and/or forecast weather conditions exceed these minimums.
Skills	The applicant demonstrates the ability to:
PA.I.C.S1	1. Use available aviation weather resources to obtain an adequate weather briefing.
PA.I.C.S2	2. Correlate weather information to determine alternate requirements.
PA.I.C.S3	3. Correlate available weather information to make a competent go/no-go or diversion decision.
PA.I.C.S4	4. Update/interpret weather in flight.
PA.I.C.S5	5. Evaluate environmental conditions using valid and reliable information sources to be able to make a competent go/no-go or diversion decision.
PA.I.C.S6	6. Given a scenario based on real time weather, where it would be appropriate, divert.
PA.I.C.S7	7. Use cockpit displays of digital weather and aeronautical information, as applicable.

I. Preflight Preparation

Task	Task D. Cross-Country Flight Planning
References	14 CFR part 91; FAA-H-8083-2, FAA-H-8083-25; Navigation Charts; Chart Supplements U.S.; AIM; NOTAMs
Objective	To determine that the applicant exhibits satisfactory knowledge, risk management, and skills associated with cross-country flights and VFR flight planning.
Knowledge	The applicant demonstrates understanding of:
PA.I.D.K1	1. Route planning, including consideration of special use airspace.
PA.I.D.K2	2. Applying universal coordinated time (UTC) to flight planning.
PA.I.D.K3	3. Converting and calculating time relative to time zones and estimated time of arrival.
PA.I.D.K4	4. Calculating time, climb and descent rates, course, distance, heading, true airspeed and ground speed.
PA.I.D.K5	5. Fuel planning.
PA.I.D.K6	6. Altitude selection accounting for terrain and obstacles, glide distance of aircraft, VFR cruising altitude, and the effect of wind.
PA.I.D.K7	7. Conditions conducive to icing.
PA.I.D.K8	8. Symbology found on VFR charts including airspace, obstructions and terrain features.
PA.I.D.K9	9. Elements of a VFR flight plan.
PA.I.D.K10	10. Procedures for activating and closing a VFR flight plan in controlled and non-controlled airspace.
PA.I.D.K11	11. Seasonal weather phenomena
Risk Management	The applicant demonstrates the ability to identify, assess and mitigate risks, encompassing:
PA.I.D.R1	1. The pilot.
PA.I.D.R2	2. The aircraft.
PA.I.D.R3	3. The environment.
PA.I.D.R4	4. External pressures.
PA.I.D.R5	5. Lack of appropriate training when flight is planned in an area different from the pilot's local area, such as in mountains, congested airspace, or location with different weather and topography.
PA.I.D.R6	6. The tendency to complete the flight in spite of adverse change in conditions.
PA.I.D.R7	7. Failure to select the appropriate VFR altitude for the direction of flight.
PA.I.D.R8	8. Limitations of ATC services.
PA.I.D.R9	9. Improper fuel planning.
PA.I.D.R10	10. A route overflying significant environmental influences, such as mountains or large bodies of water.
PA.I.D.R11	11. Flight in areas unsuitable for landing or below personal minimums.
PA.I.D.R12	12. Seasonal weather patterns.
Skills	The applicant demonstrates the ability to:
PA.I.D.S1	1. Prepare, present and explain a cross-country flight plan assigned by the evaluator including a risk analysis based on real-time weather.
PA.I.D.S2	2. Transfer knowledge used for one region to another region (given local climate, terrain, etc.).
PA.I.D.S3	3. Update fuel planning/manage fuel.
PA.I.D.S4	4. Select appropriate routes, altitudes, and checkpoints.
PA.I.D.S5	5. Recalculate fuel reserves based on a scenario provided by the evaluator.
PA.I.D.S6	6. Create a navigation log and simulate filing a VFR flight plan.
PA.I.D.S7	7. Interpret departure, en route, arrival route with reference to appropriate and current charts.
PA.I.D.S8	8. Explain or demonstrate diversion to alternate.
PA.I.D.S9	9. Apply pertinent information from Chart Supplements U.S.; NOTAMs relative to airport, runway and taxiway closures; and other flight publications.
PA.I.D.S10	10. On the day of the practical test, the final flight plan shall be to the first fuel stop, based on the maximum allowable passengers, baggage, and/or cargo loads using real-time weather and appropriate and current aeronautical charts.
PA.I.D.S11	11. Properly identify airspace, obstructions, and terrain features.
PA.I.D.S12	12. Select appropriate navigation system/facilities and communication frequencies.

I. Preflight Preparation

Task	Task E. National Airspace System
References	14 CFR parts 71, 91, 93; FAA-H-8083-2; Navigation Charts; AIM
Objective	To determine that the applicant exhibits satisfactory knowledge, risk management, and skills associated with the National Airspace System operating under VFR as a private pilot.
Knowledge	The applicant demonstrates understanding of:
PA.I.E.K1	1. Types of airspace/airspace classes and basic VFR weather minimums.
PA.I.E.K2	2. Charting symbology.
PA.I.E.K3	3. Operating rules, pilot certification, and airplane equipment requirements for flying in different classes of airspace.
PA.I.E.K4	4. Special use, special flight rules areas, and other airspace areas.
PA.I.E.K5	5. Temporary flight restrictions.
PA.I.E.K6	6. Aircraft speed limitations in various classes of airspace.
Risk Management	The applicant demonstrates the ability to identify, assess and mitigate risks, encompassing:
PA.I.E.R1	1. Various classes of airspace.
PA.I.E.R2	2. Maintaining VFR at night.
PA.I.E.R3	3. Special use airspace.
PA.I.E.R4	4. Compliance with or avoidance of specific en route airspace.
Skills	The applicant demonstrates the ability to:
PA.I.E.S1	1. Determine the requirements for basic VFR weather minimums and flying in particular classes of airspace.
PA.I.E.S2	2. Determine the requirements for flying in special use airspace (SUA), and special flight rule areas (SFRA).
PA.I.E.S3	3 Properly identify airspace and operate accordingly with regards to communication and equipment requirements.
PA.I.E.S4	4. Accounts for SUA, SFRA, and temporary flight rules (TFR).

I.   Preflight Preparation

Task	Task F. Performance and Limitations
References	FAA-H-8083-1, FAA-H-8083-2, FAA-H-8083-3, FAA-H-8083-25; POH/AFM
Objective	To determine that the applicant exhibits satisfactory knowledge, risk management, and skills associated with operating an aircraft safely within the parameters of its performance capabilities and limitations.
Knowledge	The applicant demonstrates understanding of:
PA.I.F.K1	1. Elements related to performance and limitations (e.g., takeoff and landing, crosswind, tailwind and headwind, density altitude, glide performance, weight and balance, climb, cruise, descent, powerplant considerations) by explaining the use of charts, tables, and data to determine performance.
PA.I.F.K2	2. Factors affecting performance to include atmospheric conditions, pilot technique, aircraft condition, and airport environment.
PA.I.F.K3	3. The effects of loading on performance.
PA.I.F.K4	4. The effects of exceeding weight and balance limits.
PA.I.F.K5	5. The effects of weight and balance changes over the course of the flight.
PA.I.F.K6	6. Aerodynamics.
Risk Management	The applicant demonstrates the ability to identify, assess and mitigate risks, encompassing:
PA.I.F.R1	1. Performance charts.
PA.I.F.R2	2. Limitations.
PA.I.F.R3	3. Variations in flight performance resulting from weight and balance changes during flight.
PA.I.F.R4	4. Published aircraft performance data as it relates to expected performance.
Skills	The applicant demonstrates the ability to:
PA.I.F.S1	1. Compute weight and balance for a given scenario, which includes practical techniques to resolve out-of-limit calculations and determine if the weight and balance will remain within limits during all phases of flight.
PA.I.F.S2	2. Use aircraft manufacturer's approved performance charts, tables, and data.
PA.I.F.S3	3. Evaluate takeoff and landing performance based on the values calculated.
PA.I.F.S4	4. Evaluate environmental conditions.

I. Preflight Preparation

Task	*Task G. Operation of Systems*
References	FAA-H-8083-2, FAA-H-8083-3, FAA-H-8083-25; POH/AFM
Objective	To determine that the applicant exhibits satisfactory knowledge, risk management, and skills associated with the safe operation of systems on the airplane provided for the flight test.
Knowledge	The applicant demonstrates understanding of:
PA.I.G.K1	1. Major components of the systems:
PA.I.G.K1a	a. Primary flight controls and trim
PA.I.G.K1b	b. Flaps, leading edge devices, and spoilers as appropriate
PA.I.G.K1c	c. Powerplant and propeller (basic engine knowledge)
PA.I.G.K1d	d. Landing gear
PA.I.G.K1e	e. Fuel, oil, and hydraulic
PA.I.G.K1f	f. Electrical
PA.I.G.K1g	g. Avionics
PA.I.G.K1h	h. Pitot-static, vacuum/pressure and associated flight instruments
PA.I.G.K1i	i. Environmental
PA.I.G.K1j	j. Deicing and anti-icing
PA.I.G.K2	2. Normal operation of systems.
PA.I.G.K3	3. Common errors made by pilots.
PA.I.G.K4	4. Abnormal operation of systems (recognition of system failures/malfunctions).
PA.I.G.K5	5. Systems interaction and pilot monitoring of automated systems.
Risk Management	The applicant demonstrates the ability to identify, assess and mitigate risks, encompassing:
PA.I.G.R1	1. Mishandling a system failure.
PA.I.G.R2	2. Troubleshooting system failures/malfunctions.
PA.I.G.R3	3. Mismanagement of airplane systems, which can cause a problem or system failure.
PA.I.G.R4	4. Determining and/or declaring an emergency.
PA.I.G.R5	5. Failure to identify system malfunctions or failures.
PA.I.G.R6	6. Outside/environmental factors affecting the systems, including improper fueling, carburetor ice, extremely cold temperatures, and vapor lock.
PA.I.G.R7	7. Detection and management of threats and errors.
PA.I.G.R8	8. Ineffective monitoring of automation.
Skills	The applicant demonstrates the ability to:
PA.I.G.S1	1. Explain and operate the airplane's systems.
PA.I.G.S2	2. Use checklist procedures.
PA.I.G.S3	3. Use immediate action items during emergency operations, as applicable.

I.   Preflight Preparation

Task	Task H. Human Factors
References	FAA-H-8083-2, FAA-H-8083-25; AIM
Objective	To determine that the applicant exhibits satisfactory knowledge, risk management, and skills associated with personal health, flight physiology, aeromedical and human factors, as it relates to safety of flight.
Knowledge	The applicant demonstrates understanding of:
PA.I.H.K1	1. The symptoms, recognition, causes, effects, and corrective actions associated with aeromedical and physiological issues including:
PA.I.H.K1a	a. Hypoxia
PA.I.H.K1b	b. Hyperventilation
PA.I.H.K1c	c. Middle ear and sinus problems
PA.I.H.K1d	d. Spatial disorientation
PA.I.H.K1e	e. Motion sickness
PA.I.H.K1f	f. Carbon monoxide poisoning
PA.I.H.K1g	g. Stress and fatigue
PA.I.H.K1h	h. Dehydration and nutrition
PA.I.H.K1i	i. Hypothermia
PA.I.H.K1j	j. Optical illusions
PA.I.H.K2	2. The effects of alcohol, drugs, and over-the-counter medications, and associated regulations.
PA.I.H.K3	3. The effects of dissolved nitrogen in the bloodstream of a pilot or passenger in flight following scuba diving.
PA.I.H.K4	4. The effects of hazardous attitudes on aeronautical decision-making.
PA.I.H.K5	5. Collision avoidance, scanning, obstacle and wire strike avoidance.
PA.I.H.K6	6. The pilot/airplane interface to include: pilot monitoring duties and the interaction with charts and avionics equipment.
Risk Management	The applicant demonstrates the ability to identify, assess and mitigate risks, encompassing:
PA.I.H.R1	1. The impact of environmental factors on medication's physiological effects.
PA.I.H.R2	2. Personal risk factors and the conflict between being goal oriented and adhering to personal limitations.
PA.I.H.R3	3. Optical illusions.
PA.I.H.R4	4. The circumstances of the flight (day/night, hot/cold) that affect the pilot's physiology.
PA.I.H.R5	5. Continue VFR flight into Instrument Meteorological Conditions (IMC).
PA.I.H.R6	6. Hazardous attitudes.
PA.I.H.R7	7. Failure to detect and manage threats and errors associated with human factors.
PA.I.H.R8	8. Ineffective monitoring of automation.
PA.I.H.R9	9. Distractions.
Skills	The applicant demonstrates the ability to:
PA.I.H.S1	1. Perform a self assessment including whether the pilot is fit for flight.
PA.I.H.S2	2. Show sound decision-making and judgment (based on reality of circumstances).
PA.I.H.S3	3. Demonstrate automation management and effective monitoring of automated systems.
PA.I.H.S4	4. Establish personal limitations.

II. Preflight Procedures

Task	Task A. Preflight Assessment
References	FAA-H-8083-2, FAA-H-8083-3; POH/AFM; AC 00-6
Objective	To determine that the applicant exhibits satisfactory knowledge, risk management, and skills associated with preparing for safe flight accounting for pilot, aircraft, environment, and external factors.
Knowledge	The applicant demonstrates understanding of:
PA.II.A.K1	1. Pilot self assessment.
PA.II.A.K2	2. The process to determine if the aircraft is appropriate for the mission by considering load, range, equipment and aircraft capability.
PA.II.A.K3	3. Aircraft preflight inspection including:
PA.II.A.K3a	a. Which items must be inspected
PA.II.A.K3b	b. The reasons for checking each item
PA.II.A.K3c	c. How to detect possible defects
PA.II.A.K3d	d. The associated regulations
PA.II.A.K4	4. Environmental factors that could affect the flight plan:
PA.II.A.K4a	a. Terrain
PA.II.A.K4b	b. Route selection
PA.II.A.K4c	c. Obstruction
PA.II.A.K4d	d. Weather
PA.II.A.K5	5. External pressures.
PA.II.A.K6	6. Seasonal weather phenomena.
Risk Management	The applicant demonstrates the ability to identify, assess and mitigate risks, encompassing:
PA.II.A.R1	1. Environmental factors.
PA.II.A.R2	2. External pressures.
PA.II.A.R3	3. Pilot-related factors.
PA.II.A.R4	4. Aircraft-related factors.
PA.II.A.R5	5. Aviation security concerns.
PA.II.A.R6	6. Seasonal weather patterns.
Skills	The applicant demonstrates the ability to:
PA.II.A.S1	1. Make proper use of the checklists, and systematically identify and manage pilot-related risks and personal minimums associated with the flight.
PA.II.A.S2	2. Inspect the airplane with reference to an appropriate checklist, explaining which items must be inspected, the reasons for checking each item, and how to detect possible defects.
PA.II.A.S3	3. Verify the airplane is airworthy and in condition for safe flight.
PA.II.A.S4	4. Assess the factors related to the environment (e.g., terrain, route selection, obstruction, weather).
PA.II.A.S5	5. Given the requirements of the flight the applicant uses the appropriate charts, tables, and graphs to determine performance.
PA.II.A.S6	6. Identify seasonal weather phenomena.

II.   Preflight Procedures

Task	*Task B. Cockpit Management*
References	FAA-H-8083-2, FAA-H-8083-3; POH/AFM
Objective	To determine that the applicant exhibits satisfactory knowledge, risk management, and skills associated with safe cockpit management practices.
Knowledge	The applicant demonstrates understanding of:
PA.II.B.K1	1. Pilot and passenger safety restraint systems, requirements, and operational considerations.
PA.II.B.K2	2. Oxygen use regulations, system operational guidelines, and system checks, if applicable.
PA.II.B.K3	3. Safety system rules and operational considerations.
PA.II.B.K4	4. Passenger briefing requirements and appropriate information.
PA.II.B.K5	5. PIC responsibility to have available material for the flight as planned.
PA.II.B.K6	6. The purpose of a checklist.
Risk Management	The applicant demonstrates the ability to identify, assess and mitigate risks, encompassing:
PA.II.B.R1	1. Failure to positively exchange the flight controls.
PA.II.B.R2	2. Use of portable electronic devices.
PA.II.B.R3	3. Use of automation.
PA.II.B.R4	4. Inappropriate use of technology.
PA.II.B.R5	5. The impact of reported discrepancies.
PA.II.B.R6	6. Passenger behavior that could negatively affect safety.
Skills	The applicant demonstrates the ability to:
PA.II.B.S1	1. Ensure all loose items in the cockpit and cabin are secured.
PA.II.B.S2	2. Organize, access, and determine suitability of material, equipment, and technology in an efficient manner.
PA.II.B.S3	3. Brief occupants on the use of safety belts, shoulder harnesses, doors, sterile cockpit, and flight control freedom of movement, and emergency procedures.
PA.II.B.S4	4. Properly program the navigational equipment available to the pilot on that particular aircraft.
PA.II.B.S5	5. Brief and execute positive exchange of flight controls and PIC responsibility to include identification of the PIC.
PA.II.B.S6	6. Conduct an appropriate pre take off briefing.

II. Preflight Procedures

Task	*Task C. Engine Starting*
References	FAA-H-8083-2, FAA-H-8083-3, FAA-H-8083-25; POH/AFM
Objective	To determine that the applicant exhibits satisfactory knowledge, risk management, and skills associated with recommended engine starting procedures including proper airplane positioning.
Knowledge	The applicant demonstrates understanding of:
PA.II.C.K1	1. Starting under various atmospheric conditions, using external power and hand propping safety.
PA.II.C.K2	2. Starting procedures for carbureted, fuel injected, diesel, Full Authority Digital Engine Control (FADEC), or turbine engines, as applicable.
PA.II.C.K3	3. Equipment limitations (such as starter cycles).
PA.II.C.K4	4. Proper positioning of the airplane.
Risk Management	The applicant demonstrates the ability to identify, assess and mitigate risks, encompassing:
PA.II.C.R1	1. Propeller safety and awareness to include passenger briefing and dangers associated with hand propping.
PA.II.C.R2	2. Implications of engine(s) starting with a weak or depleted battery, including considerations for use of external power.
PA.II.C.R3	3. Abnormal start.
PA.II.C.R4	4. Hot and cold weather operation.
PA.II.C.R5	5. Electrical system failure following aircraft engine starts.
PA.II.C.R6	6. Engine fires related to over priming/cold weather starting.
Skills	The applicant demonstrates the ability to:
PA.II.C.S1	1. Position the airplane properly considering structures, other aircraft, and the safety of nearby persons and property.
PA.II.C.S2	2. Utilize the checklist as appropriate during engine start.
PA.II.C.S3	3. Start the engine under various atmospheric conditions.

II.   Preflight Procedures

Task	Task D. Taxiing
References	FAA-H-8083-2, FAA-H-8083-3, FAA-H-8083-25; POH/AFM; AC 91-73; Chart Supplements U.S.; AIM
Objective	To determine that the applicant exhibits satisfactory knowledge, risk management, and skills associated with safe taxi operations, including runway incursion avoidance.
Knowledge	The applicant demonstrates understanding of:
PA.II.D.K1	1. Positioning aircraft controls for wind.
PA.II.D.K2	2. Airport markings, signs, and lights.
PA.II.D.K3	3. Aircraft lighting.
PA.II.D.K4	4. Safe taxi procedures at towered and non-towered airports:
PA.II.D.K4a	a. Maneuvering
PA.II.D.K4b	b. Maintain taxiway/runway alignment
PA.II.D.K4c	c. Situational awareness to avoid runway incursions
PA.II.D.K4d	d. Taxiing to avoid other aircraft/vehicles and hazards
PA.II.D.K5	5. Visual indicators for wind.
PA.II.D.K6	6. Airport information resources including Chart Supplements U.S., airport diagrams, and appropriate publications.
PA.II.D.K7	7. Good cockpit discipline during taxi, including maintaining a sterile cockpit, proper speed, separation between other aircraft and vehicles, and communication procedures.
PA.II.D.K8	8. Procedures for appropriate cockpit activities while taxiing including taxi route planning, briefing the location of Hot Spots, communicating and coordinating with ATC.
PA.II.D.K9	9. Rules for entering or crossing runways.
PA.II.D.K10	10. Procedures unique to night operations.
PA.II.D.K11	11. Hazards of low visibility operations.
PA.II.D.K12	12. Proper engine management including leaning, per manufacturer's recommendations.
Risk Management	The applicant demonstrates the ability to identify, assess and mitigate risks, encompassing:
PA.II.C.R1	1. Distractions during aircraft taxi.
PA.II.D.R2	2. Improper task management during taxi.
PA.II.D.R3	3. Confirmation or expectation bias as related to taxi instructions.
PA.II.D.R4	4. Taxi instructions/clearances.
PA.II.D.R5	5. Improper resource management.
Skills	The applicant demonstrates the ability to:
PA.II.D.S1	1. Perform a brake check immediately after the airplane begins moving.
PA.II.D.S2	2. Position the flight controls properly for the existing wind conditions.
PA.II.D.S3	3. Control direction and speed without excessive use of brakes.
PA.II.D.S4	4. Control the airplane during ground operations.
PA.II.D.S4a	a. Maneuvering
PA.II.D.S4b	b. Maintaining taxiway/runway alignment
PA.II.D.S4c	c. Maintaining situational awareness to avoid runway incursions
PA.II.D.S4d	d. Taxiing to avoid other aircraft/vehicles and hazards
PA.II.D.S5	5. Exhibit proper positioning of the aircraft relative to hold lines.
PA.II.D.S6	6. Exhibit procedures to ensure clearances/instructions are received, recorded, and read back correctly.
PA.II.D.S7	7. Exhibit situational awareness and taxi procedures in the event the aircraft is on a taxiway that is between parallel runways.
PA.II.D.S8	8. Use an airport diagram or taxi chart during taxi.
PA.II.D.S9	9. Comply with airport/taxiway markings, signals, ATC clearances and instructions.
PA.II.D.S10	10. Use procedures to minimize pilot workload during taxi operations.
PA.II.D.S11	11. Demonstrate briefing procedures to avoid runway incursions.

II. Preflight Procedures

Task	*Task F. Before Takeoff Check*
References	FAA-H-8083-2, FAA-H-8083-3; POH/AFM
Objective	To determine that the applicant exhibits satisfactory knowledge, risk management, and skills associated with the before takeoff check, including the reasons for checking each item, detecting malfunctions, and ensuring the airplane is in safe operating condition as recommended by the manufacturer.
Knowledge	The applicant demonstrates understanding of:
PA.II.F.K1	1. Purpose of the run up.
PA.II.F.K2	2. Aircraft performance given expected conditions.
PA.II.F.K3	3. The purpose of a checklist, to include the reasons for checking each item and how to detect malfunctions.
PA.II.F.K4	4. Wake turbulence avoidance.
PA.II.F.K5	5. An emergency locator transmitter (ELT).
Risk Management	The applicant demonstrates the ability to identify, assess and mitigate risks, encompassing:
PA.II.F.R1	1. Division of attention and scanning.
PA.II.F.R2	2. Different than expected runway.
PA.II.F.R3	3. Failure to properly exchange the flight controls.
PA.II.F.R4	4. Wake turbulence.
PA.II.F.R5	5. Improper automation management.
Skills	The applicant demonstrates the ability to:
PA.II.F.S1	1. Position the airplane properly considering other aircraft, vessels, and wind.
PA.II.F.S2	2. Divide attention between inside and outside the cockpit.
PA.II.F.S3	3. Ensure that powerplant and instrumentation are suitable for run up and takeoff, including temperature(s) and pressure(s).
PA.II.F.S4	4. Accomplish the before takeoff checklist, ensure the airplane is in safe operating condition as recommended by the manufacturer, and provide the departure briefing.
PA.II.F.S5	5. Review takeoff performance, such as airspeeds, takeoff distance, departure, and emergency procedures.
PA.II.F.S6	6. Avoid runway incursions and ensure no conflict with traffic prior to taxiing into takeoff position.

III. Airport Operations

Task	*Task A. Communications and Light Gun Signals*
References	14 CFR part 91; FAA-H-8083-2; FAA-H-8083-25; AIM
Objective	To determine that the applicant exhibits satisfactory knowledge, risk management, and skills associated with normal and emergency radio communications and ATC light gun signals to conduct radio communications safely while operating the aircraft.
Knowledge	The applicant demonstrates understanding of:
PA.III.A.K1	1. How to obtain proper radio frequencies.
PA.III.A.K2	2. Communication procedures and ATC phraseology.
PA.III.A.K3	3. ATC light signal recognition.
PA.III.A.K4	4. Transponders.
PA.III.A.K5	5. Radar assistance.
PA.III.A.K6	6. Lost communication procedures.
PA.III.A.K7	7. Use of automated weather and airport information.
Risk Management	The applicant demonstrates the ability to identify, assess and mitigate risks, encompassing:
PA.III.A.R1	1. Human factors associated with communication.
PA.III.A.R2	2. Human factors associated with declaring an emergency.
PA.III.A.R3	3. Equipment issues that could cause loss of communication.
PA.III.A.R4	4. Improper automation management.
PA.III.A.R5	5. Single-pilot resource management (SRM) and/or crew resource management (CRM).
Skills	The applicant demonstrates the ability to:
PA.III.A.S1	1. Select appropriate frequencies.
PA.III.A.S2	2. Transmit using phraseology and procedures as specified in the AIM.
PA.III.A.S3	3. Acknowledge radio communications and comply with instructions.

III. Airport Operations

Task	*Task B. Traffic Patterns*
References	14 CFR part 91; FAA-H-8083-2, FAA-H-8083-25; AIM
Objective	To determine that the applicant exhibits satisfactory knowledge, risk management, and skills associated with traffic patterns.
Knowledge	The applicant demonstrates understanding of:
PA.III.B.K1	1. Towered and non-towered airport operations and runway selection.
PA.III.B.K2	2. Airport signs and markings, lighting, and wind indicators.
PA.III.B.K3	3. Collision avoidance, scanning, obstacle and wire strike avoidance.
PA.III.B.K4	4. Right-of-way rules.
PA.III.B.K5	5. Wake turbulence recognition and resolution.
PA.III.B.K6	6. Wind shear avoidance.
PA.III.B.K7	7. Runway incursion avoidance.
PA.III.B.K8	8. Use of automated weather and airport information.
PA.III.B.K9	9. Use of radio for proper communications.
PA.III.B.K10	10. Parachuting operations.
PA.III.B.K11	11. Approach and landing considerations for different types of aircraft.
Risk Management	The applicant demonstrates the ability to identify, assess and mitigate risks, encompassing:
PA.III.B.R1	1. Collision avoidance, scanning, obstacle and wire strike avoidance.
PA.III.B.R2	2. Wake turbulence.
PA.III.B.R3	3. Failure to maintain situational awareness.
PA.III.B.R4	4. Failure to maintain separation from other aircraft.
PA.III.B.R5	5. Operating considerations of various aircraft types.
PA.III.B.R6	6. Go-around or rejected takeoff, if appropriate.
Skills	The applicant demonstrates the ability to:
PA.III.B.S1	1. Properly identify and interpret airport runways, taxiways, markings, and lighting.
PA.III.B.S2	2. Comply with proper traffic pattern procedures.
PA.III.B.S3	3. Maintain proper spacing from other aircraft.
PA.III.B.S4	4. Correct for wind drift to maintain the proper ground track.
PA.III.B.S5	5. Maintain orientation with the runway/landing area in use.
PA.III.B.S6	6. Maintain traffic pattern altitude, ±100 feet, and the appropriate airspeed, ±10 knots.
PA.III.B.S7	7. Maintain an awareness of the position of other aircraft in the pattern.

IV. Takeoffs, Landings, and Go-Arounds

Task	*Task A. Normal Takeoff and Climb*
References	FAA-H-8083-2, FAA-H-8083-3; POH/AFM
Objective	To determine that the applicant exhibits satisfactory knowledge, risk management, and skills associated with a normal takeoff, climb operations, and rejected takeoff procedures. ***Note:*** *If a crosswind condition does not exist, the applicant's knowledge of crosswind elements must be evaluated through oral testing.*
Knowledge	The applicant demonstrates understanding of:
PA.IV.A.K1	1. Takeoff distance.
PA.IV.A.K2	2. Takeoff power.
PA.IV.A.K3	3. Atmospheric conditions.
PA.IV.A.K4	4. Wind conditions and effects.
PA.IV.A.K5	5. The application of V_X or V_Y and variations with altitude.
PA.IV.A.K6	6. The manufacturer's recommended emergency procedures for relating to the takeoff sequence.
Risk Management	The applicant demonstrates the ability to identify, assess and mitigate risks, encompassing:
PA.IV.A.R1	1. Selection of runway based on wind, pilot capability, and aircraft limitations.
PA.IV.A.R2	2. The demonstrated crosswind component for aircraft.
PA.IV.A.R3	3. Windshear.
PA.IV.A.R4	4. Tailwind.
PA.IV.A.R5	5. Wake turbulence.
PA.IV.A.R6	6. Go/no-go decision-making.
PA.IV.A.R7	7. Task management.
PA.IV.A.R8	8. Low altitude maneuvering.
PA.IV.A.R9	9. Wire strikes.
PA.IV.A.R10	10. Obstacles on the departure path.
PA.IV.A.R11	11. A rejected takeoff and predetermining takeoff abort criteria.
PA.IV.A.R12	12. Handling engine failure during takeoff and climb.
PA.IV.A.R13	13. Criticality of takeoff distance available.
PA.IV.A.R14	14. Plans for engine failure after takeoff.
PA.IV.A.R15	15. Sterile cockpit environment.
Skills	The applicant demonstrates the ability to:
PA.IV.A.S1	1. Verify ATC clearance and no aircraft is on final before crossing the hold line.
PA.IV.A.S2	2. Verify aircraft is on the assigned/correct runway.
PA.IV.A.S3	3. Ascertain wind direction with or without visible wind direction indicators.
PA.IV.A.S4	4. Determine if the crosswind component is beyond the pilot's ability or aircraft manufacturer maximum demonstrated value.
PA.IV.A.S5	5. Position the flight controls for the existing wind conditions.
PA.IV.A.S6	6. Clear the area; taxi into the takeoff position and align the airplane on the runway centerline/takeoff path.
PA.IV.A.S7	7. Confirm takeoff power; and proper engine and flight instrument indications prior to rotation.
PA.IV.A.S8	8. Rotate and lift-off at the recommended airspeed and accelerate to V_Y (or other speed as appropriate for aircraft).
PA.IV.A.S9	9. Establish a pitch attitude that will maintain V_Y +10/-5 knots (or other airspeed as appropriate for aircraft).
PA.IV.A.S10	10. Retract the landing gear and flaps in accordance with manufacturer's guidance.
PA.IV.A.S11	11. Maintain takeoff power and V_Y +10/-5 knots or to a safe maneuvering altitude.
PA.IV.A.S12	12. Maintain directional control and proper wind-drift correction throughout the takeoff and climb.
PA.IV.A.S13	13. Comply with responsible environmental practices, including noise abatement and published departure procedures.
PA.IV.A.S14	14. Complete the appropriate checklist.
PA.IV.A.S15	15. Comply with manufacturer's recommended emergency procedures related to the takeoff sequence.

IV. Takeoffs, Landings, and Go-Arounds

Task	*Task B. Normal Approach and Landing*
References	FAA-H-8083-2, FAA-H-8083-3; POH/AFM
Objective	To determine that the applicant exhibits satisfactory knowledge, risk management, and skills associated with a normal approach and landing with emphasis on proper use and coordination of flight controls. ***Note:*** *If a crosswind condition does not exist, the applicant's knowledge of crosswind elements must be evaluated through oral testing.*
Knowledge	The applicant demonstrates understanding of:
PA.IV.B.K1	1. Available landing distance.
PA.IV.B.K2	2. Stabilized approach and interpretation and use of visual glide scope indicators.
PA.IV.B.K3	3. Energy management.
PA.IV.B.K4	4. Atmospheric conditions.
PA.IV.B.K5	5. Wind conditions and effects.
PA.IV.B.K6	6. Emergency procedures during approach and landing.
PA.IV.B.K7	7. Land and hold short operations (LAHSO) or option to refuse LAHSO restriction.
Risk Management	The applicant demonstrates the ability to identify, assess and mitigate risks, encompassing:
PA.IV.B.R1	1. Failure to select the appropriate runway based on wind, pilot capability, and airplane limitations.
PA.IV.B.R2	2. Exceeding the manufacturer's maximum demonstrated crosswind component.
PA.IV.B.R3	3. Windshear.
PA.IV.B.R4	4. Tailwind.
PA.IV.B.R5	5. Wake turbulence.
PA.IV.B.R6	6. Task management.
PA.IV.B.R7	7. Low altitude maneuvering.
PA.IV.B.R8	8. Collision avoidance, scanning, obstacle and wire strike avoidance.
PA.IV.B.R9	9. Failure to follow the right-of-way rules.
PA.IV.B.R10	10. Obstacles on approach and landing paths.
PA.IV.B.R11	11. Failure to recognize the need to perform a go-round/rejected landing.
PA.IV.B.R12	12. Low altitude stall/spin.
PA.IV.B.R13	13. Land and hold short operations (LAHSO).
PA.IV.B.R14	14. Failure to adhere to sterile cockpit requirement.
Skills	The applicant demonstrates the ability to:
PA.IV.B.S1	1. Ensure the aircraft is on the correct/assigned runway.
PA.IV.B.S2	2. Scan the landing runway/areas and adjoining areas for possible obstructions for landing.
PA.IV.B.S3	3. Complete the appropriate checklist.
PA.IV.B.S4	4. Consider the wind conditions, landing surface, and obstructions to select a suitable touchdown point.
PA.IV.B.S5	5. Establish the recommended approach and landing configuration and airspeed, and adjust pitch attitude and power as required.
PA.IV.B.S6	6. Maintain a stabilized approach and recommended airspeed, or in its absence, not more than $1.3 V_{SO}$, with wind gust factor applied +10/-5 knots, or as recommended by the aircraft manufacturer for the aircraft type and gust velocity.
PA.IV.B.S7	7. Make smooth, timely, and correct control applications:
PA.IV.B.S7a	a. During the round out and touchdown.
PA.IV.B.S8	8. Touch down smoothly at a speed that provides little or no aerodynamic lift.
PA.IV.B.S9	9. Touch down within the available runway area, within 400 feet beyond a specified point with no drift, and with the airplane's longitudinal axis aligned with and over the runway centerline.
PA.IV.B.S10	10. Maintain crosswind correction and directional control throughout the approach and landing sequence.
PA.IV.B.S11	11. Execute a timely go-around decision when the approach cannot be made within the tolerances specified above or for any other condition that may result in an unsafe approach or landing.
PA.IV.B.S12	12. Utilize after landing runway incursion avoidance procedures.

IV.   Takeoffs, Landings, and Go-Arounds

Task	*Task C. Soft-Field Takeoff and Climb*
References	FAA-H-8083-2, FAA-H-8083-3; POH/AFM
Objective	To determine that the applicant exhibits satisfactory knowledge, risk management, and skills associated with a soft-field takeoff, climb operations, and rejected takeoff procedures.
Knowledge	The applicant demonstrates understanding of:
PA.IV.C.K1	1. The importance of weight transfer from wheels to wings.
PA.IV.C.K2	2. P factor in turning tendencies.
PA.IV.C.K3	3. The effects of aircraft configuration.
PA.IV.C.K4	4. The effects of runway surface.
PA.IV.C.K5	5. Takeoff distance.
PA.IV.C.K6	6. Takeoff power.
PA.IV.C.K7	7. Wind conditions and effects.
PA.IV.C.K8	8. Density altitude.
PA.IV.C.K9	9. Application of V_X or V_Y.
PA.IV.C.K10	10. Emergency procedures during takeoff and climb.
PA.IV.C.K11	11. Hazards of other than a hard surfaced runway.
Risk Management	The applicant demonstrates the ability to identify, assess and mitigate risks, encompassing:
PA.IV.C.R1	1. Failure to select the appropriate runway based on wind, pilot capability, and aircraft limitations.
PA.IV.C.R2	2. Exceeding the manufacturer's maximum demonstrated crosswind component.
PA.IV.C.R3	3. Operating from other than a hard surfaced runway.
PA.IV.C.R4	4. Windshear.
PA.IV.C.R5	5. Tailwind.
PA.IV.C.R6	6. Wake turbulence.
PA.IV.C.R7	7. Failure to recognize the need to perform a go-around/rejected landing.
PA.IV.C.R8	8. Task management.
PA.IV.C.R9	9. Low altitude maneuvering.
PA.IV.C.R10	10. Wire strikes.
PA.IV.C.R11	11. Obstacles on the departure path.
PA.IV.C.R12	12. Rejected takeoffs and failure to identify a takeoff abort point.
PA.IV.C.R13	13. An engine failure during takeoff and climb.
PA.IV.C.R14	14. Failure to use a soft-field takeoff technique on an other than hard surfaced runway.
PA.IV.C.R15	15. Takeoff distance available.
PA.IV.C.R16	16. Failure to adhere to sterile cockpit requirement.

Task C continued on next page

Task C continued from previous page

Skills	The applicant demonstrates the ability to:
PA.IV.C.S1	1. Verify ATC clearance and no aircraft is on final before crossing the hold line.
PA.IV.C.S2	2. Ensure the aircraft is properly configured.
PA.IV.C.S3	3. Ensure the aircraft is on the correct takeoff runway.
PA.IV.C.S4	4. Ascertain wind direction with or without visible wind direction indicators.
PA.IV.C.S5	5. Calculate the crosswind component and determine if it is beyond the pilot ability or aircraft capability.
PA.IV.C.S6	6. Position the flight controls for the existing wind conditions to maximize lift as quickly as possible.
PA.IV.C.S7	7. Clear the area, taxi into the takeoff position and align the airplane on the runway center line without stopping while advancing the throttle smoothly to takeoff power.
PA.IV.C.S8	8. Confirm takeoff power, and proper engine and flight instrument indications prior to rotation.
PA.IV.C.S9	9. Establish and maintain a pitch attitude that will transfer the weight of the airplane from the wheels to the wings as rapidly as possible.
PA.IV.C.S10	10. Lift-off at the lowest possible airspeed consistent with safety and remain in ground effect while accelerating to V_X or V_Y, as appropriate.
PA.IV.C.S11	11. Establish a pitch attitude for V_X or V_Y, as appropriate, and maintain selected airspeed +10/-5 knots during the climb.
PA.IV.C.S12	12. Retract landing gear and flaps after a positive rate of climb has been verified or in accordance with aircraft manufacturer's guidance.
PA.IV.C.S13	13. Maintain takeoff power and V_Y +10/-5 knots to a safe maneuvering altitude.
PA.IV.C.S14	14. Maintain directional control and proper wind drift correction throughout the takeoff and climb.
PA.IV.C.S15	15. Comply with noise abatement and published departure procedures.
PA.IV.C.S16	16. Complete the appropriate checklist.
PA.IV.C.S17	17. Comply with manufacturer's recommended emergency procedures related to the takeoff sequence.

IV.   Takeoffs, Landings, and Go-Arounds

Task	**Task D. Soft-Field Approach and Landing**
References	FAA-H-8083-2, FAA-H-8083-3; POH/AFM
Objective	To determine that the applicant exhibits satisfactory knowledge, risk management, and skills associated with a soft-field approach and landing with emphasis on proper use and coordination of flight controls.
Knowledge	The applicant demonstrates understanding of:
PA.IV.D.K1	1. Landing distance.
PA.IV.D.K2	2. Hazards of other than hard surfaced runway.
PA.IV.D.K3	3. Stabilized approach.
PA.IV.D.K4	4. Energy management.
PA.IV.D.K5	5. Wind conditions and effects.
PA.IV.D.K6	6. Density altitude.
PA.IV.D.K7	7. Emergency procedures during approach and landing.
Risk Management	The applicant demonstrates the ability to identify, assess and mitigate risks, encompassing:
PA.IV.D.R1	1. Failure to select the appropriate runway based on wind, pilot capability, and aircraft limitations.
PA.IV.D.R2	2. Exceeding the manufacturer's maximum demonstrated crosswind component.
PA.IV.D.R3	3. Operating from other than a hard surfaced runway.
PA.IV.D.R4	4. Losing elevator control, sinking into the soft surface, or striking the prop if moving too slowly.
PA.IV.D.R5	5. Windshear avoidance.
PA.IV.D.R6	6. Tailwind.
PA.IV.D.R7	7. Wake turbulence.
PA.IV.D.R8	8. Task management.
PA.IV.D.R9	9. Low altitude maneuvering.
PA.IV.D.R10	10. Collision avoidance, scanning, obstacle and wire strike avoidance.
PA.IV.D.R11	11. Failure to follow the right-of-way rules.
PA.IV.D.R12	12. Obstacles on approach and landing paths.
PA.IV.D.R13	13. Failure to recognize the need for go-around/rejected landing.
PA.IV.D.R14	14. Low altitude stall/spin.
PA.IV.D.R15	15. Performing a soft-field landing after an engine failure.
PA.IV.D.R16	16. Failure to adhere to sterile cockpit requirement.
Skills	The applicant demonstrates the ability to:
PA.IV.D.S1	1. Ensure the aircraft is aligned with the correct/assigned runway.
PA.IV.D.S2	2. Scan the landing runway/area for possible obstructions for landing.
PA.IV.D.S3	3. Complete the appropriate approach and landing checklist.
PA.IV.D.S4	4. Consider the wind conditions, landing surface, and obstructions to select a suitable touchdown point.
PA.IV.D.S5	5. Establish the recommended approach and landing configuration and airspeed, and adjust pitch attitude and power as required.
PA.IV.D.S6	6. Maintain a stabilized approach and recommended airspeed, or in its absence, not more than 1.3 V_{SO}, with wind gust factor applied +10/-5 knots.
PA.IV.D.S7	7. Make smooth, timely, and correct control application during the round out and touchdown and, for tricycle gear airplanes, keep the nose wheel off the surface until loss of elevator effectiveness.
PA.IV.D.S8	8. Touch down softly with minimum sink rate and no drift, with the airplane's longitudinal axis aligned with the center of the runway.
PA.IV.D.S9	9. Maintain full up elevator during rollout and exit the "soft" area at a speed that would preclude sinking into the surface.
PA.IV.D.S10	10. Maintain crosswind correction and directional control throughout the approach and landing sequence, as required.
PA.IV.D.S11	11. Execute a timely go-around decision when the approach cannot be made within the tolerances specified above or for any other condition that may result in an unsafe approach or landing.
PA.IV.D.S12	12. Maintain proper position of the flight controls and sufficient speed to taxi on the soft surface.
PA.IV.D.S13	13. Utilize after landing runway incursion avoidance procedures.

IV. Takeoffs, Landings, and Go-Arounds

Task	*Task E. Short-Field Takeoff and Maximum Performance Climb*
References	FAA-H-8083-2, FAA-H-8083-3; POH/AFM
Objective	To determine that the applicant exhibits satisfactory knowledge, risk management, and skills associated with a short-field takeoff, maximum performance climb operations, and rejected takeoff procedures.
Knowledge	The applicant demonstrates understanding of:
PA.IV.E.K1	1. The effects of aircraft configuration.
PA.IV.E.K2	2. The effects of runway surface.
PA.IV.E.K3	3. Takeoff distance.
PA.IV.E.K4	4. Takeoff power.
PA.IV.E.K5	5. Obstruction clearance.
PA.IV.E.K6	6. Wind conditions and effects.
PA.IV.E.K7	7. Minimum safe altitude.
PA.IV.E.K8	8. Density altitude.
PA.IV.E.K9	9. Application of V_X or V_Y.
PA.IV.E.K10	10. Emergency procedures during takeoff and climb.
Risk Management	The applicant demonstrates the ability to identify, assess and mitigate risks, encompassing:
PA.IV.E.R1	1. Failure to select the appropriate runway based on wind, pilot capability, and aircraft limitations.
PA.IV.E.R2	2. Exceeding the manufacturer's maximum demonstrated crosswind component.
PA.IV.E.R3	3. Operating from other than a hard surfaced runway.
PA.IV.E.R4	4. Obstruction clearance.
PA.IV.E.R5	5. Climb attitude and stall awareness.
PA.IV.E.R6	6. Windshear.
PA.IV.E.R7	7. Tailwind.
PA.IV.E.R8	8. Wake turbulence.
PA.IV.E.R9	9. Failure to recognize the need to perform a go-around/rejected landing.
PA.IV.E.R10	10. Task management.
PA.IV.E.R11	11. Low altitude maneuvering.
PA.IV.E.R12	12. Wire strikes.
PA.IV.E.R13	13. Obstacles on the departure paths.
PA.IV.E.R14	14. Recognition of need for rejected takeoff and identification of takeoff abort criteria.
PA.IV.E.R15	15. Strategies for handling engine failure during takeoff and climb, including recognition that climb at V_X (versus V_{XSE}) may result in loss of directional control if an engine fails.
PA.IV.E.R16	16. Criticality of takeoff distance available.
PA.IV.E.R17	17. An engine failure after takeoff.
PA.IV.E.R18	18. Failure to adhere to sterile cockpit requirement.

Task E continued on next page

Task E continued from previous page

Skills	The applicant demonstrates the ability to:
PA.IV.E.S1	1. Verify proper aircraft configuration.
PA.IV.E.S2	2. Verify ATC clearance and no aircraft is on final before crossing the hold line.
PA.IV.E.S3	3. Ensure the aircraft is on the correct takeoff runway.
PA.IV.E.S4	4. Determine wind direction with or without visible wind direction indicators.
PA.IV.E.S5	5. Calculate the crosswind component and determine if it is beyond the pilot ability or aircraft capability.
PA.IV.E.S6	6. Position the flight controls for the existing wind conditions.
PA.IV.E.S7	7. Clear the area, taxi into the takeoff position utilizing maximum available takeoff area and align the airplane on the runway center line.
PA.IV.E.S8	8. Apply brakes (if appropriate), while configuring aircraft power setting to achieve maximum performance.
PA.IV.E.S9	9. Confirm takeoff power prior to brake release (if appropriate) and proper engine and flight instrument indications prior to rotation.
PA.IV.E.S10	10. Rotate and lift-off at the recommended airspeed, and accelerate to the recommended obstacle clearance airspeed or V_X.
PA.IV.E.S11	11. Establish a pitch attitude that will maintain the recommended obstacle clearance airspeed, or V_X, +10/-5 knots, until the obstacle is cleared, or until the airplane is 50 feet above the surface.
PA.IV.E.S12	12. After clearing the obstacle, establish the pitch attitude for V_Y, accelerate to V_Y, and maintain V_Y, +10/-5 knots, during the climb.
PA.IV.E.S13	13. Retract landing gear and flaps after a positive rate of climb has been verified or in accordance with aircraft manufacturer's guidance.
PA.IV.E.S14	14. Maintain takeoff power and V_Y +10/-5 knots to a safe maneuvering altitude.
PA.IV.E.S15	15. Maintain directional control and proper wind drift correction throughout the takeoff and climb.
PA.IV.E.S16	16. Comply with noise abatement and published departure procedures.
PA.IV.E.S17	17. Complete the appropriate checklist.
PA.IV.E.S18	18. Comply with manufacturer's recommended emergency procedures related to the takeoff sequence.
PA.IV.E.S19	19. Utilize runway incursion avoidance procedures.

IV.   Takeoffs, Landings, and Go-Arounds

Task	*Task F. Short-Field Approach and Landing*
References	FAA-H-8083-2, FAA-H-8083-3; POH/AFM
Objective	To determine that the applicant exhibits satisfactory knowledge, risk management, and skills associated with a short-field approach and landing with emphasis on proper use and coordination of flight controls.
Knowledge	The applicant demonstrates understanding of:
PA.IV.F.K1	1. Landing distance.
PA.IV.F.K2	2. Hazards of other than a hard surfaced runway.
PA.IV.F.K3	3. Obstruction clearance.
PA.IV.F.K4	4. Stabilized approach.
PA.IV.F.K5	5. Energy management.
PA.IV.F.K6	6. Wind conditions and effects.
PA.IV.F.K7	7. Density altitude.
PA.IV.F.K8	8. Emergency procedures during approach and landing.
PA.IV.F.K9	9. Land and hold short operations.
Risk Management	The applicant demonstrates the ability to identify, assess and mitigate risks, encompassing:
PA.IV.F.R1	1. Failure to select the appropriate runway based on wind, pilot capability, and aircraft limitations.
PA.IV.F.R2	2. Exceeding the manufacturer's maximum demonstrated crosswind component.
PA.IV.F.R3	3. Operating from other than a hard surfaced runway.
PA.IV.F.R4	4. Obstruction clearance.
PA.IV.F.R5	5. Climb attitude and stall awareness.
PA.IV.F.R6	6. Wind shear avoidance.
PA.IV.F.R7	7. Tailwind.
PA.IV.F.R8	8. Wake turbulence.
PA.IV.F.R9	9. Task management.
PA.IV.F.R10	10. Low altitude maneuvering.
PA.IV.F.R11	11. Collision avoidance, scanning, obstacle and wire strike avoidance.
PA.IV.F.R12	12. Failure to follow the right-of-way rules.
PA.IV.F.R13	13. Obstacles on approach and landing paths.
PA.IV.F.R14	14. Failure to recognize the need for a go-around/rejected landing.
PA.IV.F.R15	15. Low altitude stall/spin.
PA.IV.F.R15	16. Land and hold short operations (LAHSO).
PA.IV.F.R17	17. Failure to adhere to sterile cockpit requirement.
Skills	The applicant demonstrates the ability to:
PA.IV.F.S1	1. Ensure the aircraft is aligned with the correct/assigned runway.
PA.IV.F.S2	2. Scan the landing runway/area for possible obstructions for landing.
PA.IV.F.S3	3. Complete the appropriate approach and landing checklist.
PA.IV.F.S4	4. Consider the wind conditions, landing surface and obstructions to select a suitable touchdown point.
PA.IV.F.S5	5. Establish the recommended approach and landing configuration and airspeed, and adjust pitch attitude and power as required.
PA.IV.F.S6	6. Maintain a stabilized approach and recommended airspeed, or in its absence, not more than 1.3 V_{SO}, with wind gust factor applied +10/-5 knots or as recommended by aircraft manufacturer to a safe maneuvering altitude.
PA.IV.F.S7	7. Make smooth, timely, and correct control application during the round out and touchdown.
PA.IV.F.S8	8. Touch down smoothly at an appropriate airspeed.
PA.IV.F.S9	9. Touch down within the available runway, at or within 200 feet beyond the specified point, threshold markings or runway numbers, with no side drift, minimum float, and with the airplane's longitudinal axis aligned with and over the runway center line/landing path.
PA.IV.F.S10	10. Maintain crosswind correction and directional control throughout the approach and landing sequence, as required.
PA.IV.F.S11	11. Execute a safe and timely go-around decision when the approach cannot be made within the tolerances specified above or for any other condition that may result in an unsafe approach or landing.
PA.IV.F.S12	12. Apply brakes, as necessary, to stop in the shortest distance consistent with safety.
PA.IV.F.S13	13. Utilize after landing runway incursion avoidance procedures.

IV.   Takeoffs, Landings, and Go-Arounds

Task	*Task M. Forward Slip to a Landing*
References	FAA-H-8083-2, FAA-H-8083-3; POH/AFM
Objective	To determine that the applicant exhibits satisfactory knowledge, risk management, and skills associated with a forward slip to a landing.
Knowledge	The applicant demonstrates understanding of:
PA.IV.M.K1	1. When and why forward slips are used and differences between side and forward slips.
PA.IV.M.K2	2. How forward slips are executed.
PA.IV.M.K3	3. Landing distance.
PA.IV.M.K4	4. Stabilized approach.
PA.IV.M.K5	5. Energy management.
PA.IV.M.K6	6. The effects of forward slips affecting indicated airspeed versus true airspeed.
PA.IV.M.K7	7. Wind conditions and effects.
PA.IV.M.K8	8. Density altitude.
PA.IV.M.K9	9. Emergency procedures during approach and landing.
PA.IV.M.K10	10. Land and hold short operations.
Risk Management	The applicant demonstrates the ability to identify, assess and mitigate risks, encompassing:
PA.IV.M.R1	1. Failure to recognize the need to perform a go-around/rejected landing.
PA.IV.M.R2	2. Failure to correlate any crosswind effects with direction of forward slip.
PA.IV.M.R3	3. Failure to transition to a side slip for landing.
PA.IV.M.R4	4. Low altitude stall/spin.
PA.IV.M.R5	5. Windshear.
PA.IV.M.R6	6. Land and hold short operations (LAHSO).
PA.IV.M.R7	7. Tailwind.
PA.IV.M.R8	8. Wake turbulence.
PA.IV.M.R9	9. Task management.
PA.IV.M.R10	10. Low altitude maneuvering.
PA.IV.M.R11	11. Failure to confirm your gear position in an amphibious aircraft.
PA.IV.M.R12	12. Collision avoidance, scanning, obstacle and wire strike avoidance.
PA.IV.M.R13	13. Failure to follow the right-of-way rules.
PA.IV.M.R14	14. Obstacles on approach and landing paths.
PA.IV.M.R15	15. Aircraft systems affected by performing a forward slip to include airspeed indications and fuel flow.
PA.IV.M.R16	16. Failure to adhere to sterile cockpit requirement.
Skills	The applicant demonstrates the ability to:
PA.IV.M.S1	1. Select runway/landing area based on wind, landing surface and obstructions, pilot capability and aircraft limitations.
PA.IV.M.S2	2. Calculate the crosswind component and determine if it is beyond the pilot's ability or aircraft capability.
PA.IV.M.S3	3. Select the most suitable touchdown point.
PA.IV.M.S4	4. Establish the slipping attitude at the point from which a landing can be made using the recommended approach and landing configuration and airspeed; adjust pitch attitude as required.
PA.IV.M.S5	5. Maintain a ground track aligned with the runway/landing path centerline and an airspeed, which results in minimum float during the round out.
PA.IV.M.S6	6. Make smooth, timely, and correct control application during the recovery from the slip, the round out, and the touchdown.
PA.IV.M.S7	7. Touch down within 400 feet beyond a specified point with no drift, and with the airplane's longitudinal axis aligned with and over the runway centerline.
PA.IV.M.S8	8. Maintain crosswind correction and directional control throughout the approach and landing sequence.
PA.IV.M.S9	9. Complete the appropriate checklist.
PA.IV.M.S10	10. Execute a timely go-around decision when the approach cannot be made within the tolerances specified above.

IV. Takeoffs, Landings, and Go-Arounds

Task	*Task N. Go-Around/Rejected Landing*
References	FAA-H-8083-3, FAA-H-8083-23; POH/AFM
Objective	To determine that the applicant exhibits satisfactory knowledge, risk management, and skills associated with a go-around/rejected landing with emphasis on factors that contribute to landing conditions that may require a go-around.
Knowledge	The applicant demonstrates understanding of:
PA.IV.N.K1	1. Landing distance.
PA.IV.N.K2	2. Stabilized approach.
PA.IV.N.K3	3. Energy management.
PA.IV.N.K4	4. Wind conditions and effects.
PA.IV.N.K5	5. Communication procedures.
Risk Management	The applicant demonstrates the ability to identify, assess and mitigate risks, encompassing:
PA.IV.N.R1	1. Failure to make a timely go-around/rejected landing decision.
PA.IV.N.R2	2. Task management.
PA.IV.N.R3	3. Low altitude maneuvering.
PA.IV.N.R4	4. Slow flight.
PA.IV.N.R5	5. Collision avoidance, scanning, obstacle and wire strike avoidance.
PA.IV.N.R6	6. Failure to follow the right-of-way rules.
PA.IV.N.R7	7. Obstacles on approach and departure paths.
PA.IV.N.R8	8. Low altitude stall/spin.
PA.IV.N.R9	9. Elevator trim stalls.
PA.IV.N.R10	10. Indecision or changing the go-around/rejected landing decision.
PA.IV.N.R11	11. Failure to adhere to sterile cockpit requirement.
Skills	The applicant demonstrates the ability to:
PA.IV.N.S1	1. Make a timely decision to discontinue the approach to landing.
PA.IV.N.S2	2. Apply takeoff power immediately and transition to climb pitch attitude for V_X or V_Y as appropriate +10/−5 knots.
PA.IV.N.S3	3. Retract the flaps, as appropriate.
PA.IV.N.S4	4. Retract the landing gear after establishing a positive rate of climb and in accordance with manufacturer's guidance.
PA.IV.N.S5	5. Maneuver to the side of the runway/landing area when necessary to clear and avoid conflicting traffic.
PA.IV.N.S6	6. Maintain takeoff power V_Y +10/−5 knots or to a safe maneuvering altitude.
PA.IV.N.S7	7. Maintain directional control and proper wind-drift correction throughout the climb.
PA.IV.N.S8	8. Complete the appropriate checklist.

V. Performance Maneuvers

Task	*Task A. Steep Turns*
References	FAA-H-8083-2, FAA-H-8083-3; POH/AFM
Objective	To determine that the applicant exhibits satisfactory knowledge, risk management, and skills associated with steep turns.
Knowledge	The applicant demonstrates understanding of:
PA.V.A.K1	1. Coordinated flight.
PA.V.A.K2	2. Attitude control at various airspeeds.
PA.V.A.K3	3. Maneuvering speed, including changes in weight.
PA.V.A.K4	4. Controlling rate and radius of turn.
PA.V.A.K5	5. Accelerated stalls.
PA.V.A.K6	6. Overbanking tendencies.
PA.V.A.K6	7. Use of trim in a turn.
PA.V.A.K6	8. Aerodynamics associated with steep turns.
PA.V.A.K6	9. Aerobatic requirements and limitations.
Risk Management	The applicant demonstrates the ability to identify, assess and mitigate risks, encompassing:
PA.V.A.R1	1. Failure to divide the attention between airplane control and orientation.
PA.V.A.R2	2. Task management.
PA.V.A.R3	3. Energy management.
PA.V.A.R4	4. Accelerated stalls.
PA.V.A.R5	5. Spins.
PA.V.A.R6	6. Failure to maintain situational awareness.
PA.V.A.R7	7. Collision avoidance, scanning, obstacle and wire strike avoidance.
PA.V.A.R8	8. Failure to maintain coordinated flight.
Skills	The applicant demonstrates the ability to:
PA.V.A.S1	1. Establish the manufacturer's recommended airspeed or if one is not stated, a safe airspeed not to exceed V_A.
PA.V.A.S2	2. Roll into a coordinated 360° steep turn with a 45° bank.
PA.V.A.S3	3. Perform the Task in the opposite direction, as specified by the evaluator.
PA.V.A.S4	4. Maintain the entry altitude ±100 feet, airspeed ±10 knots, bank ±5°; and roll out on the entry heading, ±10° or as recommended by aircraft manufacturer to a safe maneuvering altitude.

V.   Performance Maneuvers

Task	*Task B. Ground Reference Maneuvers*		
References	14 CFR part 61; FAA-H-8083-2, FAA-H-8083-3		
Objective	To determine that the applicant exhibits satisfactory knowledge, risk management, and skills associated with ground reference maneuvering which may include a rectangular course, S-turns, or turns around a point.		
Knowledge	The applicant demonstrates understanding of:		
PA.V.B.K1	1.	The effects of wind on ground track and relation to a ground reference point.	
PA.V.B.K2	2.	The effects of bank angle and groundspeed on rate and radius of turn.	
PA.V.B.K3	3.	The entry/exit requirements of maneuver.	
PA.V.B.K4	4.	The relationship of rectangular course to airport traffic pattern.	
PA.V.B.K5	5.	Emergency landing considerations while conducting a ground reference maneuver.	
PA.V.B.K6	6.	S-turns and how they can be performed to increase separation from other aircraft.	
Risk Management	The applicant demonstrates the ability to identify, assess and mitigate risks, encompassing:		
PA.V.B.R1	1.	Collision avoidance, scanning, obstacle and wire strike avoidance.	
PA.V.B.R2	2.	Low altitude maneuvering.	
PA.V.B.R3	3.	Task management.	
PA.V.B.R4	4.	Failure to maintain aircraft control.	
PA.V.B.R5	5.	Failure to select a suitable emergency landing area.	
Skills	The applicant demonstrates the ability to:		
PA.V.B.S1	1.	Determine the area is clear of terrain, obstacles, and other aircraft and the aircraft will remain in the appropriate airspace.	
PA.V.B.S2	2.	Select a suitable ground reference.	
PA.V.B.S3	3.	Identify a suitable emergency landing area.	
PA.V.B.S4	4.	Plan the maneuver: ***Note:** The evaluator must select at least one maneuver for the applicant to demonstrate.*	
PA.V.B.S4a		a.	Rectangular course: enter a left or right pattern, 600 to 1,000 feet above ground level (AGL) at an appropriate distance from the selected reference area, 45° to the downwind leg
PA.V.B.S4b		b.	S-turns: enter perpendicular to the selected reference line, 600 to 1,000 feet AGL at an appropriate distance from the selected reference area
PA.V.B.S4c		c.	Turns around a point: enter at an appropriate distance from the reference point, 600 to 1,000 feet AGL at an appropriate distance from the selected reference area
PA.V.B.S5	5.	Apply adequate wind drift correction during straight and turning flight to maintain a constant ground track if around a rectangular reference area or to track a constant radius turn on each side of the selected reference line or a selected point.	
PA.V.B.S6	6.	If performing a pattern such as S-Turns, reverse the turn directly over the selected reference line; if performing turns around a point, complete turns in either direction around the selected reference point.	
PA.V.E.S7	7.	Divide attention between airplane control, traffic avoidance and the ground track while maintaining coordinated flight.	
PA.V.E.S8	8.	Maintain altitude ±100 feet; maintain airspeed ±10 knots or as recommended by aircraft manufacturer to a safe maneuvering altitude.	

VI. Navigation

Task	Task A. Pilotage and Dead Reckoning
References	14 CFR part 61; FAA-H-8083-2, FAA-H-8083-25; Navigation Charts
Objective	To determine that the applicant exhibits satisfactory knowledge, risk management, and skills associated with pilotage and dead reckoning.
Knowledge	The applicant demonstrates understanding of:
PA.VI.A.K1	1. Pilotage and dead reckoning.
PA.VI.A.K2	2. Determining heading, speed, and course.
PA.VI.A.K3	3. Estimating time, speed, and distance.
PA.VI.A.K4	4. True airspeed and density altitude.
PA.VI.A.K5	5. Wind correction angle.
PA.VI.A.K6	6. Checkpoint selection.
PA.VI.A.K7	7. Planned versus actual flight plan calculations and required corrections.
PA.VI.A.K8	8. Topography.
PA.VI.A.K9	9. Plotting a course.
PA.VI.A.K10	10. Magnetic compass errors.
PA.VI.A.K11	11. Route selection.
PA.VI.A.K12	12. Altitude selection.
PA.VI.A.K13	13. Power setting selection.
Risk Management	The applicant demonstrates the ability to identify, assess and mitigate risks, encompassing:
PA.VI.A.R1	1. Failure to select an altitude that will maintain the minimally required obstacle clearance.
PA.VI.A.R2	2. Failure to identify the correct landmarks or checkpoints.
PA.VI.A.R3	3. Bracketing strategy.
PA.VI.A.R4	4. Failure to select a suitable alternate.
PA.VI.A.R5	5. Failure to maintain situational awareness.
PA.VI.A.R6	6. Task management.
PA.VI.A.R7	7. Fuel consumption that is different than planned.
PA.VI.A.R8	8. Having to divert to an alternate airport.
PA.VI.A.R9	9. Preflight pilot/operation risk assessment and planning.
PA.VI.A.R10	10. Actual groundspeed and time en route that are different than planned.
Skills	The applicant demonstrates the ability to:
PA.VI.A.S1	1. Prepare a document or electronic equivalent to be used in flight for comparison with planned fuel consumption and times over waypoints while dead reckoning.
PA.VI.A.S2	2. Follow the preplanned course by reference to landmarks.
PA.VI.A.S3	3. Identify landmarks by relating surface features to chart symbols.
PA.VI.A.S4	4. Navigate by means of pre-computed headings, groundspeeds, and elapsed time.
PA.VI.A.S5	5. Demonstrate use of magnetic direction indicator in navigation, to include turns to headings.
PA.VI.A.S6	6. Correct for and record the differences between preflight groundspeed, fuel consumption, and heading calculations and those determined en route.
PA.VI.A.S7	7. Verify the airplane's position within 3 nautical miles of the flight planned route.
PA.VI.A.S8	8. Arrive at the en route checkpoints within 5 minutes of the initial or revised estimated time of arrival and provide a destination estimate.
PA.VI.A.S9	9. Maintain the selected altitude, ±200 feet and headings, ±15°.

VI. Navigation

Task	Task B. Navigation Systems and Radar Services
References	FAA-H-8083-2, FAA-H-8083-3, FAA-H-8083-6, FAA-H-8083-25; Navigation Equipment Manual; AIM
Objective	To determine that the applicant exhibits satisfactory knowledge, risk management, and skills associated with navigation systems and radar services.
Knowledge	The applicant demonstrates understanding of:
PA.VI.B.K1	1. Ground-based navigation (orientation, course determination, equipment, tests and regulations).
PA.VI.B.K2	2. Satellite-based navigation (e.g., equipment, regulations, authorized use of databases, Receiver Autonomous Integrity Monitoring (RAIM)).
PA.VI.B.K3	3. Radar assistance to VFR aircraft (e.g., operations, equipment, available services, traffic advisories).
PA.VI.B.K4	4. Transponder (Mode(s) A, C, and S)
Risk Management	The applicant demonstrates the ability to identify, assess and mitigate risks, encompassing:
PA.VI.B.R1	1. Failure to manage automated navigation and autoflight systems.
PA.VI.B.R2	2. Task management.
PA.VI.B.R3	3. Failure to maintain situational awareness.
PA.VI.B.R4	4. Limitations of the navigation system in use.
PA.VI.B.R5	5. Automation distractions.
Skills	The applicant demonstrates the ability to:
PA.VI.B.S1	1. Use an installed electronic navigation system.
PA.VI.B.S2	2. Locate the airplane's position using the navigation system.
PA.VI.B.S3	3. Intercept and track a given course, radial, or bearing, as appropriate.
PA.VI.B.S4	4. Recognize and describe the indication of station passage, if appropriate.
PA.VI.B.S5	5. Recognize signal loss and take appropriate action.
PA.VI.B.S6	6. Use proper communication procedures when utilizing radar services.
PA.VI.B.S7	7. Maintain the appropriate altitude, ±200 feet and headings ±15° or as recommended by aircraft manufacturer to a safe maneuvering altitude.

VI.   Navigation

Task	*Task C. Diversion*
References	FAA-H-8083-2, FAA-H-8083-25; AIM; Navigation Charts
Objective	To determine that the applicant exhibits satisfactory knowledge, risk management, and skills associated with diversion.
Knowledge	The applicant demonstrates understanding of:
PA.VI.C.K1	1. Selecting an alternate destination.
PA.VI.C.K2	2. Deviating from ATC instructions and/or the flight plan.
Risk Management	The applicant demonstrates the ability to identify, assess and mitigate risks, encompassing:
PA.VI.C.R1	1. Failure to make a timely decision to divert.
PA.VI.C.R2	2. Failure to select an appropriate airport.
PA.VI.C.R3	3. Maintaining airmanship during diversion.
PA.VI.C.R4	4. Collision avoidance, scanning, obstacle and wire strike avoidance.
PA.VI.C.R5	5. Terrain along the diversion flight path.
PA.VI.C.R6	6. Failure to manage tasks associated with diverting to another airport.
PA.VI.C.R7	7. Failure to maintain situational awareness.
PA.VI.C.R8	8. Failure to utilize all available resources while diverting (e.g., automation, ATC, and cockpit planning aids).
Skills	The applicant demonstrates the ability to:
PA.VI.C.S1	1. Select an appropriate diversion airport and route.
PA.VI.C.S2	2. Make an accurate estimate of heading, groundspeed, arrival time, and fuel consumption to the divert airport.
PA.VI.C.S3	3. Maintain the appropriate altitude, ±200 feet and heading, ±15° or as recommended by aircraft manufacturer to a safe maneuvering altitude.

VI. Navigation

Task	Task D. Lost Procedures
References	FAA-H-8083-2, FAA-H-8083-25; AIM; Navigation Charts
Objective	To determine that the applicant exhibits satisfactory knowledge, risk management, and skills associated with lost procedures and taking appropriate steps to achieve a satisfactory outcome if lost.
Knowledge	The applicant demonstrates understanding of:
PA.VI.D.K1	1. The value of recording time at waypoints.
PA.VI.D.K2	2. The assistance available if lost (radar services, communication procedures).
PA.VI.D.K3	3. The responsibility and authority of the PIC.
PA.VI.D.K4	4. Deviation from ATC instructions.
PA.VI.D.K5	5. Declaring an emergency.
Risk Management	The applicant demonstrates the ability to identify, assess and mitigate risks, encompassing:
PA.VI.D.R1	1. Failure to record times over waypoints.
PA.VI.D.R2	2. Failure to manage tasks with lost procedures.
PA.VI.D.R3	3. Situational awareness.
PA.VI.D.R4	4. Collision avoidance, scanning, obstacle and wire strike avoidance.
PA.VI.D.R5	5. Failure to seek assistance or declare an emergency in a deteriorating situation.
Skills	The applicant demonstrates the ability to:
PA.VI.D.S1	1. Select an appropriate course of action.
PA.VI.D.S2	2. Maintain an appropriate heading and climbs, if necessary.
PA.VI.D.S3	3. Identify prominent landmarks.
PA.VI.D.S4	4. Use navigation systems/facilities and/or contacts an ATC facility for assistance, as appropriate.

VII.   Slow Flight and Stalls

Task	Task A. Maneuvering during Slow Flight
References	FAA-H-8083-2, FAA-H-8083-3; POH/AFM
Objective	To determine that the applicant exhibits satisfactory knowledge, risk management, and skills associated with maneuvering during slow flight.
Knowledge	The applicant demonstrates understanding of:
PA.VII.A.K1	1. This maneuver as it applies to different phases of flight.
PA.VII.A.K2	2. The relationship between angle of attack (AOA), airspeed, load factor, aircraft configuration, aircraft weight, and aircraft attitude.
PA.VII.A.K3	3. The range and limitations of stall warning indicators (e.g., aircraft buffet, stall horn, etc.).
PA.VII.A.K4	4. The difference between AOA and aircraft attitude during all flight conditions and how it relates to aircraft performance.
PA.VII.A.K5	5. How environmental elements affect aircraft performance.
PA.VII.A.K6	6. The importance of the 1,500-foot AGL minimum altitude.
Risk Management	The applicant demonstrates the ability to identify, assess and mitigate risks, encompassing:
PA.VII.A.R1	1. The interplay of aerodynamic factors (angle of attack (AOA), airspeed, load factor, aircraft configuration, aircraft weight, and aircraft attitude).
PA.VII.A.R2	2. Range and limitations of stall warning indicators (e.g., aircraft buffet, stall horn, etc.).
PA.VII.A.R3	3. The effect of environmental elements on aircraft performance.
PA.VII.A.R4	4. Collision avoidance, scanning, obstacle and wire strike avoidance.
PA.VII.A.R5	5. Failure to react appropriately to a stall warning.
PA.VII.A.R6	6. Failure to maintain coordinated flight during the maneuver.
PA.VII.A.R7	7. Failure to manage pitch attitude and power to avoid a stall warning or a stall.
Skills	The applicant demonstrates the ability to:
PA.VII.A.S1	1. Select an entry altitude that will allow the Task to be completed no lower than 1,500 feet AGL.
PA.VII.A.S2	2. Establish and maintain an airspeed, approximately 5-10 knots above the 1G stall speed, at which the airplane is capable of maintaining controlled flight without activating a stall warning.
PA.VII.A.S3	3. Accomplish coordinated straight-and-level flight, turns, climbs, and descents with landing gear and flap configurations specified by the evaluator without activating a stall warning.
PA.VII.A.S4	4. Divide attention between airplane control, traffic avoidance and orientation.
PA.VII.A.S5	5. Maintain the specified altitude, ±100 feet; specified heading, ±10°; airspeed, +10/-0 knots; and specified angle of bank, ±10° or as recommended by aircraft manufacturer to a safe maneuvering altitude.

VII. Slow Flight and Stalls

Task	*Task B. Power-Off Stalls*
References	FAA-H-8083-2, FAA-H-8083-3; AC 61-67; POH/AFM
Objective	To determine that the applicant exhibits satisfactory knowledge, risk management, and skills associated with power-off stalls.
Knowledge	The applicant demonstrates understanding of:
PA.VII.B.K1	1. The importance of the 1,500-foot AGL minimum altitude.
PA.VII.B.K2	2. How the maneuver relates to a normal flight.
PA.VII.B.K3	3. The components of a stabilized descent.
PA.VII.B.K4	4. Approach to stall indications.
PA.VII.B.K5	5. Full stall indications.
PA.VII.B.K6	6. Which aircraft inputs are required to meet heading or bank angle requirements.
PA.VII.B.K7	7. The stall recovery procedure.
PA.VII.B.K8	8. The importance of establishing the correct aircraft configuration during the recovery process and the consequences of failing to do so.
PA.VII.B.K9	9. Aerodynamics associated with stalls and spins in various aircraft configurations and attitudes.
PA.VII.B.K10	10. The circumstances that can lead to an inadvertent stall or spin.
Risk Management	The applicant demonstrates the ability to identify, assess and mitigate risks, encompassing:
PA.VII.B.R1	1. The interplay of aerodynamic factors (angle of attack (AOA), airspeed, load factor, aircraft configuration, aircraft weight, and aircraft attitude).
PA.VII.B.R2	2. The range and limitations of stall warning indicators (e.g., aircraft buffet, stall horn, etc.).
PA.VII.B.R3	3. The effect of environmental elements on aircraft performance.
PA.VII.B.R4	4. Required actions for aircraft maximum performance and the consequences of failing to do so.
PA.VII.B.R5	5. Collision avoidance, scanning, obstacle and wire strike avoidance.
PA.VII.B.R6	6. Failure to follow the stall recovery procedure.
PA.VII.B.R7	7. Failure to maintain coordinated flight during the maneuver.
PA.VII.B.R8	8. Secondary stalls.
PA.VII.B.R9	9. Inadvertent stall or spin.
Skills	The applicant demonstrates the ability to:
PA.VII.B.S1	1. Select an entry altitude that will allow the Task to be completed no lower than 1,500 feet AGL.
PA.VII.B.S2	2. Establish a stabilized descent in the approach or landing configuration, as specified by the evaluator.
PA.VII.B.S3	3. Transition smoothly from the approach or landing attitude to a pitch attitude that will induce a stall.
PA.VII.B.S4	4. Maintain a specified heading, ±10°, if in straight flight, and maintain a specified angle of bank not to exceed 20°, ±10° if in turning flight, while inducing the stall or as recommended by the aircraft manufacturer to a safe maneuvering altitude.
PA.VII.B.S5	5. Recognize and recover promptly after a full stall has occurred.
PA.VII.B.S6	6. Retract the flaps to the recommended setting; retract the landing gear, if retractable, after a positive rate of climb is established.
PA.VII.B.S7	7. Execute a stall recovery in accordance with procedures set forth in the AFM/POH.
PA.VII.B.S8	8. Accelerates to V_X or V_Y speed before the final flap retraction and return to the altitude, heading and airspeed specified by the examiner.

VII.   Slow Flight and Stalls

Task	**Task C. Power-On Stalls**
References	FAA-H-8083-2, FAA-H-8083-3; AC 61-67; POH/AFM
Objective	To determine that the applicant exhibits satisfactory knowledge, risk management, and skills associated with power-on stalls.
Knowledge	The applicant demonstrates understanding of:
PA.VII.C.K1	1. The importance of the 1,500-foot AGL minimum altitude.
PA.VII.C.K2	2. How the maneuver relates to a normal flight.
PA.VII.C.K3	3. Rationale for power setting variances.
PA.VII.C.K4	4. Approach to stall indications.
PA.VII.C.K5	5. Full stall indications.
PA.VII.C.K6	6. Which aircraft inputs are required to meet heading or bank angle requirements.
PA.VII.C.K7	7. Determining the most efficient stall recovery procedure.
PA.VII.C.K8	8. The importance of establishing the correct aircraft configuration during the recovery process and the consequences of failing to do so.
PA.VII.C.K9	9. The aerodynamics associated with stalls and spins in various aircraft configurations and attitudes.
PA.VII.C.K10	10. The circumstances that can lead to an inadvertent stall or spin.
PA.VII.C.K11	11. The circumstances that can lead to an accelerated stall.
Risk Management	The applicant demonstrates the ability to identify, assess and mitigate risks, encompassing:
PA.VII.C.R1	1. Aerodynamic factors (angle of attack (AOA), airspeed, load factor, aircraft configuration, aircraft weight, and aircraft attitude).
PA.VII.C.R2	2. The range and limitations of stall warning indicators (e.g., aircraft buffet, stall horn, etc.).
PA.VII.C.R3	3. The effect of environmental elements on aircraft performance.
PA.VII.C.R4	4. Required actions for aircraft maximum performance and the consequences of failing to do so.
PA.VII.C.R5	5. Accelerated stalls.
PA.VII.C.R6	6. Collision avoidance, scanning, obstacle and wire strike avoidance.
PA.VII.C.R7	7. Failure to follow the stall recovery procedure.
PA.VII.C.R8	8. Failure to maintain coordinated flight during the maneuver.
PA.VII.C.R9	9. Secondary stalls.
PA.VII.C.R10	10. Inadvertent stall or spin.
Skills	The applicant demonstrates the ability to:
PA.VII.C.S1	1. Select an entry altitude that will allow the Task to be completed no lower than 1,500 feet AGL.
PA.VII.C.S2	2. Establish the takeoff, departure, or cruise configuration as specified by the evaluator.
PA.VII.C.S3	3. Set power (as assigned by the evaluator) to no less than 65 percent available power.
PA.VII.C.S4	4. Transition smoothly from the takeoff or departure attitude to the pitch attitude that will induce a stall.
PA.VII.C.S5	5. Maintain a specified heading, ±10°, if in straight flight, and maintain a specified angle of bank not to exceed 20°, ±10°, if in turning flight, while inducing the stall or as recommended by the aircraft manufacturer to a safe maneuvering altitude.
PA.VII.C.S6	6. Recognize and recover promptly after a fully developed stall occurs.
PA.VII.C.S7	7. Retract the flaps to the recommended setting; retract the landing gear if retractable, after a positive rate of climb is established.
PA.VII.C.S8	8. Execute a stall recovery in accordance with procedures set forth in the AFM/POH.
PA.VII.C.S9	9. Accelerate to V_X or V_Y speed before the final flap retraction; return to the altitude, heading, and airspeed specified by the evaluator.

VII. Slow Flight and Stalls

Task	*Task D. Spin Awareness*
References	FAA-H-8083-2, FAA-H-8083-3; AC 61-67; POH/AFM
Objective	To determine that the applicant exhibits satisfactory knowledge, risk management, and skills associated with spins, flight situations where unintentional spins may occur and procedures for recovery from unintentional spins.
Knowledge	The applicant demonstrates understanding of:
PA.VII.D.K1	1. Aerodynamics associated with stalls and spins in various aircraft configurations and attitudes.
PA.VII.D.K2	2. The circumstances that can lead to an inadvertent stall or spin.
PA.VII.D.K3	3. Spin recovery procedures.
Risk Management	The applicant demonstrates the ability to identify, assess and mitigate risks, encompassing:
PA.VII.D.R1	1. The interplay of aerodynamic factors (angle of attack (AOA), airspeed, load factor, aircraft configuration, aircraft weight, and aircraft attitude).
PA.VII.D.R2	2. The range and limitations of stall warning indicators (e.g., aircraft buffet, stall horn, etc.).
PA.VII.D.R3	3. The environmental element effects on aircraft performance.
PA.VII.D.R4	4. The required actions for aircraft maximum performance and the consequences of failing to do so.
PA.VII.D.R5	5. Uncoordinated flight.
PA.VII.D.R6	6. Hazards associated with the improper application of flight control inputs during the spin recovery.
PA.VII.D.R7	7. Collision avoidance, scanning, obstacle and wire strike avoidance.
Skills	The applicant demonstrates the ability to:
PA.VII.D.S1	1. Assess and avoid situations where unintentional spins may occur.
PA.VII.D.S2	2. Explain procedures for recovery from unintentional spins.

VIII.   Basic Instrument Maneuvers

Task	*Task A. Straight-and-Level Flight*
References	FAA-H-8083-2, FAA-H-8083-3, FAA-H-8083-15
Objective	To determine that the applicant exhibits satisfactory knowledge, risk management, and skills associated with attitude instrument flying during straight-and-level flight.
Knowledge	The applicant demonstrates understanding of:
PA.VIII.A.K1	1. Flight instrument function and operation.
PA.VIII.A.K2	2. Flight instrument sensitivity, limitations, and potential errors in unusual attitudes.
PA.VIII.A.K3	3. Flight instrument correlation (pitch instruments/bank instruments).
PA.VIII.A.K4	4. Aerodynamic factors related to maintaining straight-and-level flight.
PA.VIII.A.K5	5. Vestibular illusions (leans) and spatial disorientation.
PA.VIII.A.K6	6. Appropriate pitch, bank, and power settings for the airplane being flown.
Risk Management	The applicant demonstrates the ability to identify, assess and mitigate risks, encompassing:
PA.VIII.A.R1	1. Lack of proficiency in flight by reference to instruments.
PA.VIII.A.R2	2. Poor cockpit management.
PA.VIII.A.R3	3. Lack of awareness of the direction for the nearest VMC.
PA.VIII.A.R4	4. Continued flight into IMC or conditions outside of personal minimums.
PA.VIII.A.R5	5. Loss of situational awareness during low visibility and/or instrument conditions.
PA.VIII.A.R6	6. The hazards of abrupt control movements when flying by sole reference to instruments.
Skills	The applicant demonstrates the ability to:
PA.VIII.A.S1	1. Control the aircraft solely by reference to instruments in straight-and-level flight.
PA.VIII.A.S2	2. Perform an instrument scan and instrument cross-check.
PA.VIII.A.S3	3. Perform coordinated, smooth control application to correct for altitude, heading, airspeed, and bank deviations during straight-and-level flight.
PA.VIII.A.S4	4. Maintain altitude ±200 feet, heading ±20° and airspeed ±10 knots.

VIII. Basic Instrument Maneuvers

Task	*Task B. Constant Airspeed Climbs*
References	FAA-H-8083-2, FAA-H-8083-3, FAA-H-8083-15
Objective	To determine that the applicant exhibits satisfactory knowledge, risk management, and skills associated with attitude instrument flying during constant airspeed climbs.
Knowledge	The applicant demonstrates understanding of:
PA.VIII.B.K1	1. Flight instrument function and operation.
PA.VIII.B.K2	2. Flight instrument sensitivity, limitations, and potential errors in unusual attitudes.
PA.VIII.B.K3	3. Flight instrument correlation (pitch instruments/bank instruments).
PA.VIII.B.K4	4. Vestibular illusions (leans) and spatial disorientation.
PA.VIII.B.K5	5. Aerodynamic factors related to establishing and maintaining a constant airspeed climb, making turns while climbing, and then returning to level flight.
PA.VIII.B.K6	6. Appropriate pitch, bank, and power settings for the airplane being flown.
Risk Management	The applicant demonstrates the ability to identify, assess and mitigate risks, encompassing:
PA.VIII.B.R1	1. Lack of proficiency in flight by reference to instruments.
PA.VIII.B.R2	2. Poor cockpit management.
PA.VIII.B.R3	3. Lack of awareness of the direction for the nearest VMC.
PA.VIII.B.R4	4. Failure to descend straight ahead or make level turns under emergency instrument conditions.
PA.VIII.B.R5	5. Continued flight into IMC or conditions outside of personal minimums.
PA.VIII.B.R6	6. Loss of situational awareness during low visibility or instrument conditions.
Skills	The applicant demonstrates the ability to:
PA.VIII.B.S1	1. Control the aircraft solely by reference to instruments.
PA.VIII.B.S2	2. Perform an instrument scan and instrument cross-check.
PA.VIII.B.S3	3. Transition to the climb pitch attitude and power setting on an assigned heading using proper instrument cross-check and interpretation, and coordinated flight control application.
PA.VIII.B.S4	4. Demonstrate climbs solely by reference to instruments at a constant airspeed to specific altitudes in straight flight and turns.
PA.VIII.B.S5	5. Perform coordinated, smooth control application to correct for airspeed, heading and bank deviations during climb and then for level off.
PA.VIII.B.S6	6. Perform appropriate trimming to relieve control pressures.
PA.VIII.B.S7	7. Level off at the assigned altitude and maintain altitude ±200 feet, heading ±20° and airspeed ±10 knots.

VIII.   Basic Instrument Maneuvers

Task	Task C. Constant Airspeed Descents	
References	FAA-H-8083-2, FAA-H-8083-3, FAA-H-8083-15	
Objective	To determine that the applicant exhibits satisfactory knowledge, risk management, and skills associated with attitude instrument flying during constant airspeed descents.	
Knowledge	The applicant demonstrates understanding of:	
PA.VIII.C.K1	1.	Flight instrument function and operation.
PA.VIII.C.K2	2.	Flight instrument sensitivity, limitations, and potential errors in unusual attitudes.
PA.VIII.C.K3	3.	Flight instrument correlation (pitch instruments/bank instruments).
PA.VIII.C.K4	4.	Vestibular illusions (leans) and spatial disorientation.
PA.VIII.C.K5	5.	Aerodynamic factors related to establishing and maintaining a constant airspeed descent, making turns while descending, and then returning to level flight.
PA.VIII.C.K6	6.	Appropriate pitch, power and bank settings for the airplane being flown.
Risk Management	The applicant demonstrates the ability to identify, assess and mitigate risks, encompassing:	
PA.VIII.C.R1	1.	Lack of proficiency in flight by reference to instruments.
PA.VIII.C.R2	2.	Poor cockpit management.
PA.VIII.C.R3	3.	Lack of awareness of the direction for the nearest VMC.
PA.VIII.C.R4	4.	Failure to descend straight ahead or make level turns under emergency instrument conditions.
PA.VIII.C.R5	5.	Continued flight into IMC or conditions outside of personal minimums.
PA.VIII.C.R6	6.	Loss of situational awareness during low visibility or instrument conditions.
Skills	The applicant demonstrates the ability to:	
PA.VIII.C.S1	1.	Control the aircraft solely by reference to instruments.
PA.VIII.C.S2	2.	Perform an instrument scan and instrument cross-check.
PA.VIII.C.S3	3.	Establish the descent configuration specified by the evaluator.
PA.VIII.C.S4	4.	Transition to the descent pitch attitude and power setting on an assigned heading using proper instrument cross-check and interpretation, and coordinated flight control application.
PA.VIII.C.S5	5.	Demonstrate descents solely by reference to instruments at a constant airspeed to specific altitudes in straight flight and turns.
PA.VIII.C.S6	6.	Perform appropriate trimming to relieve control pressures.
PA.VIII.C.S7	7.	Level off at the assigned altitude and maintain altitude ±200 feet, heading ±20° and airspeed ±10 knots.

VIII. Basic Instrument Maneuvers

Task	*Task D. Turns to Headings*
References	FAA-H-8083-2, FAA-H-8083-3, FAA-H-8083-15
Objective	To determine that the applicant exhibits satisfactory knowledge, risk management, and skills associated with attitude instrument flying during turns to headings.
Knowledge	The applicant demonstrates understanding of:
PA.VIII.D.K1	1. Flight instrument function and operation.
PA.VIII.D.K2	2. Flight instrument sensitivity, limitations, and potential errors in unusual attitudes.
PA.VIII.D.K3	3. Flight instrument correlation (pitch instruments/bank instruments).
PA.VIII.D.K4	4. Vestibular illusions (leans) and spatial disorientation.
PA.VIII.D.K5	5. Aerodynamic factors related to establishing turns while maintaining level flight.
PA.VIII.D.K6	6. Appropriate pitch, power and bank settings for the airplane being flown.
Risk Management	The applicant demonstrates the ability to identify, assess and mitigate risks, encompassing:
PA.VIII.D.R1	1. Lack of proficiency in flight by reference to instruments.
PA.VIII.D.R2	2. Poor cockpit management.
PA.VIII.D.R3	3. Lack of awareness of the direction for the nearest VMC.
PA.VIII.D.R4	4. Failure to descend straight ahead or make level turns under emergency instrument conditions.
PA.VIII.D.R5	5. Continued flight into IMC or conditions outside of personal minimums.
PA.VIII.D.R6	6. Loss of situational awareness during low visibility or instrument conditions.
Skills	The applicant demonstrates the ability to:
PA.VIII.D.S1	1. Control the aircraft solely by reference to instruments.
PA.VIII.D.S2	2. Perform an instrument scan and instrument cross-check.
PA.VIII.D.S3	3. Perform coordinated, smooth flight control application to establish a standard rate turn, to correct for altitude and bank deviations, and to rollout on a specified heading.
PA.VIII.D.S4	4. Perform appropriate trimming to relieve control pressures.
PA.VIII.D.S5	5. Demonstrate turns to headings solely by reference to instruments, maintain altitude ±200 feet and maintain a standard rate turn and rolls out on the assigned heading ±10°; maintain airspeed ±10 knots.

VIII.   Basic Instrument Maneuvers

Task	*Task E. Recovery from Unusual Flight Attitudes*
References	FAA-H-8083-2, FAA-H-8083-3, FAA-H-8083-15
Objective	To determine that the applicant exhibits satisfactory knowledge, risk management, and skills associated with attitude instrument flying while recovering from unusual attitudes.
Knowledge	The applicant demonstrates understanding of:
PA.VIII.E.K1	1. Flight instrument function and operation.
PA.VIII.E.K2	2. Flight instrument sensitivity, limitations, and potential errors in unusual attitudes.
PA.VIII.E.K3	3. Flight instrument correlation (pitch instruments/bank instruments).
PA.VIII.E.K4	4. Vestibular illusions (leans) and spatial disorientation.
PA.VIII.E.K5	5. Aerodynamic factors related to unusual pitch and bank attitudes and returning to level flight.
PA.VIII.E.K6	6. The appropriate pitch, power and bank settings for airplane being flown.
PA.VIII.E.K7	7. The hazards of inappropriate control response.
Risk Management	The applicant demonstrates the ability to identify, assess and mitigate risks, encompassing:
PA.VIII.E.R1	1. Lack of proficiency in flight by reference to instruments.
PA.VIII.E.R2	2. Poor cockpit management.
PA.VIII.E.R3	3. Lack of awareness of the direction for the nearest VMC.
PA.VIII.E.R4	4. Failure to descend straight ahead or make level turns under emergency instrument conditions.
PA.VIII.E.R5	5. Operating outside of the normal operating envelope during the recovery.
Skills	The applicant demonstrates the ability to:
PA.VIII.E.S1	1. Perform timely recognition of the nature of the unusual attitude.
PA.VIII.E.S2	2. Recognize unusual flight attitudes solely by reference to instruments and perform the correct, coordinated, and smooth flight control application to resolve unusual pitch and bank attitudes while staying within the airplane's limitations and flight parameters.
PA.VIII.E.S3	3. Perform appropriate trimming to relieve control pressures.
PA.VIII.E.S4	4. When level, maintain altitude ±200 feet, heading ±20° and airspeed ±10 knots.

VIII.   Basic Instrument Maneuvers

Task	**Task F. Radio Communications, Navigation Systems/Facilities, and Radar Services**
References	FAA-H-8083-2, FAA-H-8083-3, FAA-H-8083-15, FAA-H-8083-25
Objective	To determine that the applicant exhibits satisfactory knowledge, risk management, and skills associated with radio communications, navigation systems/facilities, and radar services available for use during flight solely by reference to instruments.
Knowledge	The applicant demonstrates understanding of:
PA.VIII.F.K1	1. Flight instrument function and operation.
PA.VIII.F.K2	2. Flight instrument sensitivity, limitations and potential errors in unusual attitudes.
PA.VIII.F.K3	3. Flight instrument correlation (pitch instruments/bank instruments).
PA.VIII.F.K4	4. How to determine the minimum safe altitude for the location.
PA.VIII.F.K5	5. Radio communications equipment and procedures.
PA.VIII.F.K6	6. Air traffic control facilities and services.
PA.VIII.F.K7	7. Installed navigation equipment function and displays.
PA.VIII.F.K8	8. Pilot interface including: pilot monitoring duties and interaction with charts and avionics equipment.
Risk Management	The applicant demonstrates the ability to identify, assess and mitigate risks, encompassing:
PA.VIII.F.R1	1. Lack of proficiency in flight by reference to instruments.
PA.VIII.F.R2	2. Poor cockpit management.
PA.VIII.F.R3	3. Lack of awareness of the direction for the nearest VMC.
PA.VIII.F.R4	4. Failure to descend straight ahead or make level turns under emergency instrument conditions.
Skills	The applicant demonstrates the ability to:
PA.VIII.F.S1	1. Maintain controlled flight while selecting proper communications frequencies, identifying the appropriate facility, and setting up navigation equipment to select the desired course.
PA.VIII.F.S2	2. Maintain aircraft control while complying with ATC instructions.
PA.VIII.F.S3	3. Maintain aircraft control while navigating using radio aids.
PA.VIII.F.S4	4. Maintain altitude ±200 feet, heading ±20° and airspeed ±10 knots.

IX. Emergency Operations

Task	*Task A. Emergency Descent*
References	FAA-H-8083-2, FAA-H-8083-3; POH/AFM
Objective	To determine that the applicant exhibits satisfactory knowledge, risk management, and skills associated with an emergency descent.
Knowledge	The applicant demonstrates understanding of:
PA.IX.A.K1	1. Glide speed, distance.
PA.IX.A.K2	2. Stabilized approach.
PA.IX.A.K3	3. Energy management.
PA.IX.A.K4	4. Wind conditions and effects.
PA.IX.A.K5	5. Situations, such as depressurization, cockpit smoke and/or engine fire that require an emergency descent.
PA.IX.A.K6	6. Emergency procedures.
PA.IX.A.K7	7. Communications.
PA.IX.A.K8	8. ATC clearance deviations.
PA.IX.A.K9	9. ELTs and/or other emergency locating devices.
PA.IX.A.K10	10. Radar assistance to VFR aircraft.
PA.IX.A.K11	11. Transponder.
Risk Management	The applicant demonstrates the ability to identify, assess and mitigate risks, encompassing:
PA.IX.A.R1	1. Wind.
PA.IX.A.R2	2. Failure to select a suitable landing area.
PA.IX.A.R3	3. Failure to plan and follow a flight pattern to the selected landing area considering altitude, wind, terrain, and obstructions.
PA.IX.A.R4	4. Improper aircraft and propeller configurations.
PA.IX.A.R5	5. Improper management of tasks associated with an emergency descent.
PA.IX.A.R6	6. Low altitude maneuvering.
PA.IX.A.R7	7. Collision avoidance, scanning, obstacle and wire strike avoidance.
PA.IX.A.R8	8. Having the right-of-way in an emergency.
PA.IX.A.R9	9. Failure to maintain situational awareness during an emergency descent.
PA.IX.A.R10	10. Low altitude stalls/spins.
PA.IX.A.R11	11. Difference between using V_{NE} and V_{FE}, and when each one is appropriate.
Skills	The applicant demonstrates the ability to:
PA.IX.A.S1	1. Analyze the situation and select an appropriate course of action.
PA.IX.A.S2	2. Establish and maintain the appropriate airspeed and configuration for the emergency descent.
PA.IX.A.S3	3. Establish appropriate propeller pitch (if constant speed), flap deployment, and gear position (if retractable) relative to the distance and altitude to the selected landing area.
PA.IX.A.S4	4. Exhibit orientation, division of attention and proper planning.
PA.IX.A.S5	5. Maintain positive load factors during the descent.
PA.IX.A.S6	6. Complete the appropriate checklist.

IX. Emergency Operations

Task	*Task B. Emergency Approach and Landing (Simulated)*
References	FAA-H-8083-2, FAA-H-8083-3; POH/AFM
Objective	To determine that the applicant exhibits satisfactory knowledge, risk management, and skills associated with emergency approach and landing procedures.
Knowledge	The applicant demonstrates understanding of:
PA.IX.B.K1	1. Glide speed and distance.
PA.IX.B.K2	2. Landing distance.
PA.IX.B.K3	3. Hazards of other than hard surfaced runway.
PA.IX.B.K4	4. Stabilized approach.
PA.IX.B.K5	5. Energy management.
PA.IX.B.K6	6. Wind conditions and effects.
PA.IX.B.K7	7. Density altitude.
PA.IX.B.K8	8. Emergency procedures.
PA.IX.B.K9	9. Communications.
PA.IX.B.K10	10. ATC clearance deviations.
PA.IX.B.K11	11. Minimum fuel.
PA.IX.B.K12	12. Selecting a landing location.
PA.IX.B.K13	13. ELTs and/or other emergency locating devices.
PA.IX.B.K14	14. Radar assistance to VFR aircraft.
Risk Management	The applicant demonstrates the ability to identify, assess and mitigate risks, encompassing:
PA.IX.B.R1	1. Wind.
PA.IX.B.R2	2. Failure to select a suitable landing area.
PA.IX.B.R3	3. Failure to plan and follow a flight pattern to the selected landing area considering altitude, wind, terrain, and obstructions.
PA.IX.B.R4	4. Improper management of tasks associated with an emergency approach and landing.
PA.IX.B.R5	5. Low altitude maneuvering.
PA.IX.B.R6	6. Startle response.
PA.IX.B.R7	7. Collision avoidance, scanning, obstacle and wire strike avoidance.
PA.IX.B.R8	8. Having the right-of-way in an emergency.
PA.IX.B.R9	9. Obstacles on approach and landing paths.
PA.IX.B.R10	10. Low altitude stall/spin.
PA.IX.B.R11	11. Failure to maintain the appropriate airspeed (e.g., best glide speed, minimum sink speed) or configuration during the descent.
Skills	The applicant demonstrates the ability to:
PA.IX.B.S1	1. Analyze the situation, select an appropriate course of action, and select a suitable landing area.
PA.IX.B.S2	2. Establish and maintain the recommended best-glide airspeed, ±10 knots.
PA.IX.B.S3	3. Plan and follow a flight pattern to the selected landing area considering altitude, wind, terrain, and obstructions that would allow a safe landing.
PA.IX.B.S4	4. Prepare for landing, or go-around, as specified by the evaluator.
PA.IX.B.S5	5. Complete the appropriate checklist.
PA.IX.B.S6	6. Make appropriate radio calls, when conditions allow.

IX. Emergency Operations

Task	*Task C. Systems and Equipment Malfunction*
References	FAA-H-8083-2, FAA-H-8083-3; POH/AFM
Objective	To determine that the applicant exhibits satisfactory knowledge, risk management, and skills associated with system and equipment malfunctions appropriate to the airplane provided for the practical test and analyzing the situation and take appropriate action for simulated emergencies.
Knowledge	The applicant demonstrates understanding of:
PA.IX.C.K1	1. The elements related to system and equipment malfunctions appropriate to the airplane, including:
PA.IX.C.K1a	a. Partial or complete power loss
PA.IX.C.K1b	b. Engine roughness or overheat
PA.IX.C.K1c	c. Carburetor or induction icing
PA.IX.C.K1d	d. Loss of oil pressure
PA.IX.C.K1e	e. Fuel starvation
PA.IX.C.K1f	f. Electrical malfunction
PA.IX.C.K1g	g. Vacuum/pressure, and associated flight instruments malfunction
PA.IX.C.K1h	h. Pitot/static system malfunction
PA.IX.C.K1i	i. Landing gear or flap malfunction
PA.IX.C.K1j	j. Inoperative trim
PA.IX.C.K1k	k. Inadvertent door or window opening
PA.IX.C.K1l	l. Structural icing
PA.IX.C.K1m	m. Smoke/fire/engine compartment fire
PA.IX.C.K1n	n. Any other emergency appropriate to the airplane
PA.IX.C.K1o	o. Glass cockpit operations
PA.IX.C.K2	2. Supplemental oxygen.
PA.IX.C.K3	3. Load factors.
PA.IX.C.K4	4. High drag versus low drag.
Risk Management	The applicant demonstrates the ability to identify, assess and mitigate risks, encompassing:
PA.IX.C.R1	1. Hazardous attitudes.
PA.IX.C.R2	2. Failure to complete a preflight inspection.
PA.IX.C.R3	3. Improper maintenance.
PA.IX.C.R4	4. Failure to use the proper checklist during a system or equipment malfunction.
PA.IX.C.R5	5. Failure to recognize situations, such as:
PA.IX.C.R5a	a. Depressurization
PA.IX.C.R5b	b. Cockpit smoke
PA.IX.C.R5c	c. Fire
PA.IX.C.R6	6. Loss of orientation, failure to divide attention, and improper planning.
PA.IX.C.R7	7. Failure to properly manage the airplane's energy during a system or equipment malfunction.
Skills	The applicant demonstrates the ability to:
PA.IX.C.S1	1. Analyze the situation and take appropriate action for simulated emergencies, with reference to at least three of the systems listed in the Knowledge section above.
PA.IX.C.S2	2. Complete the appropriate checklist or procedure.

IX. Emergency Operations

Task	*Task D. Emergency Equipment and Survival Gear*
References	FAA-H-8083-2, FAA-H-8083-3; POH/AFM
Objective	To determine that the applicant exhibits satisfactory knowledge, risk management, and skills associated with emergency equipment, and survival gear appropriate to the airplane and environment encountered during flight and identifying appropriate equipment that should be onboard the airplane.
Knowledge	The applicant demonstrates understanding of:
PA.IX.D.K1	1. Emergency equipment.
PA.IX.D.K2	2. Climate extremes (hot/cold).
PA.IX.D.K3	3. The hazards of mountainous terrain.
PA.IX.D.K4	4. The hazards of overwater operations.
PA.IX.D.K5	5. Gear to meet basic physical needs until rescue.
PA.IX.D.K6	6. ELT operation, limitations and testing requirements.
Risk Management	The applicant demonstrates the ability to identify, assess and mitigate risks, encompassing:
PA.IX.D.R1	1. Being unprepared to meet basic needs (water, clothing, shelter) for 48 to 72 hours in the event of an unplanned off airport landing.
PA.IX.D.R2	2. Not knowing survival techniques, to include being located by search and rescue, in the event of an unplanned off airport landing.
Skills	The applicant demonstrates the ability to:
PA.IX.D.S1	1. Identify appropriate equipment that should be onboard the airplane.
PA.IX.D.S2	2. Identify appropriate personal gear to meet physical needs until rescue.
PA.IX.D.S3	3. Brief the proper use of the fire extinguisher and other survival equipment.

XI. Night Operations

Task	*Task A. Night Preparation*
References	FAA-H-8083-2, FAA-H-8083-3, FAA-H-8083-25; AIM; POH/AFM
Objective	To determine that the applicant exhibits satisfactory knowledge, risk management, and skills associated with night operations.
Knowledge	The applicant demonstrates understanding of:
PA.XI.A.K1	1. Physiological aspects of night flying as it relates to vision.
PA.XI.A.K2	2. Lighting systems identifying airports, runways, taxiways and obstructions, as well as pilot controlled lighting.
PA.XI.A.K3	3. Airplane equipment requirements for night operations.
PA.XI.A.K4	4. Airplane lighting systems: type, interpretation in flight, when to use each lighting system.
PA.XI.A.K5	5. Personal equipment essential for night flight.
PA.XI.A.K6	6. Night orientation, navigation, and chart reading techniques.
PA.XI.A.K7	7. Safety precautions and emergencies unique to night flying.
PA.XI.A.K8	8. Somatogravic illusion and black hole approach illusion.
PA.XI.A.K9	9. Disorientation that can be experienced in unusual attitudes at night.
PA.XI.A.K10	10. Visual scanning techniques during night operations.
PA.XI.A.K11	11. Hazards of inadvertent IMC.
Risk Management	The applicant demonstrates the ability to identify, assess and mitigate risks, encompassing:
PA.XI.A.R1	1. Collision avoidance, scanning, obstacle and wire strike avoidance.
PA.XI.A.R2	2. Improper planning to avoid terrain.
PA.XI.A.R3	3. Failure to manage Tasks during night operations.
PA.XI.A.R4	4. Failure to maintain situational awareness.
PA.XI.A.R5	5. Environmental considerations at night (e.g., IMC; terrain (roads)).
PA.XI.A.R6	6. Failure to maintain VFR.
PA.XI.A.R7	7. Physiological aspects of night flying.
Skills	*N/A* *Note: Not generally evaluated in flight. If the practical test is conducted at night, all ACS tasks are evaluated in that environment, thus there is no need for explicit task elements to exist here.*

XII. Postflight Procedures

Task	*Task A. After Landing, Parking and Securing*
References	FAA-H-8083-2, FAA-H-8083-3; POH/AFM
Objective	To determine that the applicant exhibits satisfactory knowledge, risk management, and skills associated with after landing, parking, and securing procedures.
Knowledge	The applicant demonstrates understanding of:
PA.XII.A.K1	1. Positioning aircraft controls for wind.
PA.XII.A.K2	2. Familiarity with airport markings (including hold short lines), signs, and lights.
PA.XII.A.K3	3. Aircraft lighting.
PA.XII.A.K4	4. Towered and non-towered airport operations.
PA.XII.A.K5	5. Visual indicators for wind.
PA.XII.A.K6	6. Airport information resources (Chart Supplements U.S., airport diagrams, and appropriate publications).
PA.XII.A.K7	7. Good cockpit discipline during taxi.
PA.XII.A.K8	8. Appropriate taxi speeds.
PA.XII.A.K9	9. Procedures for appropriate cockpit activities during taxiing including taxi route planning, briefing the location of Hot Spots, and communicating and coordinating with ATC.
PA.XII.A.K10	10. Procedures unique to night operations.
PA.XII.A.K11	11. Hazards of low visibility operations.
PA.XII.A.K12	12. The importance of documenting any in-flight/post-flight discrepancies.
PA.XII.A.K13	13. National Transportation Safety Board (NTSB) accident/incident reporting.
Risk Management	The applicant demonstrates the ability to identify, assess and mitigate risks, encompassing:
PA.XII.A.R1	1. Distractions during aircraft taxi and parking.
PA.XII.A.R2	2. The proximity of other aircraft, vehicles, and people when operating on airport surfaces.
PA.XII.A.R3	3. Spinning propellers.
PA.XII.A.R4	4. Failure to manage Tasks during taxi and parking.
PA.XII.A.R5	5. Confirmation or expectation bias.
PA.XII.A.R6	6. Failure to manage the automation.
PA.XII.A.R7	7. Airport security.
PA.XII.A.R8	8. Failure to maintain directional control after landing or during taxi
Skills	The applicant demonstrates the ability to:
PA.XII.A.S1	1. Maintain directional control after touchdown while decelerating to an appropriate speed.
PA.XII.A.S2	2. Utilize runway incursion avoidance procedures after landing.
PA.XII.A.S3	3. Park in an appropriate area, considering the safety of nearby persons and property.
PA.XII.A.S4	4. Plan the taxi route to the ramp.
PA.XII.A.S5	5. Follow the appropriate procedure for engine shutdown.
PA.XII.A.S6	6. Complete the after landing checklist after the airplane has stopped.
PA.XII.A.S7	7. Complete the engine shutdown checklist.
PA.XII.A.S8	8. Disembark passengers safely and remain aware of passenger movement while on the ramp area.
PA.XII.A.S9	9. Record aircraft discrepancies and notes for possible service needs before the next flight.
PA.XII.A.S10	10. Conduct an appropriate post flight inspection and secure the aircraft.

Appendix Table of Contents

Appendix 1: The Knowledge Test Eligibility, Prerequisites and Testing Centers

Knowledge Test Description

The knowledge test is an important part of the airman certification process. Applicants must pass the knowledge test before taking the practical test.

The knowledge test consists of objective, multiple-choice questions. There is a single correct response for each test question. Each test question is independent of other questions. A correct response to one question does not depend upon, or influence, the correct response to another.

Knowledge Test Tables

Test Code	Test Name	Number of Questions	Age	Allotted Time	Passing Score
PAR	Private Pilot Airplane	60	15	2.5	70
PAT	Private Pilot Airplane/Recreational Pilot - Transition	30	15	1.5	70
PBG	Private Pilot Balloon - Gas	60	14	2.5	70
PBH	Private Pilot Balloon - Hot Air	60	14	2.5	70
PCH	Private Pilot Helicopter *Canadian Conversion*	40	16	2.0	70
PCP	Private Pilot – Airplane *Canadian Conversion*	40	16	2.0	70
PGL	Private Pilot Glider	60	14	2.5	70
PGT	Private Pilot Gyroplane/Recreational Pilot - Transition	30	15	1.5	70
PHT	Private Pilot Helicopter/Recreational Pilot - Transition	30	15	1.5	70
PLA	Private Pilot Airship	60	15	2.5	70
PPP	Private Pilot Powered Parachute	60	15	2.5	70
PRG	Private Pilot Gyroplane	60	15	2.5	70
PRH	Private Pilot Helicopter	60	15	2.5	70
PWS	Private Pilot Weight-Shift-Control	60	15	2.5	70
RPA	Recreational Pilot Airplane	50	15	2.0	70
RPG	Recreational Pilot Gyroplane	50	15	2.0	70
RPH	Recreational Pilot Helicopter	50	15	2.0	70

Knowledge Test Blueprint

PAR Knowledge Areas Required by 14 CFR section 61.65 to be on the Knowledge Test	Percent of Questions Per Test
I. Regulations	5 – 15%
II. Accident Reporting	5 – 10%
III. Performance Charts	5 – 10%
IV. Radio Communications	5 – 10%
V. Weather	5 – 10%
VI. Safe and Efficient Operations	5 – 15%
VII. Density Altitude Performance	5 – 10%
VIII. Weight and Balance	5 – 10%
IX. Aerodynamics, Powerplants and Aircraft Systems	5 – 10%
X. Stalls and Spins	5 – 10%
XI. Aeronautical Decision Making (ADM)	5 – 10%
XII. Preflight actions	5 – 10%
Total Number of Questions	**60**

English Language Proficiency

In accordance with the requirements of 14 CFR part 61 and the FAA Aviation English Language Proficiency standard, throughout the application and testing process the applicant must demonstrate the ability to read, write, speak, and understand the English language. English language proficiency is required to communicate effectively with ATC, to comply with ATC instructions, and to ensure clear and effective crew communication and coordination. Normal restatement of questions as would be done for a native English speaker is permitted, and does not constitute grounds for disqualification.

Knowledge Test Requirements

In order to take the Private Pilot knowledge test, you must provide proper identification. To verify your eligibility to take the test, you must also provide one of the following in accordance with the requirements of 14 CFR, part 61:

- Section 61.35 lists the prerequisites for taking the knowledge test, to include the minimum age an applicant must be to sit for the test.

    - Received an endorsement, if required by this part, from an authorized instructor certifying that the applicant accomplished the appropriate ground-training or a home-study course required by this part for the certificate or rating sought and is prepared for the knowledge test;

    - Proper identification at the time of application that contains the applicant's—

        i)   Photograph;
        ii) Signature;
        iii) Date of birth;
        iv) If the permanent mailing address is a post office box number, then the applicant must provide a government-issued residential address

- Section 61.49 acceptable forms of retest authorization for **all** Private Pilot tests:

    - An applicant retesting **after failure** is required to submit the applicable test report indicating failure, along with an endorsement from an authorized instructor who gave the applicant the required additional training. The endorsement must certify that the applicant is competent to pass the test. The test proctor must retain the original failed test report presented as authorization and attach it to the applicable sign-in/out log.

    Note: If the applicant no longer possesses the original test report, he or she may request a duplicate replacement issued by AFS-760.

- Acceptable forms of authorization for PCP only:

    - Confirmation of Verification Letter issued by the Airman Certification Branch (Knowledge Testing Authorization Requirements Matrix).
    - Requires **no** instructor endorsement or other form of written authorization.

Knowledge Test Centers

The FAA authorizes hundreds of knowledge testing center locations that offer a full range of airman knowledge tests. For information on authorized testing centers and to register for the knowledge test, contact one of the providers listed at www.faa.gov.

Knowledge Test Registration

When you contact a knowledge testing center to register for a test, please be prepared to select a test date, choose a testing center, and make financial arrangements for test payment when you call. You may register for test(s) several weeks in advance, and you may cancel in accordance with the testing center's cancellation policy.

Appendix 2: Knowledge Test Procedures and Tips

Before starting the actual test, the testing center will provide an opportunity to practice navigating through the test. This practice or tutorial session may include sample questions to familiarize the applicant with the look and feel of the software. (e.g., selecting an answer, marking a question for later review, monitoring time remaining for the test, and other features of the testing software.)

Acceptable Materials

The applicant may use the following aids, reference materials, and test materials, as long as the material does not include actual test questions or answers:

Acceptable Materials	Unacceptable Materials	Notes
Supplement book provided by proctor	Written materials that are handwritten, printed, or electronic	Testing centers may provide calculators and/or deny the use of personal calculators
All models of aviation-oriented calculators or small electronic calculators that perform only arithmetic functions	Electronic calculators incorporating permanent or continuous type memory circuits without erasure capability	Unit Member (proctor) may prohibit the use of your calculator if he or she is unable to determine the calculator's erasure capability
Calculators with simple programmable memories, which allow addition to, subtraction from, or retrieval of one number from the memory; or simple functions, such as square root and percentages	Magnetic Cards, magnetic tapes, modules, computer chips, or any other device upon which prewritten programs or information related to the test can be stored and retrieved	Printouts of data must be surrendered at the completion of the test if the calculator incorporates this design feature
Scales, straightedges, protractors, plotters, navigation computers, blank log sheets, holding pattern entry aids, and electronic or mechanical calculators that are directly related to the test	Dictionaries	Before, and upon completion of the test, while in the presence of the Unit Member, actuate the ON/OFF switch or RESET button, and perform any other function that ensures erasure of any data stored in memory circuits
Manufacturer's permanently inscribed instructions on the front and back of such aids, e.g., formulas, conversions, regulations, signals, weather data, holding pattern diagrams, frequencies, weight and balance formulas, and air traffic control procedures	Any booklet or manual containing instructions related to use of test aids	Unit Member makes the final determination regarding aids, reference materials, and test materials

Test Tips

When taking a knowledge test, please keep the following points in mind:

- Carefully read the instructions provided with the test.
- Answer each question in accordance with the latest regulations and guidance publications.
- Read each question carefully before looking at the answer options. You should clearly understand the problem before trying to solve it.
- After formulating a response, determine which answer option corresponds with your answer. The answer you choose should completely solve the problem.
- Remember that only one answer is complete and correct. The other possible answers are either incomplete or erroneous.
- If a certain question is difficult for you, mark it for review and return to it after you have answered the less difficult questions. This procedure will enable you to use the available time to maximum advantage.
- When solving a calculation problem, be sure to read all the associated notes.
- For questions involving use of a graph, you may request a printed copy that you can mark in computing your answer. This copy and all other notes and paperwork must be given to the testing center upon completion of the test.

Cheating or Other Unauthorized Conduct

To avoid test compromise, computer testing centers must follow strict security procedures established by the FAA and described in FAA Order 8080.6 (as amended), Conduct of Airman Knowledge Tests. The FAA has directed testing centers to terminate a test at any time a test unit member suspects that a cheating incident has occurred.

The FAA will investigate and, if the agency determines that cheating or unauthorized conduct has occurred, any airman certificate or rating you hold may be revoked. You will also be prohibited from applying for or taking any test for a certificate or rating under 14 CFR part 61 for a period of one year.

Testing Procedures for Applicants Requesting Special Accommodations

An applicant with learning or reading disability may request approval from AFS-630 through the local Flight Standards District Office (FSDO) or International Field Office/International Field Unit (IFO/IFU) to take airman knowledge test using one of the three options listed below, in preferential order:

Option 1: Use current testing facilities and procedures whenever possible.

Option 2: Use a self-contained, electronic device which pronounces and displays typed-in words (e.g., the Franklin Speaking Wordmaster®) to facilitate the testing process.

> **Note:** *The device should consist of an electronic thesaurus that audibly pronounces typed-in words and presents them on a display screen. The device should also have a built-in headphone jack in order to avoid disturbing others during testing.*

Option 3: Request the proctor's assistance in reading specific words or terms from the test questions and/or supplement book. To prevent compromising the testing process, the proctor must be an individual with no aviation background or expertise. The proctor may provide reading assistance only (i.e., no explanation of words or terms). When an applicant requests this option, the FSDO or IFO/IFU inspector must contact the Airman Testing Standards Branch (AFS-630) for assistance in selecting the test site and assisting the proctor. Before approving any option, the FSDO or IFO/IFU inspector must advise the applicant of the regulatory certification requirement to be able to read, write, speak, and understand the English language.

Appendix 3: Airman Knowledge Test Report

Immediately upon completion of the knowledge test, the applicant receives a printed Airman Knowledge Test Report documenting the score with the testing center's raised, embossed seal. The applicant must retain the original Airman Knowledge Test Report. The instructor must provide instruction in each area of deficiency and provide a logbook endorsement certifying that the applicant has demonstrated satisfactory knowledge in each area. When taking the practical test, the applicant must present the original Airman Knowledge Test Report to the evaluator, who is required to assess the noted areas of deficiency during the ground portion of the practical test.

An Airman Knowledge Test Report expires 24 calendar months after the month the applicant completes the knowledge test. If the Airman Knowledge Test Report expires before completion of the practical test, the applicant must retake the knowledge test.

To obtain a duplicate Airman Knowledge Test Report due to loss or destruction of the original, the applicant can send a signed request accompanied by a check or money order for $12.00 (U.S. funds), payable to the FAA to:

> Federal Aviation Administration
> Airmen Certification Branch, AFS-760
> P.O. Box 25082
> Oklahoma City, OK 73125

To obtain a copy of the application form or a list of the information required, please see the Airman Certification Branch (AFS-760) web page.

FAA Knowledge Test Question Coding

Each Task in the Airman Certification Standard includes an Airman Certification Standards (ACS) code. This ACS code will soon be displayed on the airman test report to indicate what Task element was proven deficient on the Knowledge Exam. Instructors can then provide remedial training in the deficient areas and evaluators can re-test this element during the practical exam.

The ACS coding consists of 4 elements. For example: this code is deciphered as follows:

> PA.XI.A.K1:
>
> > PA = Applicable ACS (Private Pilot – Airplane)
> > XI = Area of Operation (Night Operation)
> > A = Task (Night Preparation)
> > K1 = Task element Knowledge 1 (Physiological aspects of night flying as it relates to vision.)

Knowledge test questions are mapped to the ACS codes, which will soon replace the system of "Learning Statement Codes." After this transition occurs, the airman knowledge test report will list an ACS code that correlates to a specific Task element for a given Area of Operation and Task. Remedial instruction and re-testing will be specific, targeted, and based on specified learning criteria. Similarly, a Notice of Disapproval for the practical test will use the ACS codes to identify the deficient Task elements.

Appendix 4: The Practical Test – Eligibility and Prerequisites

The prerequisite requirements and general eligibility for a practical test and the specific requirements for the original issuance of a private pilot certificate in the airplane category can be found in sections 61.39(a)(1) through (7) and 61.103, respectively.

For your convenience, Gleim has reproduced 14 CFR sections 61.39(a)(1) through (7) and 61.103 below.

Sec. 61.39 Prerequisites for practical tests.

a) Except as provided in paragraphs (b), (c), and (e) of this section, to be eligible for a practical test for a certificate or rating issued under this part, an applicant must:

    1) Pass the required knowledge test:

        i) Within the 24-calendar-month period preceding the month the applicant completes the practical test, if a knowledge test is required; or

        ii) Within the 60-calendar month period preceding the month the applicant completes the practical test for those applicants who complete the airline transport pilot certification training program in Sec. 61.156 and pass the knowledge test for an airline transport pilot certificate with a multiengine class rating after July 31, 2014;

    2) Present the knowledge test report at the time of application for the practical test, if a knowledge test is required;

    3) Have satisfactorily accomplished the required training and obtained the aeronautical experience prescribed by this part for the certificate or rating sought;

    4) Hold at least a third-class medical certificate, if a medical certificate is required;

    5) Meet the prescribed age requirement of this part for the issuance of the certificate or rating sought;

    6) Have an endorsement, if required by this part, in the applicant's logbook or training record that has been signed by an authorized instructor who certifies that the applicant--

        i) Has received and logged training time within 2 calendar months preceding the month of application in preparation for the practical test;

        ii) Is prepared for the required practical test; and

        iii) Has demonstrated satisfactory knowledge of the subject areas in which the applicant was deficient on the airman knowledge test; and

    7) Have a completed and signed application form.

Sec. 61.103 Eligibility requirements: General.

To be eligible for a private pilot certificate, a person must:

a) Be at least 17 years of age for a rating in other than a glider or balloon.

b) Be at least 16 years of age for a rating in a glider or balloon.

c) Be able to read, speak, write, and understand the English language. If the applicant is unable to meet one of these requirements due to medical reasons, then the Administrator may place such operating limitations on that applicant's pilot certificate as are necessary for the safe operation of the aircraft.

d) Receive a logbook endorsement from an authorized instructor who:

    1) Conducted the training or reviewed the person's home study on the aeronautical knowledge areas listed in Sec. 61.105(b) of this part that apply to the aircraft rating sought; and

    2) Certified that the person is prepared for the required knowledge test.

e) Pass the required knowledge test on the aeronautical knowledge areas listed in Sec. 61.105(b) of this part.

f) Receive flight training and a logbook endorsement from an authorized instructor who:

    1) Conducted the training in the areas of operation listed in Sec. 61.107(b) of this part that apply to the aircraft rating sought; and

    2) Certified that the person is prepared for the required practical test.

g) Meet the aeronautical experience requirements of this part that apply to the aircraft rating sought before applying for the practical test.

h) Pass a practical test on the areas of operation listed in Sec. 61.107(b) of this part that apply to the aircraft rating sought.

i) Comply with the appropriate sections of this part that apply to the aircraft category and class rating sought.

j) Hold a U.S. student pilot certificate, sport pilot certificate, or recreational pilot certificate.

Appendix 5: Practical Test Roles, Responsibilities, and Outcomes

Applicant Responsibilities

The applicant is responsible for mastering the established standards for knowledge, skill, and risk management elements in all Tasks appropriate to the certificate and rating sought. The applicant should use this ACS, its references, and the Practical Test Checklist in this Appendix in preparation to take the practical test.

Instructor Responsibilities

The instructor is responsible for training the applicant to meet the established standards for knowledge, skill, and risk management elements in all Tasks appropriate to the certificate and rating sought. The instructor should use this ACS and its references as part of preparing the applicant to take the practical test and, if necessary, in retraining the applicant to proficiency in all subject(s) missed on the knowledge test.

Evaluator Responsibilities

An Evaluator is:

- Aviation safety inspector (ASI)
- Pilot examiner (other than administrative pilot examiners) or
- Chief instructor, assistant chief instructor or check instructor of pilot school holding examining authority
- CFII conducting IPC

The evaluator who conducts the practical test is responsible for determining that the applicant meets the established standards of aeronautical knowledge, skills (flight proficiency), and risk management for each Task in the appropriate ACS. This responsibility also includes verifying the experience requirements specified for a certificate or rating.

At the initial stage of the practical test, the evaluator must also determine that the applicant meets FAA Aviation English Language Proficiency (AELP) standards by verifying that he or she can understand ATC instructions and communicate in English at a level that is understandable to ATC and other pilots. The evaluator should use AC 60-28, English Language Skill Standards required by 14 CFR parts 61, 63, and 65 (current version) when evaluating the applicant's ability to meet the standard. If, at any point during the practical test, the applicant does not meet the AELP standards, the evaluator must issue a Notice of Disapproval, FAA form 8060-5, with "NOT FAA AELP" in the comments. If there is any doubt, the evaluator should contact the local Flight Standards District Office (FSDO) for assistance.

The evaluator must develop a Plan of Action (POA), written in English, to conduct the practical test, and it must include all of the required Areas of Operation and Tasks. The POA must include a scenario that evaluates as many of the required Areas of Operation and Tasks as possible. As the scenario unfolds during the test, the evaluator will introduce problems and emergencies that the applicant must manage. The evaluator has the discretion to modify the POA in order to accommodate unexpected situations as they arise. For example, the evaluator may elect to suspend and later resume a scenario in order to assess certain Tasks.

In the integrated ACS framework, the Areas of Operation contain Tasks that include "knowledge" elements (such as K1), "risk management" elements (such as R1), and "skill" elements (such as S1). Knowledge and risk management elements are primarily evaluated during the knowledge testing phase of the airman certification process. The evaluator must assess the applicant on all skill elements for each Task included in each Area of Operation of the ACS, unless otherwise noted. The evaluator administering the practical test has the discretion to combine Tasks/elements as appropriate to testing scenarios.

The required minimum elements to include in the POA from each applicable Task are as follows:

- At least one knowledge element;
- At least one risk management element;
- All skill elements unless otherwise noted; and
- Any Task elements in which the applicant was shown to be deficient on the knowledge test.

Note: *Task elements added to the POA on the basis of being listed on the AKTR may satisfy the other minimum Task element requirements. The missed items on the AKTR are not required to be added in addition to the minimum Task element requirements.*

There is no expectation for testing every knowledge and risk management element in a Task, but the evaluator has discretion to sample as needed to ensure the applicant's mastery of that Task.

Unless otherwise noted in the Task, the evaluator must test each item in the skills section by asking the applicant to perform each one. As safety of flight conditions permit, the evaluator may use questions during flight to test knowledge and risk management elements not evident in the demonstrated skills. To the greatest extent practicable, evaluators shall test the applicant's ability to apply and correlate information, and use rote questions only when they are appropriate for the material being tested. If the Task includes sub-elements (such as PA.I.C.K4c Temperature), the evaluator may select either the primary element (such as K4) or an appropriate sub-element (such as K4c). If the broader primary element is selected, the evaluator must develop questions only from material covered in the references listed for the Task.

Possible Outcomes of the Test

There are three possible outcomes of the practical test: (1) Temporary Airman Certificate (satisfactory), (2) Notice of Disapproval (unsatisfactory), or (3) Letter of Discontinuance.

If the evaluator determines that a Task is incomplete, or the outcome is uncertain, the evaluator may require the applicant to repeat that Task, or portions of that Task. This provision does not mean that instruction, practice, or the repetition of an unsatisfactory Task is permitted during the practical test.

If the evaluator determines the applicant's skill and abilities are in doubt, the outcome is unsatisfactory and the evaluator must issue a Notice of Disapproval.

Satisfactory Performance

Satisfactory performance requires that the applicant:

- Demonstrate the Tasks specified in the Areas of Operation for the certificate or rating sought within the established standards;
- Demonstrate mastery of the aircraft by performing each Task successfully;
- Demonstrate proficiency and competency in accordance with the approved standards;
- Demonstrate sound judgment and exercise aeronautical decision-making/risk management;
- Demonstrate competence in crew resource management in aircraft certificated for more than one required pilot crew member, or, single-pilot competence in an airplane that is certificated for single-pilot operations.

Satisfactory performance will result in the issuance of a temporary certificate.

Unsatisfactory Performance

If, in the judgment of the evaluator, the applicant does not meet the standards for any Task, the applicant fails the Task and associated Area of Operation. The test is unsatisfactory, and the evaluator issues a Notice of Disapproval.

When the evaluator issues a Notice of Disapproval, he or she shall list the Area of Operation in which the applicant did not meet the standard. The Notice of Disapproval must also list the Area(s) of Operation not tested, and the number of practical test failures.

The evaluator or the applicant may end the test if the applicant fails a Task. The evaluator may continue the test only with the consent of the applicant, and the applicant is entitled to credit only those Areas of Operation and the associated Tasks satisfactorily performed. Though not required, the evaluator has discretion to reevaluate any Task, including those previously passed, during the retest.

Typical areas of unsatisfactory performance and grounds for disqualification include:

- Any action or lack of action by the applicant that requires corrective intervention by the evaluator to maintain safe flight.
- Failure to use proper and effective visual scanning techniques to clear the area before and while performing maneuvers.
- Consistently exceeding tolerances stated in the skill elements of the Task.
- Failure to take prompt corrective action when tolerances are exceeded.
- Failure to exercise risk management.

Discontinuance

When it is necessary to discontinue a practical test for reasons other than unsatisfactory performance (e.g., equipment failure, weather, illness), the evaluator must return all test paperwork to the applicant. The evaluator must prepare, sign, and issue a Letter of Discontinuance that lists those Areas of Operation the applicant successfully completed and the time period remaining to complete the test. The evaluator should advise the applicant to present the Letter of Discontinuance to the evaluator when the practical test resumes in order to receive credit for the items successfully completed. The Letter of Discontinuance becomes part of the applicant's certification file.

Practical Test Checklist (Applicant)
Appointment with Evaluator

Evaluator's Name:_____

Location:_____

Date/Time:_____

Acceptable Aircraft

- ☐ Aircraft Documents:
    - ☐ Airworthiness Certificate
    - ☐ Registration Certificate
    - ☐ Operating Limitations
- ☐ Aircraft Maintenance Records:
    - ☐ Logbook Record of Airworthiness Inspections and AD Compliance
- ☐ Pilot's Operating Handbook, FAA-Approved Aircraft Flight Manual

Personal Equipment

- ☐ View-Limiting Device
- ☐ Current Aeronautical Charts (Printed or Electronic)
- ☐ Computer and Plotter
- ☐ Flight Plan Form
- ☐ Flight Plan Form and Flight Logs (printed or electronic)
- ☐ Chart Supplements U.S., Airport Diagrams and appropriate Publications
- ☐ Current AIM

Personal Records

- ☐ Identification—Photo/Signature ID
- ☐ Pilot Certificate
- ☐ Current Medical Certificate
- ☐ Completed FAA Form 8710-1, Airman Certificate and/or Rating Application with Instructor's Signature
- ☐ Original Knowledge Test Report
- ☐ Pilot Logbook with appropriate Instructor Endorsements
- ☐ FAA Form 8060-5, Notice of Disapproval (if applicable)
- ☐ Letter of Discontinuance (if applicable)
- ☐ Approved School Graduation Certificate (if applicable)
- ☐ Evaluator's Fee (if applicable)

Additional Rating Task Table

For an applicant who holds at least a private pilot certificate and seeks an additional airplane category and/or class rating at the private pilot level, the examiner shall evaluate that applicant in the Areas of Operation and Tasks listed in the Additional Rating Task Table. Please note, however, that the evaluator has the discretion to evaluate the applicant's competence in the remaining Areas of Operation and Tasks.

If the applicant holds two or more category or class ratings at least at the private level, and the ratings table indicates differing required Tasks, the "least restrictive" entry applies. For example, if "All" and "None" are indicated for one Area of Operation, the "None" entry applies. If "B" and "B, C" are indicated, the "B" entry applies.

Addition of an Airplane Single-Engine Land Rating to an existing Private Pilot Certificate

Required Tasks are indicated by either the Task letter(s) that apply(s) or an indication that all or none of the Tasks must be tested based on the notes in each Area of Operation.

Private Pilot Rating(s) Held

Areas of Operation	ASES	AMEL	AMES	RH	RG	Glider	Balloon	Airship
I	F,G	F,G	F,G	F,G	F,G	F,G	F,G	F,G
II	D	D	D	A,C,D,F	A,D,F	A,B,C,D,F	A,B,C,D,F	A,B,C,D,F
III	None	None	None	B	None	B	B	B
IV	A,B,C,D, E,F	A,B,C,D, E,F	A,B,C,D, E,F	A,B,C,D, E,F,M,N	A,B,C,D, E,F,M,N	A,B,C,D, E,F,M,N	A,B,C,D, E,F,M,N	A,B,C,D, E,F,M,N
V	None	None	None	A,B	A	A,B	A,B	A,B
VI	None	None	None	None	None	A,B,C,D	A,B,C,D	None
VII	None	None	None	A,B,C,D	A,B,C,D	A,B,C,D	A,B,C,D	A,B,C,D
VIII	None	None	None	A,B,C,D, E,F	A,B,C,D, E,F	A,B,C,D, E,F	A,B,C,D, E,F	A,B,C,D, E,F
IX	A,B,C	A,B,C	A,B,C	A,B,C,D	A,B,C,D	A,B,C,D	A,B,C,D	A,B,C,D
X	None	None	None	None	None	None	None	None
XI	None	None	None	None	None	A	A	A
XII	A	None	A	A	A	A	A	A

Addition of an Airplane Single-Engine Sea Rating to an existing Private Pilot Certificate

Required Tasks are indicated by either the Task letter(s) that apply(s) or an indication that all or none of the Tasks must be tested based on the notes in each Area of Operation.

Private Pilot Rating(s) Held

Areas of Operation	ASEL	AMEL	AMES	RH	RG	Glider	Balloon	Airship
I	F,G,I	F,G	F,G,I	F,G,I	F,G,I	F,G,I	F,G,I	F,G,I
II	E	E	E	A,B,E,F	A,B,E,F	A,B,C,E,F	A,B,C,E,F	A,B,C,E,F
III	None	None	None	B	None	B	B	B
IV	A,B,G,H,I,J,K,L	A,B,G,H,I,J,K,L	A,B,G,H,I,J,K,L	A,B,G,H,I,J,K,L,M,N	A,B,G,H,I,J,K,L,M,N	A,B,G,H,I,J,K,L,M,N	A,B,G,H,I,J,K,L,M,N	A,B,G,H,I,J,K,L,M,N
V	None	None	None	A,B	A	A,B	A,B	A,B
VI	None	None	None	None	None	A,B,C,D	A,B,C,D	None
VII	None	None	None	None	A,B,C,D	A,B,C,D	A,B,C,D	A,B,C,D
VIII	None	None	None	A,B,C,D,E,F	A,B,C,D,E,F	A,B,C,D,E,F	A,B,C,D,E,F	A,B,C,D,E,F
IX	A,B,C	A,B,C	A,B,C	A,B,C,D	A,B,C,D	A,B,C,D	A,B,C,D	A,B,C,D
X	None	None	None	None	None	None	None	None
XI	None	None	None	None	None	A	A	A
XII	B	B	None	B	B	B	B	B

Addition of an Airplane Multiengine Land Rating to an existing Private Pilot Certificate

Required Tasks are indicated by either the Task letter(s) that apply(s) or an indication that all or none of the Tasks must be tested based on the notes in each Area of Operation.

Private Pilot Rating(s) Held

Areas of Operation	ASEL	AMES	AMES	RH	RG	Glider	Balloon	Airship
I	F,G,J	F,G,J	F,G	F,G,J	F,G,J	F,G,J	F,G,J	F,G,J
II	A,B,C,D,F	A,B,C,D,F	D	A,B,C,D,F	A,B,C,D,F	A,B,C,D,F	A,B,C,D,F	A,B,C,D,F
III	None	None	None	B	None	B	B	B
IV	A,B,E,F	A,B,E,F	A,B,E,F	A,B,E,F,N	A,B,E,F,N	A,B,E,F,N	A,B,E,F,N	A,B,E,F,N
V	A	A	None	A,B	A	A,B	A,B	A,B
VI	None	None	None	None	None	A,B,C,D	A,B,C,D	None
VII	A,B,C,D	A,B,C,D	None	A,B,C,D	A,B,C,D	A,B,C,D	A,B,C,D	A,B,C,D
VIII	None	None	None	A,B,C,D,E,F	A,B,C,D,E,F	A,B,C,D,E,F	A,B,C,D,E,F	A,B,C,D,E,F
IX	A,C,D,E,F,G	A,C,D,E,F,G	C,E,G	A,C,D,E,F,G	A,C,D,E,F,G	A,C,D,E,F,G	A,C,D,E,F,G	A,C,D,E,F,G
X	A,B,C,D	A,B,C,D	None	A,B,C,D	A,B,C,D	A,B,C,D	A,B,C,D	A,B,C,D
XI	None	None	None	None	None	A	A	A
XII	None	A	A	A	A	A	A	A

Addition of an Airplane Multiengine Sea Rating to an existing Private Pilot Certificate

Required Tasks are indicated by either the Task letter(s) that apply(s) or an indication that all or none of the Tasks must be tested based on the notes in each Area of Operation.

Private Pilot Rating(s) Held

Areas of Operation	ASES	AMEL	AMES	RH	RG	Glider	Balloon	Airship
I	F,G,I	F,G,I	F,G	F,G,I	F,G,I	F,G,I	F,G,I	F,G,I
II	E	A,B,C,E,F	A,B,C,E,F	A,B,C,E,F	A,B,C,E,F	A,B,C,E,F	A,B,C,E,F	A,B,C,E,F
III	None	None	None	B	None	B	B	B
IV	A,B,G,H, I.J,K,L	A,B,G,H, I.J,K,L	A,B,G,H, I.J,K,L	A,B,G,H, I.J,K,L,N	A,B,G,H, I.J,K,L,N	A,B,G,H, I.J,K,L,N	A,B,G,H, I.J,K,L,N	A,B,G,H, I.J,K,L,N
V	None	A	A	A,B	A	A,B	A,B	A,B
VI	None	None	None	None	None	A,B,C,D	A,B,C,D	None
VII	None	A,B,C,D	A,B,C,D	A,B,C,D	A,B,C,D	A,B,C,D	A,B,C,D	A,B,C,D
VIII	None	None	None	A,B,C D,E,F	A,B,C, D,E,F	A,B,C D,E,F	A,B,C, D,E,F	A,B,C D,E,F
IX	A,C,D, E,F,G	A,C,D, E,F,G	A,C,D, E,F,G	A,C,D, E,F,G	A,C,D, E,F,G	A,C,D, E,F,G	A,C,D, E,F,	A,C,D, E,F,G
X	None	A,B,C,D	A,B,C,D	A,B,C,D	A,B,C,D	A,B,C,D	A,B,C,D	A,B,C,D
XI	None	None	None	None	None	A	A	A
XII	B	B	None	B	B	B	B	B

Removal of the "Airplane Multiengine VFR Only" Limitation

The removal of the "Airplane Multiengine VFR Only" limitation, at the private pilot certificate level, requires an applicant to satisfactorily perform the following Area of Operation and Tasks from the Private Pilot – Airplane ACS in a multiengine airplane that has a manufacturer's published V_{MC} speed.

X.	Multiengine Operations	
	Task C:	Engine Failure During Flight (by reference to instruments) (AMEL, AMES)
	Task D:	Instrument Approach and Landing with an inoperative Engine (Simulated) (by reference to instruments) (AMEL, AMES)

Removal of the "Limited to Center Thrust" Limitation

The removal of the "Limited to Center Thrust" limitation at the private pilot certificate level requires an applicant to satisfactorily perform the following Areas of Operation and Tasks from the Private Pilot – Airplane ACS in a multiengine airplane that has a manufacturer's published VMC speed. An applicant that holds an instrument-airplane rating and has not demonstrated instrument proficiency in a multiengine airplane with a published VMC shall complete the additional Tasks listed under the ***Removal of the "Airplane Multiengine VFR Only" Limitation*** section of this Appendix.

I.	Preflight Preparation	
	Task J:	Principles of Flight – Engine Inoperative (AMEL, AMES)
IX.	**Emergency Operations**	
	Task E:	Engine Failure During Takeoff Before V_{MC} (Simulated) (AMEL, AMES)
	Task F:	Engine Failure After Lift-Off (Simulated) (AMEL, AMES)
	Task G:	Approach and Landing with an Inoperative Engine (Simulated) (AMEL, AMES)
X.	**Multiengine Operations**	
	Task A:	Maneuvering with One Engine Inoperative (AMEL, AMES)
	Task B:	V_{MC} Demonstration (AMEL, AMES)

Appendix 6: Safety of Flight

General

Safety of flight must be the prime consideration at all times. The evaluator, applicant, and crew must be constantly alert for other traffic. If performing aspects of a given maneuver, such as emergency procedures, would jeopardize safety, the evaluator will ask the applicant to simulate that portion of the maneuver. The evaluator will assess the applicant's use of visual scanning and collision avoidance procedures throughout the entire test.

Stall and Spin Awareness

During flight training and testing, the applicant and the instructor or evaluator must always recognize and avoid operations that could lead to an inadvertent stall or spin and inadvertent loss of control.

Use of Checklists

Throughout the practical test, the applicant is evaluated on the use of an appropriate checklist.

Assessing proper checklist use depends upon the specific Task. In all cases, the evaluator should determine whether the applicant appropriately divides attention and uses proper visual scanning. In some situations, reading the actual checklist may be impractical or unsafe. In such cases, the evaluator should assess the applicant's performance of published or recommended immediate action "memory" items along with his or her review of the appropriate checklist once conditions permit.

In a single-pilot airplane, the applicant should demonstrate the CRM principles described as SRM. Proper use is dependent on the specific Task being evaluated. The situation may be such that the use of the checklist while accomplishing elements of an Objective would be either unsafe or impractical in a single-pilot operation. In this case, a review of the checklist after the elements have been accomplished is appropriate.

Use of Distractions

Numerous studies indicate that many accidents have occurred when the pilot has been distracted during critical phases of flight. The evaluator should incorporate realistic distractions during the flight portion of the practical test to evaluate the pilot's situational awareness and ability to utilize proper control technique while dividing attention both inside and outside the cockpit.

Positive Exchange of Flight Controls

There must always be a clear understanding of who has control of the aircraft. Prior to flight, the pilots involved should conduct a briefing that includes reviewing the procedures for exchanging flight controls.

The FAA recommends a positive three-step process for exchanging flight controls between pilots:

- When one pilot seeks to have the other pilot take control of the aircraft, he or she will say, "You have the flight controls."
- The second pilot acknowledges immediately by saying, "I have the flight controls."
- The first pilot again says, "You have the flight controls."

Aeronautical Decision Making, Risk Management, CRM and SRM

Throughout the practical test, the evaluator must assess the applicant's ability to use sound aeronautical decision making procedures in order to identify hazards and mitigate risk. The evaluator must accomplish this requirement by reference to the risk management elements of the given Task(s), and by developing scenarios that incorporate and combine Tasks appropriate to assessing the applicant's risk management in making safe aeronautical decisions. For example, the evaluator may develop a scenario that incorporates weather decisions and performance planning.

In assessing the applicant's performance, the evaluator should take note of the applicant's use of CRM and, if appropriate, SRM. CRM/SRM is the set of competencies that includes situational awareness, communication skills, teamwork, task allocation, and decision-making within a comprehensive framework of standard operating procedures (SOP). SRM specifically refers to the management of all resources onboard the aircraft as well as outside resources available to the single pilot.

Deficiencies in CRM/SRM almost always contribute to the unsatisfactory performance of a Task. While evaluation of CRM/SRM may appear to be somewhat subjective, the evaluator should use the risk management elements of the given Task(s) to determine whether the applicant's performance of the Task(s) demonstrates both understanding and application of the associated risk management elements.

Single-Engine Considerations

VIII. Emergency Operations - Powerplant Failure—Single-Engine Airplane

For safety reasons, the evaluator will not request a simulated powerplant failure in a single engine airplane unless it is possible to safely complete a landing.

High Performance Aircraft Considerations

In some high performance airplanes, the power setting may have to be reduced below the ACS guidelines power setting to prevent excessively high pitch attitudes (greater than 30° nose up.

Appendix 7: Aircraft, Equipment, and Operational Requirements & Limitations

Aircraft Requirements & Limitations

Section 61.45 prescribes the required aircraft and equipment for a practical test. The regulation states the minimum aircraft registration and airworthiness requirements as well as the minimum equipment requirements, to include the minimum required controls.

Multiengine practical tests require normal engine shutdowns and restarts in the air, to include propeller feathering and unfeathering. The AFM must not prohibit these procedures, but low power settings for cooling periods prior to the actual shutdown in accordance with the AFM are acceptable and encouraged. For a type rating in an airplane not certificated with inflight unfeathering capability, a simulated powerplant failure is acceptable.

If the multiengine airplane used for the practical test does not publish a V_{MC}, then the "Limited to Centerline Thrust" limitation will be added to the certificate issued from this check, unless the applicant has already demonstrated competence in a multiengine airplane with a published V_{MC}.

Any equipment inoperative in an aircraft with a minimum equipment list (MEL) shall be placarded in accordance with the approved MEL procedures. The applicant shall describe the procedures accomplished, the resulting operational restrictions, and the documentation for the inoperative item(s).

Equipment Requirements & Limitations

The equipment examination should be administered before the flight portion of the practical test, but it must be closely coordinated and related to the flight portion.

This section requires the aircraft must be:

- Of U.S., foreign, or military registry of the same category, class and type, if applicable, for the certificate and/or rating for which the applicant is applying.
- The aircraft must have fully functional dual controls, except as provided for in 14 CFR section 61.45(c) and (e); and
- Capable of performing all Areas of Operation appropriate to the rating sought and have no operating limitations, which prohibit its use in any of the Area of Operation, required for the practical test.

To assist in management of the aircraft during the practical test, the applicant is expected to demonstrate automation management skills by utilizing installed equipment such as autopilot, avionics and systems displays, and/or flight management system (FMS). The evaluator is expected to test the applicant's knowledge of the systems that are installed and operative during both the ground and flight portions of the practical test.

If the practical test is conducted in an aircraft, the applicant is required by 14 CFR section 61.45(d)(2) to provide an appropriate view limiting device acceptable to the evaluator. The applicant and the evaluator should establish a procedure as to when and how this device should be donned and removed, and brief this procedure before the flight. The device must be used during all testing that requires flight "solely by reference to instruments." This device must prevent the applicant from having visual reference outside the aircraft, but it must not restrict the evaluator's ability to see and avoid other traffic.

Operational Requirements & Limitations

[Reserved]

Appendix 8: Use of Flight Simulation Training Devices (FSTD) and Aviation Training Devices (ATD): Airplane Single-Engine, Multi-Engine Land and Sea

Use of FSTDs

Section 61.4, *Qualification and approval of flight simulators and flight training devices*, states in paragraph (a) that each full flight simulator (FFS) and flight training device (FTD) used for training, and for which an airman is to receive credit to satisfy any training, testing, or checking requirement under this chapter, must be qualified and approved by the Administrator for—

(1) The training, testing, and checking for which it is used;

(2) Each particular maneuver, procedure, or crewmember function performed; and

(3) The representation of the specific category and class of aircraft, type of aircraft, particular variation within the type of aircraft, or set of aircraft for certain flight training devices.

14 CFR part 60 prescribes the rules governing the initial and continuing qualification and use of all FSTDs used for meeting training, evaluation, or flight experience requirements for flight crewmember certification or qualification.

An FSTD is defined in 14 CFR part 60 as an FFS or FTD:

Full Flight Simulator (FFS)—a replica of a specific type, make, model, or series aircraft. It includes the equipment and computer programs necessary to represent aircraft operations in ground and flight conditions, a visual system providing an out-of-the-flight deck view, a system that provides cues at least equivalent to those of a three-degree-of-freedom motion system, and has the full range of capabilities of the systems installed in the device as described in part 60 of this chapter and the QPS for a specific FFS qualification level. (part 1)

Flight Training Device (FTD)—a replica of aircraft instruments, equipment, panels, and controls in an open flight deck area or an enclosed aircraft flight deck replica. It includes the equipment and computer programs necessary to represent aircraft (or set of aircraft) operations in ground and flight conditions having the full range of capabilities of the systems installed in the device as described in part 60 of this chapter and the qualification performance standard (QPS) for a specific FTD qualification level (part 1).

The FAA National Simulator Program (NSP) qualifies Level A-D FFSs and Level 4 – 7[1] FTDs. In addition, each operational rule part identifies additional requirements for the approval and use of FSTDs in a training program.[2] Use of an FSTD for the completion of the private pilot airplane practical test is permitted only when accomplished in accordance with an FAA approved curriculum or training program.

Use of ATDs

14 CFR section 61.4(c) states the Administrator may approve a device other than an FFS or FTD for specific purposes. Under this authority, the FAA's General Aviation and Commercial Division provide approval for aviation training devices (ATD).

---

[1]The FSTD qualification standards in effect prior to part 60 defined a Level 7 FTD for airplanes (see Advisory Circular 120-45A, Airplane Flight Training Device Qualification, 1992). This device required high fidelity, airplane specific aerodynamic and flight control models similar to a Level D FFS, but did not require a motion cueing system or visual display system. In accordance with the "grandfather rights" of part 60, section 60.17, these previously qualified devices will retain their qualification basis as long as they continue to meet the standards under which they were originally qualified. There is only one airplane Level 7 FTD with grandfather rights that remains in the U.S. As a result of changes to part 60 that were published in the Federal Register in March 2016, the airplane Level 7 FTD was reinstated with updated evaluation standards. The new Level 7 FTD will require a visual display system for qualification. The minimum qualified Tasks for the Level 7 FTD are described in Table B1B of Appendix B of part 60.

[2] 14 CFR part 121, section 121.407; part 135, section 135.335; part 141, section 141.41; and part 142, section 142.59.

Advisory Circular (AC) 61-136A, *FAA Approval of Aviation Training Devices and Their Use for Training and Experience*, provides information and guidance for the required function, performance, and effective use of ATDs for pilot training and aeronautical experience (including currency). FAA issues a letter of authorization (LOA) to an ATD manufacturer approving an ATD as a basic aviation training device (BATD) or an advanced aviation training device (AATD). The LOA will be valid for a five-year period with a specific expiration date and include the amount of credit a pilot may take for training and experience.

> *Aviation Training Device (ATD)—a training device, other than an FFS or FTD, that has been evaluated, qualified, and approved by the Administrator. In general, this includes a replica of aircraft instruments, equipment, panels, and controls in an open flight deck area or an enclosed aircraft cockpit. It includes the hardware and software necessary to represent a category and class of aircraft (or set of aircraft) operations in ground and flight conditions having the appropriate range of capabilities and systems installed in the device as described within the AC for the specific basic or advanced qualification level.*

> *Basic Aviation Training Device (BATD)—provides an adequate training platform for both procedural and operational performance Tasks specific to instrument experience and the ground and flight training requirements for the private pilot certificate and instrument rating per 14 CFR parts 61 and 141.*

> *Advanced Aviation Training Device (AATD)—provides an adequate training platform for both procedural and operational performance Tasks specific to the ground and flight training requirements for the private pilot certificate, instrument rating, commercial pilot certificate, airline transport pilot (ATP) certificate, and flight instructor certificate per 14 CFR parts 61 and 141. It also provides an adequate platform for Tasks required for instrument experience and the instrument proficiency check.*

ATDs cannot be used for practical tests, aircraft type specific training, or for an aircraft type rating; therefore the use of an ATD for the private pilot airplane practical test is not permitted.

Credit for Time in an FSTD

Section 61.109 specifies the minimum aeronautical experience requirements for a person applying for a private pilot certificate. Paragraphs (a) and (b) specify the time requirements for a private pilot certificate in a single-engine airplane and a multiengine airplane, respectively.[3] These paragraphs include specific experience requirements that must be completed in an airplane. Paragraph (k) of this section specifies the amount of credit a pilot can take for time in an FFS or FTD. For those that received training in programs outside of part 142, section 61.109(k)(1).[4] For those pilots that received training through a part 142 program, section 61.109(k)(2).

Credit for Time in an ATD

Section 61.109 specifies the minimum aeronautical experience requirements for a person applying for a private pilot certificate. Paragraphs (a) and (b) specify the time requirements for a private pilot certificate in a single-engine airplane and a multiengine airplane, respectively.[5] These paragraphs include specific experience requirements that must be completed in an airplane. Paragraph (k) of this section specifies the amount of credit a pilot can take towards the private pilot certificate aeronautical experience requirements.

---

[3] The minimum aeronautical experience requirements may be further reduced as permitted in part 61, section 61.109(k)(3).

[4] As part of program approval, part 141 training providers must also adhere to the requirements for permitted time in an FFS or FTD per Appendix B to part 141.

[5] The minimum aeronautical experience requirements may be further reduced as permitted in part 61, section 61.109(k)(3).

In order to credit the time, the ATD must be FAA-approved and the time must be provided by an authorized instructor. AC 61-136A, states the LOA for each approved ATD will indicate the credit allowances for pilot training and experience, as provided under parts 61 and 141. Time with an instructor in a BATD and an AATD may be credited towards the aeronautical experience requirements for the private pilot certificate as specified in the LOA for the device used. It is recommended that applicants who intend to take credit for time in a BATD or an AATD towards the aeronautical experience requirements for the private pilot certificate obtain a copy of the LOA for each device used so they have a record for how much credit may be taken. For additional information on the logging of ATD time reference AC 61-136A, see Appendix 4.

Use of an FSTD on a Practical Test

Section 61.45 specifies the required aircraft and equipment that must be provided for a practical test unless permitted to use an FFS or FTD for the flight portion. Section 61.64 provides the criteria for using an FSTD for a practical test. Specifically, paragraph (a) states –

> *If an applicant for a certificate or rating uses a flight simulator or flight training device for training or any portion of the practical test, the flight simulator and flight training device—*
>
> *(1) Must represent the category, class, and type (if a type rating is applicable) for the rating sought; and*
>
> *(2) Must be qualified and approved by the Administrator and used in accordance with an approved course of training under part 141 or part 142 of this chapter; or under 14 CFR part 121 or 14 CFR part 135 of this chapter, provided the applicant is a pilot employee of that air carrier operator.*

Therefore, practical tests or portions thereof, when accomplished in an FSTD, may only be conducted by FAA aviation safety inspectors (ASI), aircrew program designees (APD) authorized to conduct such tests in FSTDs in 14 CFR parts 121 or 135, qualified personnel and designees authorized to conduct such tests in FSTDs for part 141 pilot school graduates, or appropriately authorized part 142 Training Center Evaluators (TCE).

In addition, 14 CFR section 61.64(b) states if an airplane is not used during the practical test for a type rating for a turbojet airplane (except for preflight inspection), an applicant must accomplish the entire practical test in a Level C or higher FFS and the applicant must meet the specific experience criteria listed. If the experience criteria cannot be met, the applicant can either—

> *(f)(1) [...] complete the following Tasks on the practical test in an aircraft appropriate to category, class, and type for the rating sought: Preflight inspection, normal takeoff, normal instrument landing system approach, missed approach, and normal landing; or*
>
> *(f)(2) The applicant's pilot certificate will be issued with a limitation that states: "The [name of the additional type rating] is subject to pilot in command limitations," and the applicant is restricted from serving as pilot in command in an aircraft of that type.*

When flight Tasks are accomplished in an airplane, certain Task elements may be accomplished through "simulated" actions in the interest of safety and practicality. However, when accomplished in an FFS or FTD, these same actions would not be "simulated." For example, when in an airplane, a simulated engine fire may be addressed by retarding the throttle to idle, simulating the shutdown of the engine, simulating the discharge of the fire suppression agent, if applicable, and simulating the disconnection of associated electrical, hydraulic, and pneumatics systems. However, when the same emergency condition is addressed in a FSTD, all Task elements must be accomplished as would be expected under actual circumstances.

Similarly, safety of flight precautions taken in the airplane for the accomplishment of a specific maneuver or procedure (such as limiting altitude in an approach to stall or setting maximum airspeed for an engine failure expected to result in a rejected takeoff) need not be taken when a FSTD is used. It is important to understand that, whether accomplished in an airplane or FSTD, all Tasks and elements for each maneuver or procedure shall have the same performance standards applied equally for determination of overall satisfactory performance.

Appendix 9: References

This ACS is based on the following 14 CFR parts, FAA guidance documents, manufacturer's publications, and other documents.

Reference	Title
14 CFR part 39	Airworthiness Directives
14 CFR part 43	Maintenance, Preventive Maintenance, Rebuilding and Alteration
14 CFR part 61	Certification: Pilots, Flight Instructors, and Ground Instructors
14 CFR part 71	Designation of Class A, B, C, D and E Airspace Areas; Air Traffic Service Routes; and Reporting Points
14 CFR part 91	General Operating and Flight Rules
14 CFR part 93	Special Air Traffic Rules
AC 00-6	Aviation Weather
AC 00-45	Aviation Weather Services
AC 60-28	English Language Skill Standards Required by 14 CFR parts 61, 63 and 65
AC 61-67	Stall and Spin Awareness Training
AC 91-73	Parts 91 and 135 Single Pilot, Flight School Procedures During Taxi Operations
AIM	Aeronautical Information Manual
Chart Supplements U.S.	Chart Supplements U.S. (previously Airport/Facility Directory or A/FD)
FAA-H-8083-1	Aircraft Weight and Balance Handbook
FAA-H-8083-2	Risk Management Handbook
FAA-H-8083-3	Airplane Flying Handbook
FAA-H-8083-6	Advanced Avionics Handbook
FAA-H-8083-15	Instrument Flying Handbook
FAA-H-8083-23	Seaplane, Skiplane, and Float/Ski Equipped Helicopter Operations Handbook
FAA-H-8083-25	Pilot's Handbook of Aeronautical Knowledge
FAA-P-8740-19	Flying Light Twins Safely
POH/AFM	Pilot's Operating Handbook/FAA-Approved Airplane Flight Manual
Other	Navigation Charts
	Navigation Equipment Manual
	USCG Navigation Rules, International-Inland
	NOTAMs

Note: *Users should reference the current edition of the reference documents listed above. The current edition of all FAA publications can be found at www.faa.gov.*

Appendix 10: Abbreviations and Acronyms

The following abbreviations and acronyms are used in the ACS.

Abb./Acronym	Definition
14 CFR	Title 14 of the Code of Federal Regulations
AATD	Advanced Aviation Training Device
AC	Advisory Circular
ACS	Airman Certification Standards
AD	Airworthiness Directive
ADF	Automatic Direction Finder
ADM	Aeronautical Decision-Making
AFS	Flight Standards Service
AELP	Aviation English Language Proficiency
AFM	Airplane Flight Manual
AFS	Flight Standards Service
AGL	Above Ground Level
AIM	Aeronautical Information Manual
AKTR	Airman Knowledge Test Report
ALD	Available Landing Distance
AMEL	Airplane Multiengine Land
AMES	Airplane Multiengine Sea
AOA	Angle of Attack
AOO	Area of Operation
ASEL	Airplane Single Engine Land
ASES	Airplane Single Engine Sea
ASI	Aviation Safety Inspector
ATC	Air Traffic Control
ATD	Aviation Training Device
ATP	Airline Transport Pilot
BATD	Basic Aviation Training Device
CDI	Course Deviation Indicator
CFIT	Controlled Flight Into Terrain
CFR	Code of Federal Regulations
CG	Center of Gravity
CP	Completion Phase
CRM	Crew Resource Management
CTP	Certification Training Program
DA	Decision Altitude
DH	Decision Height
DME	Distance Measuring Equipment
DP	Departure Procedures
DPE	Designated Pilot Examiner
ELT	Emergency Locator Transmitter
FAA	Federal Aviation Administration

Abb./Acronym	Definition
FADEC	Full Authority Digital Engine Control
FFS	Full Flight Simulator
FMS	Flight Management System
FSB	Flight Standardization Board
FSDO	Flight Standards District Office
FSTD	Flight Simulation Training Device
FTD	Flight Training Device
GBAS	Ground Based Augmentation System
GBAS GLS	Ground Based Augmentation Landing System
GNSS	Global Navigation Satellite System
GPS	Global Positioning System
HAT	Height Above Threshold (Touchdown)
HSI	Horizontal Situation Indicator
IA	Inspection Authorization
IAP	Instrument Approach Procedure
IFO	International Field Office
IFR	Instrument Flight Rules
IFU	International Field Unit
ILS	Instrument Landing System
IMC	Instrument Meteorological Conditions
IPC	Instrument Rating – Airplane *Canadian Conversion*
IPC	Instrument Proficiency Check
IR	Instrument Rating
IRA	Instrument Rating – Airplane
KOEL	Kinds of Operation Equipment List
LAHSO	Land and Hold Short Operations
LDA	Localizer-Type Directional Aid
LOA	Letter of Authorization
LOC	ILS Localizer
LPV	Localizer Performance with Vertical Guidance
MAP	Missed Approach Point
MDA	Minimum Descent Altitude
MEL	Minimum Equipment List
MFD	Multi-functional Displays
NAS	National Airspace System
NOD	Notice of Disapproval
NOTAMs	Notices to Airmen
NSP	National Simulator Program
NTSB	National Transportation Safety Board
PA	Private Airplane
PAR	Private Pilot Airplane
PAT	Private Pilot Airplane/Recreational Pilot – Transition
PCP	Private Pilot Canadian Conversion

Abb./Acronym	Definition
PFD	Primary Flight Display
PIC	Pilot-in-Command
POA	Plan of Action
POH	Pilot's Operating Handbook
PTS	Practical Test Standards
QPS	Qualification Performance Standard
RAIM	Receiver Autonomous Integrity Monitoring
RMP	Risk Management Process
RNAV	Area Navigation
RNP	Required Navigation Performance
SAE	Specialty Aircraft Examiner
SFRA	Special Flight Rules Area
SIAP	Standard Instrument Approach Procedure
SMS	Safety Management System
SOP	Standard Operating Procedures
SRM	Single-Pilot Resource Management
SRM	Safety Risk Management
STAR	Standard Terminal Arrival
SUA	Special Use Airspace
TAEA	Track Advisory Environmental Assessment
TAF	Terminal Forecast
TAS	True Airspeed
TCH	Threshold Crossing Height
TEM	Threat and Error Management
TFR	Temporary Flight Restrictions
UTC	Coordinated Universal Time
V_A	Maneuvering speed
VDP	Visual Descent Point
V_{FE}	Maximum flap extended speed
VFR	Visual Flight Rules
VMC	Visual Meteorological Conditions
V_{MC}	Minimum Control Speed with the Critical Engine Inoperative
V_{NE}	Never exceed speed
VOR	Very High Frequency Omnidirectional Range
V_S	Stall Speed
V_X	Best Angle of Climb Speed
V_Y	Best Rate of Climb Speed
V_{SSE}	Safe, intentional one-engine-inoperative speed. Originally known as safe single-engine speed
V_{XSE}	Best angle of climb speed with one engine inoperative
V_{YSE}	Best rate of climb speed with one engine inoperative
V_{SO}	Stalling Speed or the Minimum Steady Flight Speed in the Landing Configuration

AIRCRAFT INFORMATION

AIRPLANE MAKE/MODEL _____

WEIGHT		AIRSPEEDS		FUEL			

WEIGHT

Gross _____

Empty _____

Pilot/Pasngrs _____

Baggage _____

Fuel (gal × 6) _____

AIRSPEEDS

V_{SO} _____

V_{S1} _____

V_X _____

V_Y _____

V_A _____

V_{NO} _____

V_{NE} _____

V_{FE} _____

V_{LO} _____

V_R _____

FUEL

Capacity L ___ gal R ___ gal

Current Estimate L ___ gal R ___ gal

Endurance (Hr.) _____

Fuel-Flow -- Cruise (GPH) _____

CENTER OF GRAVITY

Fore Limit _____

Aft Limit _____

Current CG _____

PERFORMANCE DATA

	Airspeed	Power* MP	RPM
Takeoff Rotation	_____	_____	_____
Climbout	_____	_____	_____
Cruise Climb	_____	_____	_____
Cruise Level	_____	_____	_____
Cruise Descent	_____	_____	_____
Approach to Land (Visual)	_____	_____	_____
Landing Flare	_____	_____	_____

* If you do not have a constant-speed propeller, ignore manifold pressure (MP).

AIRCRAFT MAINTENANCE RECORDS

Date of Most Recent Annual Inspection [91.409(a)] _____

Date of Most Recent 100-Hour Inspection [91.409(b)] _____

Tachometer Time at Most Recent 100-Hour Inspection _____

Current Tachometer Time _____ Date _____

Date of Most Recent ATC Transponder Tests and Inspections (91.413) _____

Date of Most Recent ELT Inspection [91.207(d)] _____

FAA PRIVATE PILOT
ORAL EXAM GUIDE

Aircraft Information

The previous page has a blank form for you to write in information pertaining to the aircraft you will specifically use during the practical test. This page helps you (1) put this information into your long-term memory and (2) get organized and know whether your aircraft is airworthy.

Sample Examiner Questions

The following sections contain questions that may be asked by your evaluator during the oral exam portion of your private pilot practical test.

Part I covers Single-Pilot Resource Management. Because determining an applicant's ability to make sound decisions, even though (s)he is fully capable of flying an airplane, can be difficult, evaluators will emphasize this topic during your practical test through oral questioning. Evaluators must ensure that pilots are capable of managing risks according to specific scenario-based examples. Since it is impossible to cover every possible scenario, this section emphasizes processes you should be able to apply to a variety of situations. Below is a listing of the airplane tasks and the pages on which the related questions start.

Part II covers the Airman Certification Standards (ACS) Tasks. We present the related questions in the order in which their associated subjects are listed in the ACS. However, your evaluator may ask these questions (or questions that are very similar) in any order (s)he wishes. Below is a listing of the airplane tasks and the pages on which the related questions start. All answers are from the perspective of a single-engine oral exam because this book is geared toward the airplane single-engine land (ASEL) practical test. In addition, seaplane- and multiengine-specific tasks are not included because they are not relevant to ASEL.

The questions contained in this oral exam guide primarily cover the oral tasks listed in the ACS. Be confident; you will do fine. You can never be totally prepared. If you have studied this book, you will pass with confidence. This book contains the answer to virtually every question, issue, and requirement that is possible on the oral exam portion of the private pilot practical test. Good luck!

PART I: SINGLE-PILOT RESOURCE MANAGEMENT (SRM)

1. Aeronautical Decision Making

1.	What are the components of the 3P model used in Aeronautical Decision Making?	Perceive, process, and perform are the three components of the 3P model.
2.	How would the 3P model come into play if you suspected an instrument failure in flight?	Perceive; I would recognize if a conflict existed between supporting instruments that suggested a potential failure. Process; I would determine how significant an effect this potential failure would have on flight safety. For instance, if the failure is in the VSI, it would be a minor issue, but if the failure is of the altimeter, that would be significantly more important. Perform; I would verify the failure and implement the best possible course of action to either continue the flight safely or terminate the flight early in the interest of safety.
3.	The 3P model is associated with another acronym, PAVE. What does PAVE indicate?	PAVE is a reminder that makes it possible for the pilot to evaluate the various aspects that make up a successful flight. PAVE is a means of evaluating the Pilot, Aircraft, enVironment, and External Pressures associated with the flight in an organized manner.
4.	In respect to PAVE, what is the question we want to ask ourselves as it pertains to each point?	For each element of PAVE, the pilot should ask, "What could hurt me, my passengers, or my aircraft?" PAVE is a defensive tool.
5.	What is the rule of thumb when working with the processing phase of the 3P model?	If you find yourself thinking that you'll probably be okay on a given flight, that is a good indication that you really need to take time out for a reality check. "Probably" being okay is not a good starting point for any flight, nor is it an effective approach to risk management.
6.	Is there a reminder associated with the Perform element of the 3P model?	Yes, it's ME. That stands for Mitigate (or eliminate) the risk, then Evaluate the outcome of your actions.
7.	How would you describe the DECIDE model of aeronautical decision making?	The DECIDE model is a six-step process that allows the pilot to use a logical progression when involved in aeronautical decision making.
8.	What are the six elements of the DECIDE model?	Detect, Estimate, Choose, Identify, Do, and Evaluate.
9.	Does the DECIDE model scenario end with Evaluate?	No, DECIDE is a looping process of thoughts and actions that repeats. After completing the Evaluate element, the PIC would typically run through the process again, starting with Detect each time a change is recognized.

10.	Can you explain the function of each element of the DECIDE model?	Detect recognizes that the pilot in command has detected that a change has occurred. Estimate acknowledges the PIC's need to react to the change. Choose suggests the PIC should select a desirable outcome for the flight. Identify deals with the PIC identifying the steps necessary to successfully deal with the change. Do is the action step, where the PIC actually performs the steps necessary for the situation. And Evaluate is the point where the PIC will evaluate the result of his or her actions.
11.	How many recognized hazardous attitudes do pilots need to concern themselves with?	There are five hazardous attitudes that have been identified. They are anti-authority, impulsivity, invulnerability, macho, and resignation.
12.	What is resignation?	That is a passive hazardous attitude. If the pilot takes the attitude, "What's the use?," (s)he will not deal with problems effectively or in a timely manner.
13.	Explain the macho attitude.	The catch phrase is, "I can do it." This is the belief that above all odds, regardless of how significant the issue, I can rise above the problem and save the day. This attitude is dangerous because the pilot assumes (s)he is better than any other pilot, which may lead to taking unnecessary risks.
14.	Are female pilots immune from the macho attitude?	No, the term "macho" is not literal; it merely describes a thought process. Women are equally susceptible to the dangers of the macho attitude.
15.	Why is impulsivity dangerous to a pilot?	The tendency to deal with problems quickly can be taken too far. If the goal is to do something, anything, as quickly as possible, the chances of doing the wrong thing due to a lack of consideration before taking action increases. Impulsivity can lead to accidents that could have been prevented if more time and care had been taken when making decisions.
16.	What is the danger involved in the anti-authority attitude?	Anti-authority runs counter to the concept of cockpit resource management. Rather than availing himself or herself of all the information and assistance available to him or her, the anti-authority pilot shuts out all outside information and aid in order to handle the situation entirely on his or her own. This self-imposed isolation is not conducive to safe flight.
17.	If a pilot was taxiing out to the runway with frost on the wings and shrugged off any suggestions to clear the airplane's surfaces first, what attitude might that indicate?	That would suggest Invulnerability. The pilot knows that frost can be dangerous but has convinced himself or herself that, "It won't happen to me." In truth, frost is an equal opportunity enemy of lift. The pilot should recognize the error of his or her ways, stop, and clean the wings before attempting a departure.

18.	At the halfway point of a cross-country flight, you recognize that headwinds have caused a significantly slower groundspeed than anticipated. Your arrival time will now be 1 hour and 10 minutes later than planned. What concern might you have with that realization?	If my flight time will be extended for 1 hour and 10 minutes, I have to consider my fuel reserves. If I have enough fuel to reach my destination, I very likely would not have enough to meet my reserve needs. My best course of action would be to identify an airport along my route where I could stop for fuel, then make plans to divert to that airport. It is better to be late on arrival with sufficient fuel than to be on time with empty tanks.
19.	While flying a C-172 in high humidity, you notice your RPMs are dropping. Your fuel gauges show more than half tanks available. Oil pressure and temperature are in the green. It is 55°F. What might you do?	With a temperature of 55°F while flying in visible moisture, I would suspect carburetor ice. I would apply carburetor heat in an effort to regain normal power. But while I was waiting for the carb heat to take effect, I would identify the nearest field to divert to should that become necessary. If the carb heat worked, I would apply it periodically to prevent carb ice buildup en route. If it did not work, I would plan a diversion to the airport I had previously identified.
20.	Where should you plan to touch down when landing behind a large aircraft that has just landed on the same runway?	Stay above the preceding aircraft's flight path. Observe where the large aircraft's nose touches down and plan to touch down well beyond that point.
21.	What should you do when landing behind a large aircraft that has just taken off on the same runway?	Take note of the location of the large aircraft's rotation point and plan to land well before that point.
22.	How can a risk management assessment benefit you as a pilot?	The PAVE checklist is appropriate for every flight operation. Pilot, Aircraft, enVironment, and External Pressures all come into play when planning, conducting, and concluding a flight. Because my workload is known to rise during the approach and landing phase of flight, it is important that I use a tool that will help assure the balance of safety remains on my side throughout the flight.

2. Risk Management

23.	What are the four fundamental risk elements associated with any flight?	The pilot, the aircraft, the environment, and the type of operation.
24.	What concerns might you have about yourself, the pilot?	I have to be on guard to evaluate my competency to safely conduct the flight. This includes my health, the level of physical and mental stress I am experiencing, my fatigue level, and even my emotional state. Each of these factors has to be considered when I make my go/no-go decisions.
25.	What concerns might we have about the aircraft?	It is my responsibility to consider the limitations of the aircraft, including inoperative components that may be present. I have to be confident that the aircraft's performance capabilities exceed what will be asked of it during the flight and that it complies with airworthiness requirements.

26.	When we think of the environment, are we considering weather alone?	Not at all. Weather is a significant factor when we consider the environment, but we also have other considerations. The term environment is all encompassing. We consider every aspect of the environment, from weather, to terrain, to ATC services available to us during the flight.
27.	Why are external pressures of significance to our planning processes?	Because external pressures can cause a pilot to make decisions based on factors that can degrade the safety margin of the flight. Meeting deadlines, pleasing people, and accomplishing secondary tasks can push a pilot to take risks that were unnecessary and may be to the detriment of the safety of the flight.
28.	A flight is scheduled for 6:00 a.m. Among the factors to consider are – the pilot completed his or her previous flight at 1:30 a.m. after a full day of flying.	The Pilot element of PAVE encourages us to examine pilot fitness to fly. This pilot has not had adequate rest to safely conduct the flight. Consequently, this flight should be postponed until the pilot has had sufficient rest.
29.	A flight is scheduled for 6:00 a.m. The aircraft has been tied down on the ramp overnight. It rained until past midnight, the temperature has dropped throughout the night, and it is currently 28°F.	The Aircraft element of PAVE encourages us to consider the airworthiness and condition of the aircraft. In this case, moisture on the airframe may have frozen in areas that are difficult to see but may affect aircraft performance. The aircraft should be moved to a heated hangar where the ice can thaw and flow out of the aircraft, or the flight should be postponed until the ambient temperatures allow the ice to thaw. Trapped ice that could inhibit free movement of flaps, ailerons, rudder, or elevator could affect the safety of flight.
30.	The same flight as described in the previous question is scheduled to depart at 6:00 a.m. Light freezing rain has begun to fall. The aircraft has no deice or anti-ice capabilities.	The enVironment element of PAVE encourages us to consider all aspects of the environment that aircraft will be operating in. With no means of deicing wings or propellers, and freezing rain falling, the flight would violate regulations that prohibit flight into known icing by aircraft that are unequipped to deal with those conditions. The safety of this flight would be compromised. The flight should be postponed until more reasonable weather conditions exist.
31.	After explaining that the flight will be delayed because of freezing rain, your passenger insists that he must leave promptly, or an important business deal will fall through. He offers to pay you a considerable amount of money for making the flight.	External pressures can cause a pilot to make poor decisions that may affect the safety of flight. In this case, neither the importance of the business deal or the money for making the flight negate the fact that freezing rain is falling and your aircraft is not capable of flying in known icing conditions. Regardless of the incentives, the flight must be postponed until conditions improve. Further, private pilots cannot legally accept compensation for performing a flight.
32.	How can a tool like the I'M SAFE checklist help pilots maintain a high level of safety?	Using the I'M SAFE checklist gives pilots a standardized approach to evaluating their fitness for flight, which provides for a more thorough self-examination of our condition.
33.	What are the elements of the I'M SAFE checklist?	Illness, Medication, Stress, Alcohol, Fatigue, and Emotion/Eating.

34.	If you have had an upsetting argument with your spouse just before leaving home for the airport, what element of I'M SAFE would that fall under?	The Stress element. An upsetting argument with your spouse could cause you to be distracted, or agitated. Neither is a desirable condition for a pilot who is preparing to initiate a flight.
35.	Why is Eating an issue?	In addition to being healthy and well rested, it is equally important for pilots to be adequately nourished so that their thought processes can function normally and their motor skills are well maintained.
36.	What weather phenomenon is suggested by the approach of a fast-moving cold front?	Squall lines can lead fast-moving cold fronts by a significant margin. Although the current weather may be excellent, the squall line can bring violent weather to the area quickly.
37.	When can you expect to encounter hazardous wind shear?	Hazardous wind shear is commonly encountered near the ground during periods of strong temperature inversion and near thunderstorms.
38.	What is a microburst?	Microbursts are small-scale intense downdrafts that, on reaching the surface, spread outward in all directions from the downdraft center.
39.	What effect does encountering a microburst have on an airplane which traverses it?	First the aircraft could see an increase in indicated airspeed (performance gained) from the headwind. Then the wind will switch to a tailwind (performance lost), which could cause contact with terrain.
40.	Under what conditions are microbursts likely?	Microbursts commonly occur within the heavy rain portion of thunderstorms, but also in much weaker, benign-appearing convective cells that have little or no precipitation reaching the ground.
41.	How long do microbursts normally last?	Microbursts seldom last longer than 15 min. from the time they strike the ground.
42.	If the winds are light and the temperature and dew point are 5° or less apart, and closing at your destination airport, what weather phenomenon might this indicate is possible?	When temperature and dew point are within 5° and winds are light, fog and low clouds may form.
43.	Why is fog particularly dangerous to pilots?	Because it hugs the ground, fog may give the appearance of being very thin and easy to see through when viewed from above. On an approach, fog may reduce visibility to near zero, however.
44.	What are the two conditions that can cause fog to form?	Cooling air until the temperature equals the dew point, or adding moisture to an air mass.
45.	How can a thunderstorm be identified in flight?	Lightning flashes are an excellent indicator of a thunderstorm. However, if the thunderstorms are embedded it may be impossible to determine where the thunderstorm is specifically located.

46.	What is one way of avoiding thunderstorms when they are embedded?	The best course of action is not to fly in those conditions. Embedded thunderstorms are an extreme hazard to aircraft and should be avoided at all times.
47.	What resource will provide the most accurate indication of turbulence along your route?	Pilot reports are the most accurate indication of turbulence in flight.
48.	What is the 5P model?	The 5P model is a method of systematically assessing risk in five specific areas that are pertinent to flight.
49.	What are the five areas associated with the 5P model?	Plan, Plane, Pilot, Passengers, and Programming.
50.	How does Plan relate to the 5P model?	Plan relates to the planning of the flight. It is a reminder to take care and gather all pertinent information for the flight as it relates to the route, fuel requirements, the weather, NOTAMs, etc.
51.	How does Plane figure into the 5P model?	The airworthiness of the aircraft is critical to safety, so the Plane heading reminds pilots to verify the aircraft's mechanical fitness for flight, be familiar with its systems and their operation, and ensure that all required paperwork is in order.
52.	Other than being present, how is the Pilot aspect of the 5P model important?	Showing up for the flight is important, but the pilot also has to realistically self-evaluate his or her health, fatigue and stress levels, and any medications (s)he may have taken. The I'M SAFE checklist can be a great aid to the pilot in making these determinations.
53.	How does Passengers relate to safety in terms of the 5P model?	Passengers come in all types. Some are experienced pilots who may be able to help in an emergency. Others are noticeably uncomfortable with the idea of flying and may need to be reassured in turbulence or if an unexpected occurrence should rattle them. Knowing what sort of passengers you have on board, and recognizing how to deal with them in various flight situations can positively affect the safety of flight.
54.	The last P in the 5P model is Programming. What does Programming have to do with the flight?	As cockpits transition to glass panels, automated systems become more common, and GPS navigation becomes a primary navigation tool, the importance of verifying the integrity and currency of databases and software is increased. The Programming line item in the 5P model literally refers to the programming that runs so many of the tools that a pilot may make use of today, and the importance of verifying that it is accurate and appropriate for the flight.

3. Task Management

55.	Are there situations before the flight departs when prioritization might be important?	Yes, when acting as PIC, it is always important to recognize the need to prioritize. Even before leaving the ground, it is possible that a passenger might want to ask questions while ATC is passing along instructions. It would be my responsibility to recognize that the ATC communication is the priority task. I would indicate to the passenger that I needed to focus my attention on ATC momentarily and would be free to answer questions afterward.
56.	Give me an example of where the ability to prioritize tasks might be important in flight.	If I had been cleared by ATC to proceed to a visual checkpoint, for instance, and had a map light go out while I was nearing the checkpoint. The priority would be to proceed as instructed, then deal with the map light issue. If I attempted to deal with the light first, I might miss the checkpoint and cause a safety issue to other aircraft, and increase the workload for ATC.
57.	What about a situation in which there are no apparent problems, such as when entering the airport traffic pattern. Is there any need to prioritize your planning or your actions then?	Yes. Although everything is going according to plan, my priority is to set myself and the aircraft up for the next phase of the flight, prior to reaching that point. For pattern entry, I want to have reviewed the airport diagram and have become familiar with the airport area well in advance of arrival. I would have my radio set up for the airport early. By prioritizing the need to prepare, my flight will be less stressful and safety will be enhanced.

4. Situational Awareness

58.	What is situational awareness?	Situational awareness refers to the pilot's accurate perception of the operational and environmental factors that affect the flight. It is about being aware. That awareness includes everything from the position of the aircraft in relation to other aircraft, its position in relation to a fix or a given runway, recognition of the terrain the aircraft is flying over, current weather conditions, resources available the pilot, and even the type and use of the instrumentation available in the cockpit.
59.	Why is good situational awareness so important?	A pilot who has a high level of situational awareness can make better decisions than one who is less aware. Situational awareness allows the pilot to make better decisions, earlier, than the pilot who is struggling to see how the flight, and the available resources, fit into any given scenario.

60.	Can you give me an example of when situational awareness is beneficial to a pilot?	When entering the airport traffic pattern, good situational awareness will allow the pilot to have a sense of where (s)he is in relation to the runway and airport. That situational awareness will prevent him or her from being surprised or caught off guard when unforeseen circumstances occur. The pilot will also be more confident in his or her awareness if familiar with the physical environment (s)he is flying in, with knowledge of the current weather, obstacle heights, and the location and intention of other traffic.
61.	Can you give me an example where a lack of situational awareness could be a problem while in flight?	Perhaps the most obvious example would be the pilot who enters the approach and landing phase of flight without adequate preparation and planning. Poor situational awareness might cause him or her to violate airspace, cause a collision hazard, or result in forgotten or skipped steps that could lead to an accident. This lack of basic situational awareness can lead to tragic results.
62.	What is fixation?	Fixation is the tendency to focus on one instrument, or a single issue, to the exclusion of everything else.
63.	Why is fixation such a serious issue in instrument or visual flight?	Fixation is a potential problem for any pilot, but it is especially important for visual pilots to guard against because we need to incorporate all the information available to us in order to maintain flight safety. As an example, if I was to focus on just the altimeter, my heading would tend to wander. If I was to focus on just the GPS ground track, my altitude might vary enough to create a problem. All the while my focus would be inside the cockpit rather than outside, itself a serious hazard to flight safety.
64.	Can you give me a real world example of how serious fixation can be?	Perhaps the best known example was Eastern Airlines Flight 401. The entire crew became fixated on a burned out gear indicator light, which prevented them from noticing that the aircraft was descending over terrain with no lights. By the time they recognized the problem, there was no time left to correct it. More than 100 passengers and crew were killed in that case, in large part due to the fixation of the crew.

5. Controlled Flight into Terrain Awareness

65.	What does the acronym TAWS stand for?	TAWS is an abbreviation of Terrain Awareness and Warning System.
66.	What does the abbreviation GPWS stand for?	GPWS refers to the Ground Proximity Warning System.
67.	Do all aircraft have TAWS or GPWS installed?	No, but it is the pilot's responsibility to understand the specific system if it is installed and be able to use it correctly in order to enhance safety.

68.	Are there similarities between the TAWS and the GPWS?	Yes, both systems are designed to give the pilot warnings meant to prevent accidents due to an excessive sink rate or flight into terrain.
69.	Can a TAWS or GPWS always prevent controlled flight into terrain accidents?	No, there are limitations to aircraft performance that must be understood and planned for when flying in mountainous or other potentially hostile environments. Good planning and a high level of situational awareness are necessary to ensure safe flight, regardless of instrumentation and equipment available on board.
70.	Can you give me an example of a CFIT accident scenario that could be prevented through good planning and maintaining situational awareness?	The classic example may be the poor decision to fly into a box canyon. With insufficient room to turn around, and insufficient performance to climb above the walls of the canyon, the accident becomes unavoidable as soon as the pilot enters the canyon, regardless of how long or far (s)he can fly before running out of clear airspace.
71.	Are there other circumstances where CFIT accidents can be prevented?	Yes, the Steve Fossett crash is a good example of a good pilot who suffered a serious accident due to performance issues. The NTSB found that Fossett's Bellanca was forced into the ground by winds that exceeded his airplane's ability to overcome them. His crash is a good reminder that wind and weather can cause a controlled flight into terrain accident. It is for that exact reason that it is so important that pilots maintain a sense of situational awareness and plan flights in such a way that the performance of their aircraft can deal with the situations that may arise during any given flight.
72.	Is CFIT as much of a danger for VFR operations as it is for IFR operations?	It could be argued that Controlled Flight into Terrain is a greater danger for VFR operations because the pilot feels more visually aware of the outside world. It is the risk of CFIT that makes it imperative that pilots maintain an awareness of risk elements like minimum altitudes, go-around procedures, and rising terrain in the vicinity of their departure/destination airports. While the see-and-avoid concept is certainly important, adherence to established information and practices is equally imperative.

6. Automation Management

73.	How can you verify the mode of operation your autopilot is in?	The specific method differs from unit to unit, based on manufacturer, but in general there is an enunciation on the display that reads out the mode.
74.	If you were tracking a VOR with the autopilot, what mode would you be using?	NAV mode would be the appropriate choice when tracking a VOR radial.

75.	How can I manually transition from one mode to another?	The specific process varies by manufacturer and model, but in general you can manually transition from one mode to another by using a selector button located on the panel. Mode buttons are typically labeled HDG, NAV, and APR, although there may also be additional modes for reverse course and/or altitude.
76.	Can you give me an example of a situation that might surprise a pilot with an unanticipated mode change on the autopilot?	Unanticipated mode changes can catch a pilot by surprise and are often self-induced. Input errors, or misunderstanding how the autopilot works in various modes, can result in the pilot issuing a command to do something other than that which (s)he intended.
77.	How would the Garmin G1000 indicate that it was using the GPS or VOR information for navigation?	The HSI needle is magenta when the unit is using GPS information. It switches to green when it is tracking the localizer. Other cockpit automation systems use a similar color scheme, but it is important to fully understand new equipment when transitioning to it for the first time.

PART II: AIRMAN CERTIFICATION STANDARDS (ACS) TASKS

AREA OF OPERATION I: PREFLIGHT PREPARATION

Task A: Pilot Qualifications

1.	What certificates and documents must be on board the aircraft for it to be considered legal?	Remember **A.R.R.O.W.**: **A**irworthiness certificate, **R**egistration, **R**adio station license (if you are flying outside the U.S.), **O**perating limitations, and **W**eight and balance.
2.	What are the items required to be carried with you in order to act as pilot in command (PIC)?	To act as PIC of an aircraft, you are required to carry your pilot's certificate and medical certificate or driver's license, whichever is appropriate. All pilots acting as PIC must carry a government-issued photo ID as a means of positively identifying themselves.
3.	What are the limitations regarding flying for hire as a private pilot?	A private pilot cannot act as a pilot in command of an aircraft that is carrying passengers or property for compensation or hire. A private pilot must pay at least an equal (pro rata) share of the operating expenses of a flight carrying passengers.
4.	What documents should you carry on your person when operating the airplane in flight?	A valid pilot certificate, a current and valid medical certificate, and a government-issued photo ID (a driver's license satisfies this requirement).
5.	Must you notify the FAA of a change of address?	Yes. If your address changes, you must notify the FAA in writing within 30 days, or you may not exercise the privileges of your pilot certificate.
6.	Where can pilot certification requirements be found?	Pilot certification requirements can be found in 14 CFR Part 61.
7.	What is an advisory circular (AC)?	ACs are documents used by the FAA as a means of issuing nonregulatory information to pilots, mechanics, and manufacturers.

8.	Define the responsibility and authority of the pilot in command.	The pilot in command is the final authority as to the operation of the aircraft. (S)he is responsible for the safety of the crew and all passengers on board the aircraft.
9.	Can a private pilot tow a glider?	Yes, provided (s)he obtains specific experience and training required by 14 CFR Part 61.69, which includes 100 hours of pilot-in-command time in the category and class and type of aircraft being used to tow gliders.
10.	When would you need to obtain a flight review to remain legal to act as pilot in command?	Within 24 months of successfully completing my private pilot practical test. I would then need to complete a flight review every 24 months with a certified flight instructor or a designated pilot examiner.
11.	What is the minimum age requirement to qualify for a private pilot certificate for a single-engine airplane?	To be eligible for a private pilot certificate, a person must be at least 17 years old for a rating in other than a glider or a balloon.
12.	As PIC (pilot in command), what is your responsibility to your passengers with regard to safety belts?	As PIC, you must brief your passengers on the operation of the safety belts and notify your passengers when belts must be worn.
13.	How long is a third-class medical certificate valid?	A third-class medical certificate is valid until the end of the 60th calendar month following the date of the examination if you were under 40 years of age on the day of the medical exam. If you were 40 years old or older on the day of the exam, then the certificate is valid until the end of the 24th calendar month following the date of the examination.
14.	How long is a second-class medical certificate valid?	A second-class medical certificate is valid for 12 months. However, since private pilots cannot operate an aircraft for hire, a private pilot need not have a second-class certificate and must only carry a third-class medical certificate. If a private pilot receives a second-class medical certificate, it will effectively become a third-class medical certificate after the 12-month period, and it remains valid for as long as a third-class medical certificate is valid. Therefore, a private pilot holding a second-class medical certificate holds a valid medical certificate for 60 months if the pilot was under 40 years old on the date of the examination. If the pilot was 40 years old or over on the date of the examination, a second-class medical certificate is valid for 24 months after the month the medical examination was conducted.

15.	How long is a first-class medical certificate valid?	A first-class medical certificate is valid for 12 months if the pilot is under the age of 40. For private pilots who are age 40 and over, first-class medical certificates are valid for 6 months. However, since private pilots cannot operate an aircraft for hire, a private pilot need not have a first-class certificate and must only carry a third-class medical certificate. Therefore, a private pilot holding a first-class medical certificate holds a valid medical certificate for 60 months if the pilot was under 40 years old on the date of the examination. If the pilot was 40 years old or over on the date of the examination, a first-class medical certificate is valid for 24 months after the month the medical examination was conducted.
16.	What class of medical certificate must a private pilot hold?	A private pilot must carry at least a third-class medical certificate that is valid and current.
17.	What flight experience must be entered into a pilot's logbook?	The only flight experience that is required to be entered into a pilot logbook is the experience that is required for obtaining a certificate or rating, completing a flight review, or meeting recency of experience requirements.
18.	Can you give me an example of an endorsement that is required in your pilot logbook in order for you to take this practical test?	I have a solo endorsement from my flight instructor that allows me to operate the aircraft in solo flight. I also have an endorsement recommending me for this practical test.
19.	Are there established airworthiness requirements for pilots?	Yes, there are a number of requirements a pilot must meet in order to be considered current. These include a flight review every 24 months, and three takeoffs and landings within 90 days to be current to carry a passenger.
20.	How would a pilot show that (s)he meets those currency requirements required of pilots in order to act as PIC?	A pilot can show currency through logbook records and endorsements. Landings and the dates they occurred should be recorded in the pilot's logbook, and an endorsement acknowledging the successful completion of a flight review should also be included in the pilot's logbook.
21.	What is a flight review?	A flight review is a mandatory period of instruction and evaluation that pilots must successfully complete within a 24-calendar-month period in order to act as pilot in command (PIC). The flight review must include a minimum of 1 hour of ground instruction and 1 hour of flight instruction.
22.	Who can provide the services required for a flight review?	An appropriately rated Certified Flight Instructor (CFI) or a designated pilot examiner can each conduct a flight review.
23.	If you do not obtain a flight review within 24 calendar months, how can you become legal to act as PIC again?	If I do not successfully complete a flight review within 24 calendar months, I can seek out flight and ground instruction as necessary to become proficient again and complete a flight review with a CFI or a designated pilot examiner.

24.	Can the CFI you took instruction from provide you with a flight review?	Yes. A flight review can be completed with any appropriately rated Certified Flight Instructor, or a designated pilot examiner.
25.	If you have completed your flight review and are current to act as PIC, are you automatically current to carry passengers as PIC?	No. In order to act as PIC when carrying passengers, I must make three takeoffs and three landings every 90 days, in addition to completing a flight review. If the airplane is a tailwheel type, the landings must be to a full stop in a tailwheel-type airplane. To carry passengers at night, I would need to make three landings within 90 days, to a full stop, at night.
26.	Is there any exception for carrying passengers that requires full-stop landings during daylight hours?	Yes, if the pilot wishes to carry passengers in a tailwheel type airplane, the three landings must be to a full stop and made in a tailwheel-type airplane, regardless of whether the flights will be made during the daylight or night hours.
27.	What is required to act as PIC of a complex, high-performance, or tailwheel airplane?	To act as PIC of a complex, high-performance, or tailwheel airplane, you are required to receive and log ground and flight training and obtain a logbook endorsement from an appropriately rated CFI.
28.	What is required to act as PIC of a turbojet-powered aircraft, or one with a gross weight over 12,500 lb?	To act as PIC of a turbo-jet powered aircraft, or one with a gross weight of over 12,500 lb, you are required to have a type rating.
29.	Give me an example of an aircraft category.	Category is a broad classification of aircraft that includes airplane, rotorcraft, and lighter-than-air.
30.	Give me an example of an aircraft class.	Class is used to describe aircraft that fall into a similar classification, such as landplane, seaplane, single-engine, or multi-engine.
31.	Give me an example of an aircraft type.	Type refers to a specific make and model of aircraft. A Piper Cub is a type. A Cessna 172 is another type.
32.	Where is the registration located in your aircraft?	NOTE: The location of the registration may vary from one aircraft to another, even when referencing aircraft of the same type. Typically the registration is displayed in a clear plastic holder mounted in the cockpit. Be sure to cover the exact location of required documents with your instructor, using the actual aircraft you will be taking your practical test in.
33.	How long is an aircraft's registration certificate valid?	An aircraft's registration is valid until the aircraft is destroyed or scrapped, the owner loses his or her U.S. citizenship, ownership is transferred, the owner requests the cancelation of the registration, or 30 days have elapsed since the death of the certificate holder. (The registration must be renewed every three years.)
34.	Does the airworthiness certificate alone guarantee that the aircraft is airworthy?	There are inspections and maintenance requirements that must be done on a regular basis in order for the airplane to continue to be airworthy. The annual inspection or the 100-hour inspection are good examples of inspections that must be completed in order to maintain the aircraft's airworthiness.

35.	Where would I find a copy of the operating limitations for your aircraft?	The Pilot's Operating Handbook (POH) and/or Airplane Flight Manual (AFM) include the operating limitations, although the placards in the aircraft that establish limits are also considered a part of the operating limitations.
36.	Can you give me an example of a placard in the aircraft that would be considered an operating limitation?	A placard that is mounted to the instrument panel that prohibits intentional spins would be considered an operational limitation.
37.	Where would I find performance charts that are appropriate to the aircraft we will be flying today?	The POH/AFM will have the appropriate charts for takeoff and landing distances, weight and balance information, time, and fuel and distance charts, along with other pertinent information specific to this airplane.
38.	Where would I find a listing for the best glide speed in this airplane?	In the POH/AFM for the aircraft.
39.	How can we determine V_A for today's flight?	V_A, or maneuvering speed, varies with the weight of the aircraft. The POH/AFM will specify what V_A is at a given weight.
40.	Which color code on the airspeed indicator shows us what maneuvering speed is?	Maneuvering speed is also known as V_A. It is not shown on the airspeed indicator because V_A changes with the weight of the aircraft. We have to look to our performance charts in the POH/AFM to find the appropriate V_A speed for the aircraft as it is loaded for that flight.
41.	What does the green arc on the airspeed indicator tell us?	The green arc indicates the normal operating range for the aircraft.
42.	What does the bottom of the green arc indicate?	The bottom of the green arc indicates the stall speed with flaps retracted.
43.	What does the white arc on the airspeed indicator tell us?	The white arc indicates the full flap operating range.
44.	What does the bottom of the white arc suggest?	The bottom of the white arc is the power-off stalling speed with flaps set to the landing position.
45.	What does the top of the white arc indicate?	The top of the white arc is the maximum speed that we should fly with full flaps extended. When decelerating for landing, it is the speed where it becomes safe to extend the flaps.
46.	What is V_{NO}?	V_{NO} is the maximum structural cruising speed.
47.	How can we identify V_{NO} on the airspeed indicator?	V_{NO} is identified by the airspeed at the top of the green arc as shown on the airspeed indicator.
48.	How do we know if the aircraft is loaded within its CG limit when we fly today?	I calculated a weight and balance problem using both pilot and passenger weights in the aircraft, as well as our fuel load. We will be safely within the CG envelope for the aircraft. (NOTE: Show the examiner your calculations.)

49.	Where did you find the numbers (or charts) that you made your calculations with?	The weight and balance charts are included in the POH/AFM for the aircraft. I used those numbers for a starting point, then included our weights and the weight of our fuel load to calculate an accurate CG location for today's flight.
50.	Other than CG, what other issue is of importance when doing a weight and balance calculation?	We need to verify the total weight of the loaded aircraft. We need to be sure that we do not overload the aircraft. My calculations for today's flight indicate that we are within the CG envelope and below the maximum weight for the loaded aircraft.
51.	How do you calculate the CG of an aircraft?	The POH/AFM includes weight and balance graphs, which can be used to determine the moment of each weight loaded into the aircraft. By adding together all the weights and adding together all the moments, then dividing the total moment by the total weight, the resulting number represents the CG of the aircraft. If a Center of Gravity Moment Envelope is included in the POH/AFM, we can verify that the CG falls within limits by finding the intersection of the total weight of the aircraft with the total moment of the loaded aircraft. As long as the intersection of the two lines is within the envelope, the aircraft's CG is within limits.
52.	If there is no Center of Gravity Moment Envelope in the POH/AFM, how can we be sure we are within CG and weight limits then?	The POH/AFM will list a range that the CG must fall into. If our calculated number falls within that range, we are safely within CG limits. The POH/AFM also lists a maximum gross weight for the aircraft. If our weight is below that number and the CG is within limits, we have loaded the airplane appropriately for the flight.
53.	If the owner of the aircraft installed a new radio last week, would we have to include that in our weight and balance calculations?	No. The mechanic who installed the radio would have amended the aircraft's paperwork to reflect the new empty weight and moment of the aircraft. We can make our calculations based on the information provided in the aircraft's records, which are kept current as they are required to be.
54.	How much does aviation gasoline weigh?	Avgas weighs 6 pounds per gallon.
55.	Why does the weight of gasoline matter to us?	Because the fuel is being consumed during our flight. We need to be sure that our weight and CG are acceptable before taking off. But we should also calculate an estimated fuel burn for the flight and verify that the fuel we burn during our flight is not going to cause our CG to shift forward or aft of the limits en route.

Task B: Airworthiness Requirements

| 56. | What instruments and equipment are required for day VFR flights? | Tachometer, MAP gauge (if equipped), oil pressure gauge, oil temp, fuel gauge, altimeter, airspeed indicator, magnetic direction indicator, anticollision light, ELT, seatbelts, flotation gear (if over water), and landing gear indicator lights (if equipped). |

57.	When is a transponder with Mode C required for VFR flight?	A working transponder with Mode C is required any time you are above 10,000 ft. MSL; inside Class B or Class C airspace, and above Class B or Class C airspace up to 10,000 ft. MSL; or within 30 NM of a Class B primary airport.
58.	When are safety belts required to be worn by all occupants?	Safety belts and shoulder harnesses, if installed, are required to be worn by all occupants during taxi, takeoff, and landing.
59.	Is the VSI a required instrument for VFR flight during nighttime hours?	No, the VSI (vertical speed indicator) is not a required instrument during VFR for day or nighttime hours.
60.	Is a radio required equipment for VFR flight?	It depends on the type of airspace you intend to fly in. If you will be flying into Class B, Class C, or Class D airspace, a radio will be a requirement. However, if your flight is entirely in Class G airspace, there is no requirement to make radio contact with ATC during your flight.
61.	Is a landing light a requirement for night VFR flight?	A landing light is only required for night VFR if the flight is conducted for hire.
62.	Can you give me an example of some other equipment requirements that pertain to night VFR?	The pilot is required to have access to spare fuses of each type required to operate the systems on board. The aircraft must also have position lights installed, and the airplane must have a source of electrical power.
63.	Can we legally fly an aircraft if the installed VSI does not work?	It is not legal to fly in an aircraft with inoperative instruments or equipment unless the specific actions listed in 14 CFR 91.213 are performed.
64.	Can you give me an example of how we could legally fly an aircraft with an installed instrument that is not working?	If the pilot or a maintenance person deems that the inoperative equipment does not present a hazard, we can fly with it. The instrument/equipment must be removed, deactivated, or labeled "inoperative" for us to fly the aircraft without violating the regulations.
65.	If we remove inoperative equipment or instruments, do we have to do anything else before flying?	Whenever a piece of equipment or an instrument is removed from the aircraft, the weight and balance information included with the aircraft must be amended to reflect the change in empty weight and the empty-weight CG.
66.	What is the purpose of an MEL (minimum equipment list)?	The MEL is designed to provide aircraft owners and operators with the authority to operate an aircraft with certain items or components inoperative.
67.	Are there requirements for operating an aircraft when an item or items on the MEL are inoperative?	Yes, the pilot must observe appropriate operating limitations, or the function of the inoperative item must be transferred to another instrument or component that will provide the required information or operational function.
68.	Is an MEL a requirement?	No, most general aviation airplanes operate without an MEL.

69.	How do you know if it is acceptable to fly with inoperative equipment if your airplane does not have an MEL?	We can continue to fly an airplane with inoperative equipment, even without an MEL, provided the equipment that is inoperative is not included on the required VFR instrument and equipment list or the aircraft's equipment list and provided it is not required by any FAR or by an airworthiness directive (AD).
70.	When would a special flight permit be required?	If the airplane has inoperable instruments or equipment and it needs to be moved to a location where the repair work can be performed, a special flight permit would be required.
71.	What is implied when a special flight permit is requested?	The implication is that the airplane does not meet the current airworthiness requirements but that it can be flown safely in order to get it to an airport where repairs can be made.
72.	Who would you request a special flight permit from?	The FAA issues special flight permits. I would contact my local FSDO to make the request.
73.	What information would you provide when requesting a special flight permit?	I would provide information about the purpose of the flight, the itinerary, and the crew required to operate the airplane. I would also provide information regarding how the airplane is currently deficient in meeting the airworthiness standards, as well as any restrictions I consider necessary for the safe operation of the aircraft.
74.	Is a special flight permit requested verbally or in writing?	It is requested in writing, and all the information required to complete the request is included in writing as well.
75.	What is an airworthiness directive (AD) and why are they issued?	An AD is issued by the FAA when there is a safety issue with a particular type of aircraft, engine, or appliance. ADs are mandatory and must be complied with within a certain time frame unless the AD specifically indicates otherwise.
76.	How is an emergency AD different from a less urgent AD?	Emergency ADs may require inspection or repair before another flight can be made. Less urgent ADs often allow for a longer compliance period, which will allow the owner/operator to continue flying the aircraft until a future inspection or maintenance procedure is scheduled.
77.	Are ADs mandatory or voluntary?	ADs are mandatory. The AD is a written regulation that requires action within a specific time period, unless a specific exemption is granted.
78.	How do you know if an AD has been issued for your airplane?	ADs are listed on the FAA website, which allows for an easy search to see if any ADs exist for my airplane. An AD search is a required part of any 100-hour or annual inspection. The mechanic who endorses the logbooks for my airplane would have recorded any ADs that pertained to my airplane, along with the method of compliance that was employed.

79.	How can we tell if an airworthiness directive (AD) that was issued for your aircraft has been complied with?	There will be an entry in the appropriate maintenance log that reflects the work being performed.
80.	How can we be sure an AD that requires ongoing inspections will be complied with in a timely manner?	A record will be included in the maintenance logs by the mechanic doing the work. The record will include the next time or date that work is required in order to comply with the AD.
81.	If an AD does not require recurring action, how would we be able to determine that it had been complied with in the past?	A record of the AD and the method of compliance would be included in the aircraft's maintenance logs.
82.	Are there established airworthiness requirements for aircraft?	Yes, there are a number of requirements that aircraft owners and operators must comply with to maintain their aircraft in airworthy condition. These requirements include maintenance, record keeping, and compliance with airworthiness directives.
83.	What type of airframe inspections is an aircraft required to have undergone to be considered airworthy?	An aircraft must have undergone an annual inspection within the preceding 12 calendar months to be considered airworthy. If an aircraft is used for commercial operations, it is also required to have undergone an inspection within the preceding 100 hr. of operation, or it must be included in a progressive inspection program.
84.	Is the annual inspection required just for the airframe?	No, the entire aircraft must be included in the annual inspection, including the condition of the engine and propeller.
85.	How often must a transponder be tested and inspected to be considered airworthy?	You may not operate a transponder unless it has been inspected and tested within the preceding 24 calendar months.
86.	Who is responsible for keeping the airplane in an airworthy condition?	The owner or operator is responsible for making sure the airplane is kept in an airworthy condition.
87.	How do we establish a record that indicates if an aircraft is airworthy?	By keeping maintenance logbooks that detail inspections and maintenance done to the aircraft throughout its life.
88.	Are all the inspections and maintenance recorded in the same log?	No, there are typically three maintenance logbooks for an aircraft. There is an airframe logbook, a powerplant logbook, and a logbook for the propeller.
89.	What type of maintenance records is the owner required to keep for an aircraft?	Maintenance records must be kept for the current status of life-limited parts (propeller, engine, etc.), the current status of all ADs, and any preventive maintenance done by the pilot.
90.	What are the required inspections for an ELT?	An ELT must have been inspected in the preceding 12 calendar months to be legal. Also, the ELT battery must be replaced after 1 hr. of cumulative use or after 50% of its useful life has expired.

91.	How is an ELT activated?	An ELT can be activated either manually by flipping the switch on the physical unit, or automatically by an impact to the airplane.
92.	If you hear an ELT distress signal when tuned to 121.5 at 13:02, what does that indicate?	It may indicate an emergency, or it may indicate a mechanic, aircraft owner, or pilot is testing an ELT nearby. ELTs may be tested in the first 5 minutes after the hour. To verify, it would be wise to monitor 121.5 to see if the signal continues. If it does, the appropriate action would be to report the ELT signal to the authorities.
93.	What signal does an ELT emit?	ELTs emit a distress signal on 121.5 MHz or 406 MHz for newer ELTs. The signal itself sounds like a pulsing siren, much like a laser gun in an old-fashioned video game. The FAA describes the sound as a "downward swept audio tone."
94.	Must your airplane be equipped with a working ELT before beginning a flight?	Yes. ELTs are always required unless exempt under FAR Part 91.207. An example of when an aircraft is not required to have an ELT is if that aircraft is used for flight instruction within 50 NM of the home airport.
95.	What is the recommended duration for an ELT test?	The *Aeronautical Information Manual* suggests no more than three audible sweeps of the alarm when testing.
96.	Is an airplane owner who is not an Aviation Maintenance Technician (AMT) allowed to perform any type of maintenance on his or her airplane?	Yes. An airplane owner who is not a certificated mechanic is allowed to perform preventive maintenance, such as oil changes.
97.	Who is qualified to perform and make a logbook endorsement for a 100-hour inspection?	An Aviation Maintenance Technician (AMT).
98.	Who is qualified to perform and make a logbook endorsement for an annual inspection?	An AMT with inspection authorization (IA).
99.	Why are some aircraft required to undergo a 100-hour inspection and an annual inspection, while others are only required to undergo an annual inspection?	Aircraft used in commercial operations are required to undergo 100-hour inspections in addition to the annual inspections all aircraft are required to undergo.
100.	Is there any other option besides the 100-hour and annual inspections?	Yes, you can enroll the airplane in a progressive inspection program that meets or exceeds the requirements for the 100-hour and annual inspections.
101.	What is the difference between a 100-hour inspection and an annual inspection?	The only difference between a 100-hour inspection and an annual inspection is the requirement for who makes the logbook endorsement. An AMT can make logbook endorsements for a 100-hour inspection. Only an AMT with inspection authorization (IA) can make the logbook endorsements for an annual inspection.

102.	If you were 5 hours away from home when you realized that your airplane was 3 hours overdue for a 100-hour inspection, could you legally fly home to get the work done?	Yes. It is permissible to fly up to 10 hours past the point of the 100-hour inspection, provided the aircraft is being flown to a place where the inspection can be completed.
103.	If you do fly beyond the 100-hour time limit by 10 hours, when is the next 100-hour inspection due?	The aircraft would be due for inspection immediately, and the 10 hours would be deducted from the next 100-hour inspection period. The 100-hour inspection requirement is not extended by flying past the 100-hour limit.
104.	Who is primarily responsible for maintaining accurate records pertaining to maintenance on the aircraft?	The owner or operator is primarily responsible for maintaining appropriate maintenance records.
105.	As the PIC, are you involved in the process of keeping maintenance records?	Yes, the PIC can be construed as one of the operators of the aircraft.
106.	How would you locate the most recent 100-hour or annual inspection in the aircraft's logbooks?	I would go to the most recent entry and work backwards until I found the endorsement for the most current 100-hour or annual inspection.
107.	Can you give me a couple of examples of mandatory inspections that we might find records for in the aircraft logbooks?	All the mandatory inspections and required maintenance should be included in the aircraft's logbooks. This would include any ADs issued for the airframe, engine, or appliances; 100-hour inspections; annual inspections; and ELT inspections; as well as transponder and static system inspections.

Task C: Weather Information

108.	What is a METAR?	A METAR is a current weather observation that is updated at a regular interval and applies to a 5-mile radius around the observation point (usually at any airport) reporting wind, visibility, storm activity, ceilings, temperature, altimeter setting, and remarks.
109.	What is a TAF?	A TAF is a forecast of conditions expected over the next 24 hr. within a 5-mile radius around an airport. It reports wind, visibility, significant weather, sky condition, and possible wind shear.
110.	How often are TAFs updated?	TAFs are updated four times a day.
111.	How do TAFs indicate wind shear?	TAFs indicate forecast wind shear with the code WS after the sky conditions segment.
112.	What is a PIREP?	A PIREP is a Pilot Weather Report. PIREPs are important sources of observed weather aloft.
113.	How is a PIREP submitted?	PIREPs are submitted by pilots to an FSS.
114.	How can a pilot receive a PIREP?	PIREPs can be received from an FSS or ATC.

115.	What is an area forecast (FA)?	An area forecast (FA) is a forecast of clouds and general weather conditions over an area that includes several states.
116.	How often is an area forecast updated?	Area forecasts are updated three times a day.
117.	What type of information can be found in an area forecast (FA)?	An FA contains four sections: the communication and product header, precautionary statement, synopsis, and VFR clouds/weather section. The communication and product header indicates the date and time of issuance, valid times, and area of coverage. The precautionary statement indicates icing, low-level wind shear, and IFR conditions, and non-MSL heights are denoted by AGL or CIG. The synopsis is a brief summary of the location and movement of fronts, pressure systems, and circulation patterns. The VFR clouds/weather section contains a 12-hr. specific forecast and a 6-hr. outlook and covers possible weather hazards such as IFR conditions, icing, thunderstorms, and wind shear.
118.	What is standard sea level temperature and pressure?	Standard sea level temperature is 15°C (59°F) Standard sea level pressure is 29.92" Hg. These numbers are important for completing important calculations, such as true airspeed, current lapse rate, and density altitude.
119.	What is the standard lapse rate?	The standard lapse rate is 2°C per 1,000 ft. of altitude gained.
120.	What is the Coriolis force?	The Coriolis force is a theory that explains how wind, pressure, and general weather patterns deflect to the right in the Northern Hemisphere. The Coriolis force is the reason wind and weather patterns generally move from west to east (left to right) in the United States.
121.	Why is wind shear dangerous?	Wind shear is dangerous because it is unpredictable and can cause significant changes in heading, airspeed, and altitude, especially close to the ground.
122.	What is the significance of a close temperature-dew point spread?	A close temperature-dew point spread indicates the probable formation of visible moisture in the form of dew, mist, fog, or clouds. The decrease in temperature (most frequently at night) can result in a close temperature-dew point spread and fast-forming fog.
123.	What are the characteristics of stable air?	Stable air is characterized by continuous precipitation, smooth air, and poor visibility.
124.	What are the characteristics of unstable air?	Unstable air is characterized by showery precipitation, rough air, and good visibility.
125.	What is clear air turbulence (CAT)?	Clear air turbulence (CAT) is turbulence not associated with thunderstorms. It usually occurs along an upper-level temperature inversion.

126.	Why is clear air turbulence (CAT) dangerous?	It is dangerous because it is often unexpected, and it can be severe.
127.	What are three types of structural icing?	Clear ice, rime ice, and mixed ice. Clear ice forms when drops are large, as in rain or cumuliform clouds. It is hard, heavy, and unyielding. Rime ice forms as a result of small drops found in stratified clouds and drizzle. Air becomes trapped in between the drops and makes the ice appear white. Mixed ice is a combination of clear and rime ice.
128.	How much can ice or frost degrade performance?	It is important not to operate with frost on the wings because even a seemingly thin coating of frost can degrade performance by up to 40%.
129.	Where is weather information available on the ground?	Weather information is available on the ground from a Flight Service Station (FSS), Direct User Access Terminal System (DUATS), and Telephone Information Briefing Service (TIBS). You can speak to a preflight briefer at an FSS and/or receive recorded weather information from TIBS by calling 1-800-WX-BRIEF anywhere in the country. DUATS is a free service available to pilots on the Internet. With DUATS, you can receive weather information and file a flight plan.
130.	Where is weather information available in-flight?	Weather information is available in-flight with • HIWAS (Hazardous Inflight Weather Advisory Service) • FSS (Flight Service Station) • ATIS (Automatic Terminal Information Service) • ASOS (Automated Surface Observing System) • AWOS (Automated Weather Observing System) You can file a PIREP and obtain numerous types of weather information with FSS. HIWAS is a recorded briefing of hazardous weather over select VOR frequencies. FSS may be contacted at 122.2 MHz. Additional frequencies are shown on navigational charts. ATIS is recorded weather information for a terminal area. AWOS and ASOS are automated weather reporting stations found at many airports.
131.	What is a SIGMET?	SIGMETs are issued for all aircraft and may include severe icing not associated with thunderstorms, clear air turbulence, dust storms, and volcanic eruptions.
132.	What is a convective SIGMET?	Convective SIGMETs are issued for severe thunderstorms, embedded thunderstorms, lines of thunderstorms, and tornadoes, all of which imply severe or greater turbulence, severe icing, and low-level wind shear.
133.	What is an AIRMET?	AIRMETs are issued for moderate icing, moderate turbulence, IFR conditions over 50% of an area, sustained surface winds of 30 kt. or greater, nonconvective low-level wind shear, and mountain obscuration.

134.	What do winds and temperatures aloft forecasts indicate?	Winds and temperatures aloft forecasts indicate the wind speed and direction, as well as temperature, at various altitudes.
135.	What can a pilot determine from these forecasts?	Pilots can make decisions regarding cruise altitudes and route selection that will make the best use of the most favorable winds and temperature inversions when planning flights.
136.	What is a Center Weather Advisory?	A Center Weather Advisory is an advisory provided by ATC for potentially hazardous weather expected to happen within the next 2 hr.
137.	What are the four types of fronts and of what significance is this to aviation?	The four types of fronts are cold, warm, stationary, and occluded. Each front indicates a different type of weather.
138.	What type of weather is associated with a cold front?	Cold fronts usually contain the most volatile weather. Because cold air replaces warm air quickly, the difference in pressure is the greatest, with the potential for violent weather.
139.	What type of weather is associated with a warm front?	The weather associated with a warm front is usually relatively mild. Warm front weather is usually much more widespread and longer lasting than that of cold front weather.
140.	What type of weather is associated with a stationary front?	A stationary front is when warm and cold air masses meet but do not mix. Wind always blows along the frontal boundary of a stationary front, and in some cases, embedded storms occur.
141.	What is an occluded front?	An occluded front is a combination of cold, warm, and cool air. Thus, weather in occluded fronts is a combination of cold and warm front weather.
142.	What are the types of fog and how are they formed?	Fog types include radiation, advection, precipitation-induced, upslope, and ice. Radiation fog forms when the air close to the ground is cooled faster than the air above it. It usually forms at night or near daybreak. Advection fog forms along coastal areas when the water is warmer than the air around it. Precipitation-induced fog forms when relatively warm rain or drizzle falls through cool air and evaporation from the precipitation saturates the cool air. Upslope fog forms as a result of moist, stable air being cooled adiabatically as it moves up sloping terrain. Ice fog occurs in cold weather when the temperature is well below freezing and water vapor sublimates directly as ice crystals.
143.	What conditions must be present for a thunderstorm to form?	Formation of a thunderstorm requires a lifting action, an unstable lapse rate, and sufficient water vapor.
144.	What is a microburst?	A microburst is a heavy downdraft occurring within a thunderstorm.

145.	Why is a microburst hazardous to aircraft?	Microbursts are hazardous to aircraft because of the extreme downforce of the oncoming winds forming the downdraft. Downdrafts become stronger as they encounter the surface and begin to move horizontally, flowing outward from the base of the thunderstorm. The vertical speed of the downdraft may exceed the aircraft's ability to climb. Surface winds can be strong enough to cause significant degradation of performance to aircraft in flight.
146.	How long does a microburst typically last?	A microburst usually lasts for a total of 10 minutes with the maximum intensity winds lasting for 2 to 4 minutes.
147.	What type of flying weather do low-pressure systems present?	Low-pressure systems are often regions of poor flying weather.
148.	What type of flying weather do high-pressure systems present?	High-pressure systems are predominantly regions of favorable flying weather.
149.	What direction does air flow around a high-pressure system?	Air currents move clockwise around a high-pressure system.
150.	What direction does air flow around a low-pressure system?	Air currents move counter-clockwise around a low-pressure system.
151.	Is there a good method of remembering which way the air currents move around high- or low-pressure systems?	If you think of the short arm of the L being an arrow, you can use that memory aid to help remember that the air moves counter-clockwise around the low-, and in the opposite direction around a high-pressure system.
152.	What does a radar summary chart show us?	A radar summary chart displays areas of precipitation, as well as information about the type, intensity, configuration, coverage, echo top, and cell movement of that precipitation.
153.	What is the abbreviation we use to identify radar weather reports?	We use the two-letter abbreviation SD to identify radar weather reports. The radar summary chart is made up of a collection of SDs included together in one graphic display.
154.	Does radar detect clouds?	No, radar primarily detects particles of precipitation in a cloud or falling from a cloud.
155.	Does the radar summary chart only show information gathered by radar?	The radar summary chart can also include severe weather watch areas, which are plotted if they are in effect when the chart is valid.
156.	How many different types of winds and temperatures aloft charts are there?	There are two types of winds and temperatures aloft charts: forecast and observed.
157.	What is the primary difference between the two types of winds and temperatures aloft charts?	The forecast winds and temperatures aloft charts include expected conditions, while the observed winds and temperatures aloft charts include information that reflects the actual conditions.
158.	How are wind direction and speed indicated on a winds and temperatures aloft chart?	An arrow indicates the direction of the wind, while barbs on the tail of the arrow indicate wind speed.

159.	How is temperature indicated on the winds and temperatures aloft charts?	It is printed out in Celsius, just above and to the right of the circle that indicates the reporting station.
160.	How does the winds and temperatures aloft chart indicate a calm wind?	Calm winds are indicated by the number "99," which is printed to the lower left of the circle that identifies the reporting station.
161.	There are two types of significant weather prognostic charts. What is the difference between them?	Significant weather prognostic charts are presented as either high-level or low-level versions. Pilots flying piston engine airplanes are primarily concerned with the low-level version because they cover the altitudes we generally operate in.
162.	What is the distinguishing characteristic of the significant weather prognostic charts?	They contain four panels. The lower two panels show 12- and 24-hour prognostic charts for the surface, while the upper two charts show the 12- and 24-hour prognostic charts for the surface up through 24,000 ft. MSL.
163.	Do the significant weather prognostic charts show weather reports or weather forecasts?	The significant weather prognostic charts are forecasts of what weather conditions are expected to be at the valid time of the charts.
164.	How often are significant weather prognostic charts updated?	Significant weather prognostic charts are issued four times a day, based on the synoptic data at 0000Z, 0600Z, 1200Z, and 1800Z.
165.	What information do the upper panels of the significant weather prognostic charts depict?	The upper panels show forecasts for IFR and MVFR, as well as turbulence and freezing levels.
166.	What major weather information is provided on the surface prognostic charts?	The surface prog charts show high- and low-pressure centers, fronts, and significant troughs, as well as forecast precipitation and/or thunderstorms.
167.	What would indicate an area of MVFR weather?	A scalloped line encloses an area of forecast MVFR weather on the upper panels of the significant weather prognostic charts.
168.	What would indicate an area of IFR weather?	A smooth line encloses an area of forecast IFR weather on the upper panels of the significant weather prognostic charts.
169.	What does a number expressed as a fraction indicate on the prog charts?	The upper number indicates the anticipated top of a turbulent layer in hundreds of feet MSL, while the bottom number indicates the forecast base of that turbulent layer.
170.	Does the significant weather prognostic chart indicate areas of icing?	No. While it does indicate areas of precipitation and freezing levels, it does not indicate icing directly.
171.	What is the purpose of the convective outlook chart?	The convective outlook chart is a 48-hr. outlook for thunderstorm activity presented in two panels.
172.	What geographic area is shown in the convective outlook chart?	The convective outlook chart indicates possible thunderstorm and severe thunderstorm activity for the continental United States.

173.	What is the difference between the information included in the left-hand panel and the information presented in the right-hand panel?	The left-hand panel covers the first 24-hr. period starting from 1200Z. The right-hand panel shows the forecast thunderstorm activity for the following 24-hr. period.
174.	What are the risk categories used to indicate the possibility of severe thunderstorm activity in an area?	The risk categories are slight, moderate, and high. There is also a note that reads "See Text" that indicates a slight risk may exist, but the risk was not enough to warrant including the notation in the forecast with the current information. Pilots should refer to the textual convective outlook for additional information when "See Text" is included in a convective outlook chart.
175.	If a thunderstorm that does not meet the definition of a severe thunderstorm is expected, is a risk category assigned to that area on the convective outlook chart?	No. If forecast thunderstorms are not expected to be severe, there is no risk category included for that area in the convective outlook chart.
176.	What is an AWOS?	AWOS stands for Automated Weather Observing System. It is an older automated reporting system that might provide only basic weather information, or it might provide a complete automated METAR. AWOS capabilities vary from location to location.
177.	What is ASOS?	ASOS is also an automated system. The abbreviation stands for Automated Surface Observing System. The ASOS is being phased in, replacing the older and more limited AWOS.
178.	What is ATIS?	The Automatic Terminal Information Service is a continuous broadcast of recorded information pertinent to a specific terminal area. Winds and runway information are commonly included in ATIS broadcasts to inform pilots and lower the workload on controllers.
179.	How are AWOS, ASOS, or ATIS of value to a pilot in the air who is approaching an airport with the intention of landing?	By listening to the broadcast prior to entering the pattern, or prior to contacting the tower at a controlled airport, the pilot can become familiar with a wide assortment of pertinent information regarding field conditions, winds, active runway information, and NOTAMs.
180.	Do AWOS, ASOS, and ATIS have any value to a pilot on a cross-country flight whose route of flight takes him or her near an airport where these services are available?	Even en route a pilot can monitor these broadcasts to be aware of the current altimeter setting and possible NOTAMs that are being broadcast.
181.	What is the limitation of AWOS, ASOS, and ATIS broadcasts that pilots should be aware of?	Because they are automated, the information being broadcast may not be entirely current. In the case of the ATIS recorded broadcasts, the information broadcast can be as much as an hour old. Pilots should be aware of that limitation and plan accordingly.

182.	If we were at an airport with only one runway, and you calculated a crosswind component of 15 knots, would that affect your decision to take off?	I would make my go/no-go decision based on the maximum crosswind component listed for my aircraft in the POH/AFM. If the crosswind were above that maximum crosswind component, I would not fly. If it were below the maximum crosswind component, I would base my decision on my level of experience, the terrain, and the existence of obstacles in the area that might cause a safety issue. If in doubt, I would not fly.
183.	If you were planning a flight on a day with light rain forecast, would that affect your plans?	If the ceiling were high enough to allow for adequate cloud clearance and if the visibility were above VFR minimums, a light rain forecast would not automatically cause me to cancel the flight.
184.	If you were planning a flight on a day with light rain forecast and the freezing level was at 1,000 feet, would that affect your plans?	Yes, I would cancel the flight. Even light rain can cause a rapid and dangerous build-up of ice when flying above the freezing level.
185.	If your destination airport were reporting visibility below VFR minimums due to fog, but your navigation log suggested the flight would take 75 minutes, would you depart as planned or wait?	I would probably wait. If I had sufficient fuel, I could legally make the flight and opt not to land if the fog had not cleared. But the fog could also lift into a low layer of clouds. Until I had a better indication that the conditions would be above VFR minimums at my arrival time, I would delay my takeoff.
186.	If you had not flown in 11 weeks and intended to take a passenger flying, but found the weather to be MVFR at the time of your intended departure, would you fly?	Not under those conditions. If I had flown recently and was sure of having sharp skills, I would consider MVFR weather for a local flight or when flying cross-country into improving weather. But after more than 2 months away from the cockpit, I would want to fly under good VFR conditions until I felt comfortable and competent enough to add to my workload by flying in less than VFR weather.
187.	A pilot report from a B-737 indicates moderate turbulence in your area at an altitude you intend to fly. How would this affect your decision-making process?	That pilot report would make me reconsider my flight, my route of flight, or the altitude I intend to fly. Pilot reports are subjective, based on the type of aircraft being flown. If a B-737 is reporting moderate turbulence, I may very well experience that to a much greater degree.
188.	What are three weather conditions that would absolutely make you cancel or postpone a cross-country flight?	Without a doubt, I would not fly into an area with a fast-moving cold front, embedded thunderstorms, or reports of fog at my destination airport. Any of those conditions would make me delay my flight until conditions improved, or cancel it altogether.
189.	In the future, would you be inclined to limit your flying to days and times when the weather is clear and calm?	No. I certainly would enjoy flying under those conditions, but I would base my decision of when and where to fly on my competence, the type of equipment I would be flying with (including the aircraft), and the weather conditions. Over time, I expect my increased experience to enhance my abilities and my judgment, allowing me to fly safely when the conditions are less than ideal.

Task D: Cross-Country Flight Planning

190.	What is the first step when diverting to a new destination?	The first step to take when diverting to a new destination is to turn to the approximate heading of the new destination. This will allow you to be flying toward the destination while you are figuring out the exact heading and distance. Moreover, in the event that the diversion is due to an emergency, it is vital to divert to the new course as soon as possible.
191.	What are the important calculations needed for a safe, successful diversion?	When diverting to an alternate airport, it is important to calculate the exact heading and distance to the alternate airfield. Then calculate groundspeed, arrival time, and fuel needed to get there.
192.	What errors are magnetic compasses subject to?	Magnetic compasses are subject to northerly and southerly turning and acceleration errors. Unlike a gyroscopic heading indicator, they are not subject to compass card oscillation errors.
193.	What is magnetic variation?	Magnetic variation is the difference in degrees between true north and magnetic north. Although the magnetic field of the Earth lies roughly north and south, the Earth's magnetic poles do not coincide with its geographic poles, which are used in construction of aeronautical charts.
194.	What is magnetic dip?	Magnetic dip is the tendency of the compass needles to point down as well as point to the magnetic pole. The resultant error is known as dip error, greatest at the poles and zero at the magnetic equator. It causes northerly and southerly turning errors as well as acceleration and deceleration errors.
195.	What is northerly and southerly turning error?	If the airplane is on a northerly heading and turns east or west, the compass will lag. If the airplane is on a southerly heading and turns east or west, the compass will lead the actual airplane heading. REMEMBER: North Lags, South Leads. Northerly and southerly turning error is the most pronounced of the dip errors.
196.	What is compass card oscillation?	Compass card oscillation error results from erratic movement of the compass card, which may be caused by turbulence or abrupt flight-control movement.
197.	What is acceleration error?	When on east or west headings, acceleration causes compasses to indicate a turn to the north. Deceleration causes compasses to indicate a turn to the south. REMEMBER: Accelerate North, Decelerate South (ANDS). Acceleration error is in part due to the dip of the Earth's magnetic field. Because the compass is mounted like a pendulum, the aft end of the compass card is tilted upward when accelerating and downward when decelerating during changes of airspeed.
198.	What type of information do sectional charts provide?	Sectional charts provide topographical, physical (roads, railroad tracks, etc.), airport, NAVAID, and airspace information for a specific geographic location.

199.	We will be simulating a cross-country flight to KABC during our flight. How will you be monitoring our route of flight en route?	Produce the appropriate sectional chart and indicate to your examiner the route and checkpoints you have chosen for the flight.
200.	How can we be sure that the sectional chart we use today is current and valid?	The effective date and the expiration date are both printed on the sectional chart right under its name.
201.	Since we are making this flight under VFR conditions, is it acceptable to use a road map to assist in our navigation?	There is no rule that prevents us from using road maps as a navigational aid, but a sectional chart would be a better choice. The road map does not include much of the information we need to fly safely. Radio frequencies, the location and height of obstructions, and airport locations are generally not included on road maps.
202.	If we were flying into a satellite airport located inside Class B airspace, which VFR navigational chart would we use?	The sectional chart is a good reference for a wider area. But if we were flying into a satellite airport that is located within the boundaries of Class B airspace, we would be better off using a VFR terminal area chart. The scale is 1:250,000, which will give us much better indications of specific landmarks that will be important when operating in the confines of the Class B airspace.
203.	Which chart can be used to find the recommended route when planning a flight through a terminal area?	We would used a VFR Flyway Planning Chart found on the back of selected Terminal Area Charts. The scale is 1:250,000, and the coverage is the same as the associated TAC. Flyway Planning Charts depict flight paths and altitudes recommended for bypassing areas heavily traversed by large turbine-powered aircraft. Ground references on these charts provide a guide for visual orientation. The charts are designed for use in conjunction with TACs and are not to be used for navigation.
204.	How is a Class B airport depicted on the sectional chart?	Class B airspace is indicated by heavy blue circular lines. The floor and ceiling of each layer of the Class B airspace is included.
205.	How is Class C airspace depicted on a sectional chart?	Class C airspace is shown as solid magenta lines. The floor and ceiling of each layer of the Class C airspace is included.
206.	If the chart shows a number written like a fraction, with 40 over 12, what does that mean?	The fraction indicates that the altitude of the depicted airspace extends from 1,200 feet MSL to 4,000 feet MSL.
207.	What does a dashed magenta line surrounding an airport located in Class D airspace indicate?	The dashed magenta line indicates Class E airspace that extends up from the surface.
208.	What does a light magenta-shaded line indicate?	The light magenta-shaded line indicates Class E airspace that extends upward from 700 ft. AGL. Outside the line, the Class E airspace extends upward from 1,200 ft. AGL.

209.	How is Class G airspace depicted on sectional charts?	Class G airspace is not depicted on sectional charts. It is implied to exist everywhere that controlled airspace does not exist, extending upward from the surface to the floor of overlying controlled airspace.
210.	Can you show me a maximum elevation figure on the sectional chart and tell me what it indicates?	The maximum elevation figure (MEF) is shown as a large, bold, two-digit number, indicating the highest elevation in a given quadrangle. The MEF indicates altitude in thousands and hundreds of feet (e.g., 1^2 means 1,200 ft. MSL).
211.	What steps should you take to determine your position if you suspect you are lost?	First, if conditions permit, initiate a climb. Climbing will allow you to see farther so that you might identify a prominent landmark. If you cannot verify your position visually, you can triangulate using VORs, ask ATC for help, or utilize GPS if it is available.
212.	What determines a good visual checkpoint when planning a flight?	Visual checkpoints should be distinctive and easily recognizable. A large lake, a very tall or large building, an intersection of two highways, or something similarly unique makes a good visual checkpoint.
213.	How far apart would you select checkpoints when flying cross-country?	I would select my first checkpoint within 5 miles of my departure point to verify that I am on my route. Subsequent checkpoints would be approximately 10 miles apart.
214.	What is the risk when using lakes as checkpoints?	Depending on the area and the season, they may change size or shape or even disappear depending on whether the season is particularly wet or dry. When using lakes as checkpoints in an unfamiliar area, it is a good idea to have a secondary landmark to verify your position.
215.	Define the different types of altitude.	Altitude types include indicated, true, pressure, absolute, and density. 1) Indicated altitude is read directly from the altimeter after it is set to the local altimeter setting. 2) True altitude is the vertical distance of the aircraft above sea level. 3) Pressure altitude is the altitude indicated on the altimeter when the altimeter setting is adjusted to standard pressure. Pressure altitude is indicated altitude adjusted for nonstandard pressure. 4) Absolute altitude is the vertical distance of the aircraft above the ground. 5) Density altitude is pressure altitude corrected for nonstandard temperature.
216.	When flying in an area with no tall ground-based obstructions, would you rather cruise at 1,500 ft. AGL or 3,500 ft. AGL?	It would depend on the reason for the flight. If it were a local flight, I might fly lower rather than burn the fuel to climb higher on a short flight. But if I were flying cross-country, I would rather fly at a higher altitude to take advantage of the better visibility, a longer range of radio communications, and navigation.

217.	Other than obstructions, what would be a consideration when selecting a cruise altitude for a cross-country flight?	I would be aware of the winds aloft and try to select an altitude that would provide me with either the most beneficial winds (tailwind) or least detrimental winds (headwind) for the trip.
218.	If flying cross-country at a higher altitude is better than flying at a low altitude, would it be reasonable to plan all our cross-country flights at 8,500 or 9,500 ft. MSL?	Not necessarily. The airplane's performance decreases as altitude increases. Also, for short trips, the time to climb to high altitudes is often inefficient. Planning a 50-mile flight at 8,500 feet MSL might be impractical since we would spend the majority of the flight climbing and descending. On the other hand, if the flight required a greater ground distance, flying at a higher altitude would be a better choice.
219.	What is groundspeed?	Groundspeed is the actual speed at which the aircraft is moving over the ground.
220.	How do you determine an accurate groundspeed?	We can calculate an estimated groundspeed by using the E6B (flight computer) to show the relationship between the true airspeed and any head, cross, or tailwind component. In flight, we can measure an actual groundspeed by timing ourselves as we pass two points over a known distance and by using the E6B to indicate our groundspeed.
221.	What is true airspeed?	True airspeed is calibrated airspeed, or indicated airspeed corrected for nonstandard temperature and pressure. True airspeed at higher altitudes is greater than indicated airspeed due to the less-dense air at higher altitudes.
222.	How will you verify that you are completing all the appropriate steps for the various phases of flight, from takeoff through landing?	I will be using the checklists included in the POH/AFM for this specific aircraft type throughout the flight to verify that the aircraft is always configured appropriately and that I have completed all the necessary steps suggested for each phase of flight.
223.	What information do you need to have in order to accurately estimate your fuel requirements for a cross-country flight?	I would need to know the distance between my departure point and my destination, the estimated fuel burn for the aircraft, and the winds aloft. This would allow me to determine an accurate estimate of how long the flight would be and how much fuel I would be likely to use during the trip.
224.	If your aircraft burns 6 gallons of fuel per hour, would it be acceptable to depart on a 2-hour flight with 15 gallons of fuel on board?	No, that would be an insufficient fuel load. Because all fuel tanks contain a certain amount of unusable fuel that cannot be delivered to the engine, 15 gallons would not allow us enough range to complete the flight and still fulfill the required 30-minute additional fuel supply required for daytime VFR flights.
225.	How do you use VORs to triangulate your position?	First, tune in and identify a nearby VOR station (you may need to climb to pick up the signal). Center the CDI with a FROM indication. Draw a line on the chart indicating the radial you are on. Repeat this process for another neighboring VOR. The point where the lines intersect is your position.

226.	Why do we identify NAVAIDs like VORs and NDBs by Morse code when we first tune them in?	NAVAIDs can share frequencies, just like airports without an operating control tower can share common CTAF frequencies. We need to identify a NAVAID to know that it is working properly and that it really is the NAVAID we want, located in the place we expect it to be.
227.	What is one reason a VOR might not be broadcasting its identifier?	The facility may be undergoing maintenance. The identifier may not be broadcast in that case because the signal may be unreliable.
228.	Can we still navigate using a NAVAID that is not broadcasting an identifier?	If no identifier is being broadcast, we have no way of knowing if we are tuned into the correct NAVAID or if the signal being broadcast is reliable and accurate. If we cannot positively identify a NAVAID, we should not navigate by it.
229.	Is it legal to use a handheld GPS to navigate a cross-country flight?	Yes, it is legal. But in the interest of safety, it would be advisable to work out a navigation log and use pilotage and/or dead reckoning to verify our position throughout the flight.
230.	What is one advantage of navigating with a GPS unit as opposed to another type of navigational aid?	The GPS allows the pilot to navigate directly to the destination. There is no need to navigate in a zig-zag pattern from one NAVAID to another in order to reach your destination.
231.	Why is it a good idea not to rely too heavily on a GPS unit, or any single NAVAID, for navigation?	The unit in the aircraft could fail, obstructions might interrupt the signal, or the ground-based NAVAID could fail or go down for maintenance. We should always have a backup plan when flying, especially when flying cross-country.
232.	Are weather updates on your GPS unit always available?	XM weather updates are available for many GPS units on a subscription basis.
233.	How would you make use of weather updates on your GPS, if they are available?	If an active subscription allows for accurate weather updates on the unit in my aircraft, I would use the weather information for avoidance only, by altering my route to skirt thunderstorms that are indicated to exist on my route of flight.
234.	Can you give me an example how a GPS might be an asset if the weather suddenly worsened, or mechanical difficulties occurred in flight?	The GPS offers a "nearest" function that can be very helpful in an emergency situation or when the conditions of flight change significantly. Pressing a single key will provide me with the course and distance to the nearest airport, which lessens the workload while providing important information quickly.
235.	How will you find the appropriate radio frequencies for your departure airport?	The radio frequencies are listed on the sectional chart, as well as in the Chart Supplement.

236.	If the Chart Supplement lists a tower frequency and a CTAF for your destination airport, which would be the appropriate frequency to use?	The Chart Supplement would list the hours of operation for the tower. If I had any doubts, I could monitor the frequency inbound to determine whether the tower was operating or pilots were self-announcing on the CTAF. And I could always call the airport to confirm the tower's hours of operation before departing.
237.	How could you get pertinent weather and airport information prior to arriving at your destination airport?	I could tune to the ASOS, AWOS, or ATIS frequency before making my initial call to the destination tower or CTAF, depending on which service the airport offers.
238.	What information do Chart Supplements provide?	Chart Supplements provide all the information needed for an airport or radio navigation aid (NAVAID). They also provide published NOTAMs and areas of parachute and aerobatic activity.
239.	What information does the *Aeronautical Information Manual (AIM)* provide?	The *AIM* provides information regarding airport operations, navigation aids, airspace, flight operations, and ATC procedures.
240.	Where can regulatory information such as fuel requirements, airspace, and flight rules be found?	All flight rules that apply to general aviation are in FAR Part 91.
241.	How can we be sure that the runway at KABC is long enough for us to land on safely?	Produce a Chart Supplement and show the examiner the information pertinent to your destination airport. Also assure the examiner that you have used the landing distance performance chart included in your POH/AFM to verify that the runway at your destination is sufficiently long to accommodate your aircraft based on the current weather conditions for that airport.
242.	Which publication would I go to if I needed to be sure fuel would be available at my destination?	The Chart Supplement would tell us what types of fuel are available at the airport. If the airport symbol included on the sectional chart includes ticks, that would indicate that fuel is available, too.
243.	What is a NOTAM?	NOTAM is an acronym that stands for Notice To Airmen. NOTAMs are aeronautical information that could affect the decision to make a flight.
244.	How would you become aware of a NOTAM that might affect your flight?	The NOTAM information would be available through a standard weather briefing.
245.	Can you request information regarding a specific NOTAM from a weather briefer?	Yes, the database is available to weather briefers, and I could request specific NOTAM information using the appropriate airport or NAVAID identifier.
246.	How would you file a VFR flight plan?	I would file a VFR flight plan with the FSS by phone, using the information pertinent to my specific flight, as filled out on the FAA Flight Plan Form. I could also file by radio, or via the Internet with DUAT.
247.	What is a NASA Aviation Safety Reporting Program (ASRP) report?	The NASA ASRP is a voluntary program designed to gather information about deficiencies in the aviation system.

248.	When should a NASA Aviation Safety Reporting Program report be filed?	When a Federal Aviation Regulation is violated inadvertently without involving a criminal offense, filing a NASA ASRP report within 10 days may prevent an enforcement action.
249.	Should we always complete a navigation log for a cross-country flight?	Yes. It is important that pilots do not become overconfident and embark on cross-country flights without doing the necessary cross-country flight planning.
250.	Is filing a VFR flight plan mandatory?	No, but it is a good idea. Filing a VFR flight plan is the only way to be sure that search and rescue crews will be dispatched if we do not show up at our destination as expected.
251.	When will a search begin for a flight that has filed a VFR flight plan?	A search will begin 30 minutes after your scheduled arrival time at your destination. This is why it is important to close a VFR flight plan: to prevent an unnecessary search from being launched.

Task E: National Airspace System

252.	What are the minimum VFR cloud clearance and visibility requirements for Class A airspace?	VFR minimums do not apply in Class A airspace. VFR flight is not normally permitted in Class A airspace, although there are exceptions if approval is granted prior to flight.
253.	What are the minimum VFR cloud clearance and visibility requirements for Class B airspace?	The minimum VFR cloud clearance and visibility requirements in Class B airspace are clear of clouds and 3 miles visibility.
254.	What are the minimum VFR cloud clearance and visibility requirements for Class C airspace?	The minimum VFR cloud clearance and visibility requirements in Class C airspace are identical to those that affect Class D airspace. They are 500 ft. below clouds, 1,000 ft. above clouds, 2,000 ft. horizontally from clouds, and 3 miles visibility.
255.	What are the minimum VFR cloud clearance and visibility requirements for Class D airspace?	The minimum VFR cloud clearance and visibility requirements in Class D airspace are identical to those that affect Class C airspace. They are 500 ft. below clouds, 1,000 ft. above clouds, 2,000 ft. horizontally from clouds, and 3 miles visibility.
256.	What are the minimum VFR cloud clearance and visibility requirements for Class E airspace below 10,000 ft. MSL?	The minimum VFR cloud clearance and visibility requirements in Class E airspace below 10,000 ft. MSL are 500 ft. below clouds, 1,000 ft. above clouds, 2,000 ft. horizontally from clouds, and 3 miles visibility.
257.	What are the minimum VFR cloud clearance and visibility requirements for Class G airspace at 1,200 ft. AGL or less, during daylight hours, regardless of MSL altitude?	One statute mile visibility and clear of clouds is the VFR minimum for Class G airspace that is above 1,200 ft. AGL, regardless of MSL altitude, during daylight hours.

258.	What are the minimum VFR cloud clearance and visibility requirements for Class G airspace at 1,200 ft. AGL or less, at night, regardless of MSL altitude?	The VFR minimums are 500 ft. below, 1,000 ft. above, and 2,000 ft. horizontally from clouds, with 3-statute mile visibility, in Class G airspace as you described it.
259.	What are the minimum VFR standards for flight in Class G airspace above 1,200 ft. MSL?	If we remain below 10,000 ft. MSL, the minimums are 500 ft. below, 1,000 ft. above, and 2,000 ft. horizontally from clouds. During daylight hours, 1-statute mile visibility is required. At night, 3-statute miles visibility is the minimum.
260.	Are there any other VFR minimums that pertain to Class G airspace?	Yes, if we are more than 1,200 ft. AGL, and at or above 10,000 ft. MSL, the VFR minimums increase to 5-statute mile visibility with cloud clearances of 1,000 ft. below, 1,000 ft. above, and 1 statute mile horizontally.
261.	What is the base and the ceiling of Class A airspace?	Class A airspace ranges from 18,000 ft. MSL up to and including 60,000 ft. MSL (FL 600).
262.	Does Class A airspace end at the coastline of the continental United States?	No, Class A airspace includes the airspace above Alaska, as well as the waters within 12 NM of the coastline of the 48 contiguous states and Alaska.
263.	What are the requirements to act as PIC in Class A airspace?	A pilot must be instrument rated to act as PIC in Class A airspace.
264.	What equipment is required to operate in Class A airspace?	Two-way radio communication, appropriate navigational capability, and a Mode C transponder are required.
265.	What class of airspace requires a clearance prior to entry?	Class B airspace requires a clearance prior to entry.
266.	What constitutes a clearance?	When air traffic control (ATC) responds to my radio call and uses the word "cleared" to describe an action, such as "November-123, cleared into Bravo airspace."
267.	If the controller in Class B airspace responds to your call with a vector that will put you into the Class B airspace, does that constitute a clearance to enter Class B?	No, if the controller does not use the word "cleared" in his call, I am not cleared and must not enter the Class B airspace until the clearance is received.
268.	Can you fly an aircraft without a working transponder into Class B airspace?	No, the aircraft is required to have an operating Mode C transponder when within or above the lateral limits of Class B airspace and within 30 NM of the primary airport.
269.	Before today, could you land at any airport that lies within any Class B airspace?	No. There are several especially busy airports located in Class B airspace that require the PIC to hold at least a private pilot certificate to land or take off.
270.	To what altitude does Class B airspace typically extend?	Class B airspace surrounds the nation's busiest airports, and the airspace can be modified in size and shape to accommodate the unique needs of the traffic and the geographic area. However, Class B airspace generally extends from the surface up to 10,000 ft. MSL.

271.	How many layers are generally included in an area designated as Class B airspace?	There are generally three layers that expand in size as the altitude increases. It looks a bit like an upside-down wedding cake.
272.	Is a Mode C transponder required only when you are within the boundaries of the Class B airspace?	No, Mode C is required within 30 NM of a Class B airport. The Mode C ring is depicted on sectional charts as a magenta circle surrounding the Class B airspace.
273.	What are the dimensions of Class C airspace?	Class C airspace normally includes two layers. The lower layer extends from the surface to 4,000 ft. above airport elevation. That lower layer, which is known as the inner circle, has a 5-NM radius. The shelf area has a 10-NM radius and extends from 1,200 ft. to 4,000 ft. above airport elevation.
274.	When should you contact ATC after leaving from an uncontrolled satellite airport located inside Class C airspace?	After departing an uncontrolled satellite airport in Class C airspace, contact ATC as soon as practicable.
275.	Can you fly into or out of that satellite airport located within Class C airspace without an operating Mode C transponder?	No, a Mode C (altitude encoding) transponder is required equipment when within or above Class C airspace.
276.	What is required before entering Class C airspace?	The requirement is for the pilot to establish two-way radio communication prior to entering into Class C airspace.
277.	Does making a radio call constitute establishing two-way radio communication?	No. Two-way radio communication has been established when ATC responds to your call, using your correct call sign.
278.	What is required before entering Class D airspace?	The requirement is for the pilot to establish two-way radio communication prior to entering into Class D airspace.
279.	What are the typical dimensions of Class D airspace?	Class D airspace typically extends upward from the surface to 2,500 ft. AGL and outward to a 5-SM radius from the primary airport. Airspace dimensions may vary according to local requirements, however.
280.	When should you contact ATC after leaving from an uncontrolled satellite airport located inside Class D airspace?	After departing an uncontrolled satellite airport in Class D airspace, contact ATC as soon as practicable.
281.	Can you fly into or out of that satellite airport located inside Class D airspace in an aircraft that is not equipped with an operating Mode C transponder?	Yes, there is no requirement for a Mode C transponder in Class D airspace.
282.	How is Class E airspace that extends to the surface depicted on sectional charts?	Class E airspace that extends to the surface is depicted on sectional charts by a dashed magenta line surrounding the airport. Class E airspace that extends to the surface of an airport signifies that the airport has instrument approach procedures.

283.	How is Class E to 700 ft. AGL depicted?	Class E that begins at 700 ft. AGL is indicated by a shaded magenta ring. Class E airspace that begins at 700 ft. AGL is used for transitioning aircraft operating under IFR to/from the terminal or en route environment.
284.	What airspace designation do federal airways have?	Federal airways are an example of Class E airspace.
285.	What are the dimensions of a federal airway?	A federal airway extends from 1,200 ft. up to, but not including, 18,000 ft. MSL.
286.	Victor airways are federal airways. What NAVAID might you find defining a Victor airway?	Victor airways lead to and from VORs.
287.	How are Victor airways depicted on sectional charts?	Victor airways are shown as light blue lines that radiate out from VORs. They are identified by the letter V followed by a number.
288.	Is there a general rule about the vertical dimensions of Class E airspace?	Class E airspace generally extends upward from the surface or a specified altitude to the overlying controlled airspace. If no Class B or Class C airspace overlies the Class E airspace, it would extend upward to 18,000 ft. MSL where Class A airspace begins.
289.	What equipment must your airplane be equipped with to operate in Class E airspace?	There are no equipment requirements to operate VFR in Class E airspace.
290.	What are the minimum VFR cloud clearance and visibility requirements for Class G airspace below 1,200 ft. AGL during the day?	The minimum VFR cloud clearance and visibility requirements in Class G airspace below 1,200 ft. AGL during the day are clear of clouds and 1 mile visibility.
291.	What are the minimum VFR cloud clearance and visibility requirements for Class G airspace above 1,200 ft. AGL but below 10,000 ft. MSL during the day?	The minimum VFR cloud clearance and visibility requirements in Class G airspace above 1,200 ft. AGL but below 10,000 ft. MSL during the day are 500 ft. below clouds, 1,000 ft. above clouds, 2,000 ft. horizontally from clouds, and 1 mile visibility.
292.	What procedure should a pilot use to depart the traffic pattern of a non-tower airport?	At an airport without an operating control tower, you should depart the pattern straight out or with a 45° turn in the direction of traffic after reaching pattern altitude. You should state which departing procedure you intend to use when you make your takeoff call on the CTAF frequency.
293.	What procedure should a pilot use to enter the traffic pattern of an airport that does not have an operating control tower?	Inbound pilots are expected to observe other aircraft in the pattern to conform to the traffic pattern in use. If there is not any traffic in the pattern, the pilot should overfly the airport at least 500 ft. above pattern altitude to observe traffic and wind indicators on the ground. All entries to a non-tower airport's traffic pattern should be a 45° turn to the downwind entry.
294.	What constitutes Class G airspace?	Class G airspace is any airspace that is not designated as Class A, Class B, Class C, Class D, or Class E airspace.

295.	What are the radio communication rules when operating in Class G airspace?	Radio communications are not required in Class G airspace. However, if the aircraft has an operational radio installed or the pilot has access to a handheld radio, it is advisable to monitor the appropriate frequency and make position calls in the interest of the safe and expedient flow of traffic.
296.	What is a TRSA?	TRSA stands for Terminal Radar Service Area. TRSAs are established around Class D airports that have radar service capability but do not meet all of the criteria to be designated as Class C airspace. Participation in TRSA service is voluntary (though it is recommended), but two-way radio communication must still be established prior to entering Class D airspace.
297.	What is a prohibited area?	Prohibited areas are established for reasons of national security. Flight is prohibited at all times within them.
298.	What is a restricted area?	Restricted areas are established to contain unusual, often invisible hazards to aircraft, such as aerial gunnery or missile tests. Flight is restricted within a restricted area when that area is active.
299.	What is a military operations area?	Military operations areas (MOAs) are established to separate IFR and military traffic. VFR flight is always permitted within MOAs.
300.	What is an alert area?	Alert areas are established to notify pilots of unusual aerial activity, such as a high volume of flight training, but flight is always permitted within them.
301.	What is a warning area?	Warning areas are located offshore and are established to alert pilots of activity that may be hazardous to nonparticipating aircraft. A warning area can be thought of as a restricted area that is located outside the borders of the United States and the U.S. airspace system.
302.	What is a military training route (MTR)?	Military training routes are depicted on sectional charts to establish flight paths used for military training, usually occurring at high speeds and low altitudes.
303.	What type of airspace is often surrounded by large temporary flight restrictions (TFRs)?	Prohibited areas are often surrounded by large TFRs.
304.	Why are TFRs put into effect around prohibited areas?	Prohibited areas protect areas where the President often visits. TFRs are in place when the President is present at these locations.
305.	Are TFRs only put into effect in places where the President is located?	No, TFRs can be put into effect for reasons of national security or national welfare. They may also be put into effect in the vicinity of any incident or event that may result in a high degree of public interest and cause hazardous congestion of air traffic.
306.	How are TFRs different from other forms of airspace?	Unlike other forms of airspace, TFRs are often created, canceled, moved, or changed.

307.	How can you become aware of the existence of a TFR?	A NOTAM is created when a TFR is implemented. The NOTAM contains a description of the area where the restrictions apply.
308.	Can aircraft operate in a TFR?	Only with a waiver or permission obtained in advance from the FAA can an aircraft operate in a TFR.

Task F: Performance and Limitations

309.	How does weight affect aircraft performance?	The airplane is designed to use a specific wing, with a specific engine and propeller, to produce a known amount of thrust and lift. That design is based on the airplane's ability to lift a given amount of weight. Loading the airplane outside the CG limits or beyond the maximum weight allowances will adversely affect aircraft performance regardless of weather or other variables that can affect aircraft performance.
310.	What structural danger is a result of overloading the airplane?	When loaded properly, the airplane will stall before the load factor can increase enough to do damage to its structure. When the airplane is overloaded, that is not the case. Structural damage may result from steep turns or encounters with turbulence that would not have occurred if the airplane had been loaded properly within published weight limits.
311.	How does the condition and length of a runway factor into your flight planning?	The performance charts in the POH/AFM assume a paved, flat runway. If the performance charts suggest we have sufficient length to takeoff or land safely, we can operate out of runways that allow for that amount of distance plus a reasonable amount of extra length for safety. However, if the runway is grass or loose dirt, if it runs uphill, or if the pavement is broken and rough, all these factors will lead to a longer takeoff roll than the POH/AFM indicates.
312.	Why might you want to choose a runway that is longer than the POH/AFM indicates you need for takeoff or landing?	Safety is the primary responsibility of the PIC. I would be disinclined to put myself into a position where I have to be perfect, the weather has to be perfect, and the airplane has to perform perfectly in order to conduct a successful flight. I would much rather select runways that will allow me a reasonable margin for error when landing or taking off.
313.	What is the leading cause of general aviation in-flight accidents?	Fuel starvation is the leading cause of general aviation in-flight accidents.
314.	How can you prevent yourself from being a victim of a fuel exhaustion accident?	By visually checking the fuel before every flight, establishing reasonable minimums for myself, and monitoring my fuel burn on all flights, I can increase my level of safety significantly. It is important that I adhere to VFR minimum fuel requirements and do not exceed the length of time in flight that is appropriate for the amount of fuel I departed with.

315.	If headwinds cause your groundspeed to be considerably lower than expected, and your cross-country flight time to your destination has expanded to much longer than you anticipated, what caution might you take?	I would plan a diversion from my destination for a fuel stop. It is better to have a longer flight that is safe, due to an unanticipated fuel stop, than it is to try to stretch my fuel reserves to reach my original destination and potentially run my tanks dry in the process.
316.	When preparing for a cross-country flight, what special considerations would you have pertaining to weight and balance computations?	I would compute weight and balance for our takeoff, as well as weight and balance for our anticipated weight and CG at landing. This is especially important on a longer flight when fuel will be burning off, changing the weight and CG of the airplane. I would do the extra calculations to be sure that I wasn't taking off within weight and CG limits but inadvertently allowing the airplane to shift out of CG limits as the fuel burns off.
317.	Why is knowing your estimated landing weight important?	Some aircraft list a maximum landing weight in the POH/AFM. If we were to land at a weight above the listed limit, we would risk damaging the aircraft.
318.	Is it still necessary to compute a full weight and balance and calculate the CG if you are just going on a short local flight?	It is necessary to compute a full weight and balance and calculate the CG for any flight.
319.	Which of the performance charts will you use for today's flight?	I will use all the appropriate charts for every flight. In the interest of safety, I want to calculate weight and balance, and I need to estimate takeoff and landing distances based on my current loading of the airplane. I also need to consider the time, fuel, and distance chart as I calculate fuel use in order to be sure that I have a sufficient fuel supply for every flight.
320.	What tools do you need in order to accurately use the performance charts and tables in your POH/AFM?	A sharp pencil and a straightedge are helpful with some of the more intricate charts. I often use a calculator, too, as a means of making some of the calculations more expedient.
321.	If you found that your POH/AFM was missing a performance chart, would that keep you from flying?	It would keep me from flying until I could find a replacement book or an accurate replication of the chart that I could include in my POH/AFM until I could obtain a new replacement book.
322.	Why is density altitude a factor in aircraft performance?	Density altitude is a description of how dense the air is that the aircraft is operating in. More dense air can improve aircraft performance. Less dense air can decrease aircraft performance.
323.	Can you give me an example of how weather can adversely affect airplane performance?	Density altitude is weather dependent. A high density altitude will degrade performance by slowing the airplane's rate of climb and limiting the maximum power output of the engine (assuming a non-turbocharged engine).

324.	Why are turbocharged engines not affected as negatively as non-turbocharged engines in high density altitude conditions?	Turbocharged engines have the ability to maintain their rated power as density altitude increases, to a point, because they have the ability to increase air pressure on the intake side of the engine. Non-turbocharged engines do not have that ability.
325.	Can you give me an example of how weather can positively affect airplane performance?	Colder, denser air will improve the airplane's performance. In very cold air, the airplane will have a higher rate of climb than the same plane at the same weight on a hot day.
326.	What specific performance is affected by air density?	Lift, power, and thrust are all affected by air density. In less dense air, the wing produces less lift, the engine produces less power, and the propeller produces less thrust. In higher density air, all three aspects of aircraft performance would increase.
327.	Flying from a low temperature area to a higher temperature area, would the density altitude increase or decrease?	As air temperature increases, density altitude increases. A higher density altitude indicates less dense air, which degrades airplane performance.
328.	If you fly from an area of low pressure to an area of higher pressure, how would that change affect density altitude?	Moving from a lower pressure area to an area of higher pressure would cause a decrease in density altitude. This denser air would improve aircraft performance somewhat.
329.	If there is no automatic leaning control on the aircraft's engine, why do we need to manually lean the engine when in cruise flight at altitude?	As the air becomes thinner at altitude, the fuel/air mixture becomes richer. We need to lean out the mixture to prevent it from becoming excessively rich.

Task G: Operation of Systems

330.	Can you name three primary flight controls?	Ailerons, rudder, and elevator.
331.	What is the function of the ailerons?	The ailerons are the primary flight controls that affect the aircraft's ability to roll. One aileron deflects upward while the other deflects downward. The down aileron creates more lift by affecting the chord line of the airfoil. As the wing with greater lift rises, the opposite wing, which is producing less lift, descends. The ability to roll, when used in conjunction with the rudder, allows the airplane to make coordinated turns.
332.	Which axis of control do the ailerons affect?	The ailerons affect roll around the longitudinal axis. But it is equally correct to say that ailerons affect roll along the lateral axis.
333.	What effect does the elevator have on the airplane?	The elevator controls pitch. By pulling back on the stick (or yoke), the elevator deflects upward. This movement changes the chord line of the airfoil and decreases lift. As the tail loses lift, the aircraft pivots around the CG, raising the nose. The opposite is true when pitching the nose downward.

334.	Which axis does the elevator affect?	The elevator affects pitch around the lateral axis, although that same effect can be described as the elevator controlling pitch along the longitudinal axis.
335.	What does the rudder do?	The rudder controls yaw, which allows the nose to move from side to side. Pushing on the left rudder pedal will move the nose of the aircraft to the left. Pushing on the right rudder pedal will have the opposite effect.
336.	Which axis does the rudder affect?	The rudder controls yaw about the vertical axis.
337.	What does the term "coordinated" mean in reference to flight controls?	All three primary flight controls (aileron, elevator, and rudder) should be used together in order to keep the aircraft in coordinated flight. To initiate a turn, pressure is applied to both ailerons and rudder in the same direction, while the elevator pressure is increased slightly to maintain altitude. This is a coordinated use of the flight controls.
338.	What is the purpose of trim?	Trim devices are commonly used to relieve the pilot of the need to maintain continuous pressure on the primary controls.
339.	How can you tell if your aircraft is properly trimmed?	A properly trimmed aircraft can be flown hands-off.
340.	How many flight controls have trim devices installed?	Typically, small general aviation aircraft only have trim installed on the elevator. But trim devices can be installed to relieve control pressures in all three axes.
341.	What is the purpose of flaps?	Flaps have two functions. They allow for a decrease in stall speed, and they allow the aircraft to descend at a steeper angle.
342.	Aerodynamically, what effect do flaps have?	When deployed, flaps can increase lift, but they also increase drag.
343.	How are flaps deployed?	Flaps are usually deployed incrementally, using a lever with stops that represent specific flap settings. Each setting is generally identified by the number of degrees of flap being deployed, but pilots often refer to these settings as "first notch," "second notch," and so on.
344.	Can you give me an example of when flaps might be employed?	Most commonly, flaps are used on landing, where they can be deployed incrementally, depending on the conditions. But flaps can also be used on takeoff to enhance lift and shorten the takeoff distance.
345.	Would it be advisable to attempt a landing with full flaps?	Depending on the conditions, that might be a normal landing. Full flaps would create additional lift to steepen our approach and enough drag to help slow the aircraft. But flaps positions have to be evaluated based on the conditions. In a strong headwind, the use of full flaps might be counter-productive, requiring a considerable amount of power for the aircraft to make it to the runway threshold. In that case, a lesser quantity of flaps would be preferable.

346.	Would it be advisable to attempt a takeoff with full flaps?	No, full flaps creates too much drag to make that position useful during takeoff.
347.	What are spoilers?	Spoilers are devices that can be deployed to spoil lift. They are used in some high-performance airplanes to allow them to descend while maintaining a relatively high speed. Gliders also make use of spoilers.
348.	What are leading edge devices?	Leading edge devices, like slats or slots, accelerate air over the wing, increasing lift. Some aircraft have full-span leading-edge slats. Others have slots that affect airflow over the ailerons. Most general aviation aircraft do not use slats or slots.
349.	What are the four cycles of a reciprocating engine?	Intake, compression, power, and exhaust.
350.	How do air-cooled and liquid-cooled engines differ?	Air-cooled engines rely on air flowing over the cylinders to carry away heat. Oil flow aids in cooling air-cooled engines as well. Liquid-cooled engines utilize a coolant system that pumps fluid through the cylinder heads and back to a radiator to dissipate the heat generated by the engine. Air flow and oil circulation also aid in the cooling of liquid-cooled engines.
351.	What is the purpose of a magneto?	A magneto provides electrical current to the spark plugs.
352.	Why are there usually two magnetos in airplane engines?	Most general aviation engines have two magnetos for redundancy. There are also two spark plugs per cylinder. Each magneto provides current to one set of spark plugs, assuring that the engine will continue to run even if one magneto fails.
353.	What is the risk of idling for extended periods of time on the ground, or idling with the carburetor heat in the "on" position?	The risk is that running such a rich mixture at low RPMs for an extended period of time might tend to foul the spark plugs, leading to a rough-running engine that is not able to produce full power.
354.	Describe the engine installed in your aircraft.	Many older aircraft use four-cylinder, four-stroke, opposed, air-cooled, normally aspirated, direct drive engines, manufactured by Continental or Lycoming. Many newer aircraft have Rotax 912 engines installed. The Rotax 912 is a 100-HP, four-cylinder, four-stroke, air-and-liquid-cooled, geared drive engine.
355.	What does the term, "direct drive" mean in reference to an aircraft engine?	The propeller is attached directly to the engine's crankshaft on a direct drive engine. This means the propeller turns at the same speed as the engine's crankshaft.

356.	What does the term, "geared drive" mean in reference to an aircraft engine?	The propeller is connected to the engine via a gearbox on a geared drive engine. This design is normally used to allow the propeller to turn at a lower, more efficient speed than the engine's crankshaft. The Rotax 912 is a good example of an engine that develops power at an RPM that would be too high for the propeller to operate effectively if it were connected to the crankshaft directly.
357.	Why is it important to verify oil capacity before flight?	Low oil capacity can lead to engine damage or failure. The oil provides necessary lubrication for the internal workings of the engine and plays an important role in cooling the engine, regardless of whether it is an air-cooled or liquid-cooled engine.
358.	What is the purpose of the propeller on your aircraft?	The propeller is an airfoil that converts power produced by the engine into thrust that propels the aircraft.
359.	What does the term "normally aspirated" mean when used in reference to an engine?	A normally aspirated engine is not turbocharged or supercharged.
360.	How is your engine cooled?	Older aircraft engine designs, such as Lycoming or Continental or Franklin's, are air-cooled. Air is directed over the cylinder heads to carry heat away as the airplane flies. Newer engine designs, such as the Rotax 912, are oil-and-air-cooled. Air cools the cylinder heads as on the older engine designs, but oil is routed through a radiator that helps discharge engine heat into the atmosphere.
361.	How do hydraulic brakes work on your aircraft?	Toe brakes activated with the rudder pedals allow me to apply pressure to the brake system, which actuates independent brake assemblies on each wheel. This allows me to apply brakes to one or both wheels as necessary.
362.	What is the advantage of conventional landing gear?	Conventional gear is lighter than tricycle gear because the tailwheel can be much smaller and lighter than a nosewheel would be. The conventional gear also has less drag, which allows the aircraft to cruise faster using the same power.
363.	What is the disadvantage of conventional gear?	Ground handling takes more care. Because the center of gravity is behind the main wheels, the aircraft will have a tendency to want to ground loop (the tail rotates toward the direction of travel), which requires the pilot to take much greater care and make constant rudder adjustments to control the aircraft on the ground.
364.	When taxiing, does a conventional-gear aircraft present any other problems?	Visibility can be difficult because the nose is higher than it would be for a similar aircraft with tricycle gear. If visibility is restricted, the pilot can perform a series of S turns while taxiing to allow him or her to see out one side window, then the other, to verify a clear path.

365.	What are the advantages of tricycle gear on an aircraft?	The center of gravity is ahead of the main wheels on a tricycle-gear airplane. This tends to make the aircraft track straight when on the ground.
366.	What are the disadvantages of tricycle gear on an aircraft?	The parts for a tricycle-gear aircraft are heavier and more complex than those for a conventional-gear aircraft. The nosewheel has to be able to swivel freely or have a steering mechanism installed, and it requires a damper to prevent shimmy when the wheel touches down at high speed.
367.	Why is taxi speed important in reference to steering?	A tricycle-gear airplane may tend to develop a potentially damaging shimmy in the nosewheel if taxied too fast with excessive weight on the nosewheel. Both conventional and tricycle-gear airplanes can suffer from control issues in a taxi turn if entered at too high a speed.
368.	What does the term "fixed gear" mean?	Most general aviation airplanes have fixed gear. The term means that the landing gear cannot be retracted during flight.
369.	How does the fuel system work on your airplane?	High-wing airplanes tend to have gravity feed fuel systems. Low-wing airplanes require an electrically driven fuel pump to push fuel uphill from the wing tanks to the engine so that the engine can be started, at which point the mechanically driven fuel pump takes over. Many manufacturers recommend using the electrically driven fuel pump when the engine is run at low RPMs, too.
370.	Is using all the fuel from one tank before switching to another a good practice?	No, using all the fuel from one tank is not a good practice because it may cause vapor lock in the fuel line. It also tends to cause an imbalance as one wing lightens as the tank is emptied, while the tank in the opposite wing remains full.
371.	What is a risk of using all the fuel in one tank before switching to a tank that is full of fuel?	Draining a tank may result in engine failure due to fuel starvation. With air in the fuel lines, it may be impossible to restart the engine inflight with the limited time available as the aircraft descends to the ground.
372.	What is the function of the mixture control?	On Lycoming and Continental aircraft engines, the mixture controls the amount of fuel going to the carburetor or cylinders. It makes for better fuel efficiency, less build-up on the spark plugs, and a more efficient engine. Rotax engines adjust the mixture automatically and do not include a manual mixture control.
373.	What does the throttle control?	The throttle controls the amount of air being allowed into the intake system. The fuel is automatically metered to be in a proper proportion to the amount of air the throttle is allowing into the intake.
374.	What is the purpose of a carburetor?	The carburetor is where the fuel mixes with the air before it is sent to the cylinders.

375.	What is one of the limitations of a carburetor?	It is subject to carburetor induction icing, which can starve the engine of fuel and cause an engine failure if the icing isn't addressed in a timely manner.
376.	What does applying carburetor heat do to the fuel/air mixture?	Applying carburetor heat causes the fuel/air mixture to become enriched. This is because the hot air being routed to the carburetor intake is less dense than the colder ambient air.
377.	What is fuel injection?	Fuel injection systems inject fuel directly into the cylinders or the induction manifold at high pressure through nozzles.
378.	What is the advantage of fuel injection?	Fuel injection systems are less susceptible to induction system icing than carburetor installations are.
379.	What is the disadvantage of fuel injection systems?	They can be difficult to start when the engine has been heated up and then shut down for a short time. This can cause vapor lock, where the fuel in the lines has vaporized from the heat and cannot be delivered effectively to the cylinders.
380.	How can you monitor the oil system in flight?	The oil temperature and oil pressure gauge give me a good indication of the oil system's operation while in flight.
381.	How can you tell if your oil level is low in flight?	The oil temperature will tend to rise and the oil pressure will tend to fall if the oil level is too low. If this occurs, it is a good idea to land in order to fill the oil reservoir and verify that the aircraft does not have an oil leak.
382.	What major components are included in a typical aircraft electrical system?	A typical training aircraft would have a battery, a starter, an alternator or generator, a voltage regulator, an ammeter, and various electrical devices including lights, radios, and perhaps an electric fuel pump.
383.	What does the battery do during the start procedure?	The battery stores the electrical energy necessary to start the engine. Once the engine starts, the battery becomes a back-up electrical source and is used to excite the magnetic field in the alternator.
384.	What does the master switch do?	The master switch brings the electrical system online, providing power to the system for engine starting and running the electrical loads of the aircraft.
385.	If the alternator or generator on your aircraft fails, what will happen?	The battery will take up the electrical load and supply power for a period of time. I would turn off all non-essential electrical devices to extend the amount of time the battery could supply power, and I would make a decision on whether to land at the first possible opportunity or continue to my home airport.
386.	How can you monitor the condition of your electrical system while in flight?	You can monitor the electrical system with the ammeter, to be sure the electrical power being supplied is greater than the amount of electrical power being consumed.

387.	What is the advantage of an alternator over a generator?	An alternator will produce power even at idle speeds, while a generator requires a higher RPM in order to produce power.
388.	What is a disadvantage of an alternator as compared to a generator?	The alternator requires power from the battery to excite the field that allows it to produce power. A generator does not require an outside power source to produce power.
389.	What does the term "avionics" refer to?	Avionics refers to electrical devices used in the aircraft. Normally it is used in reference to communication and navigation aids.
390.	How do hand-held avionics differ from panel-mount avionics?	They are used for the same functions and often have similar levels of functionality. The only real difference is that hand-held avionics are easily portable, while panel-mount avionics are fixed in the aircraft.
391.	What are the benefits of avionics to the private pilot?	Safety, primarily. They allow for communications with facilities on the ground, and they provide important options for navigation that can help keep me out of airspace I do not want to stray into or find a nearby landing spot in an emergency.
392.	What is GPS?	The Global Positioning System (GPS) is a satellite-based navigation system operated and maintained by the U.S. Department of Defense. GPS allows for point-to-point navigation with great reliability and accuracy.
393.	Can you tell me how GPS navigation works?	The GPS receiver in the aircraft determines its position using a constellation of satellites in orbit. The receiver computes the distance from each satellite based on signal travel time. With input from three satellites, the unit can determine its lateral position on the globe. With input from four satellites, the unit can approximate its altitude above sea level.
394.	How is GPS typically used to navigate?	Most commonly, pilots use GPS to navigate from point to point, plotting a direct route to their destination without the need to fly a zig-zag pattern from one NAVAID to another that lies near their route of flight.
395.	What is a concern that pilots using a hand-held GPS unit would have that users of panel-mount GPS units do not have?	Pilots using a hand-held GPS unit need to be sure they have an adequate power supply. Whether that means carrying extra batteries or having an electrical source supplied by the aircraft itself, the unit is only a useful tool when it has sufficient power.
396.	What does the term "EFIS" relate to?	EFIS is an acronym that stands for Electronic Flight Information System. These units combine the information provided by analog flight instruments into a single electronic display.
397.	What is an Engine Monitoring System (EMS)?	An EMS provides a digital display of a variety of engine parameters to the pilot. This allows a single screen to provide important information like RPM, cylinder head temperature, oil temperature, oil pressure, and fuel flow.

398.	If navigating by VOR, with the CDI centered on 090 and a TO indication, are you east or west of the station?	I would be west of the station. If I fly 090° (with a wind correction if necessary), I would eventually fly over the station.
399.	If navigating by VOR, with the CDI centered on 090 and a FROM indication, are you east or west of the station?	I would be east of the station. If I were to fly the reciprocal of the radial indicated on the VOR (270°), I would eventually fly over the station.
400.	Which flight instruments are part of the pitot-static system?	Typically, the airspeed indicator, vertical speed indicator, and altimeter are the flight instruments in the pitot-static system.
401.	Which instrument uses air pressure from the pitot tube?	The airspeed indicator is the only instrument that makes use of the air pressure taken from the pitot tube.
402.	If the pitot tube became blocked, what would the airspeed indicator read?	Zero. With no ram-air pressure to compare to the static pressure, the airspeed indicator would stop working and read zero until the blockage was cleared.
403.	What will the airspeed indicator read if the static port becomes blocked?	With the static pressure trapped in the system, the airspeed indicator will show a higher airspeed as the aircraft descends and a lower airspeed as the aircraft climbs, regardless of the aircraft's actual airspeed.
404.	Which instruments are driven by a vacuum pump?	Typically, the gyros in the attitude indicator and heading indicator are driven by the vacuum system.
405.	What is indicated airspeed?	Indicated airspeed is what is read on the airspeed indicator.
406.	What is calibrated airspeed?	Calibrated airspeed is indicated airspeed corrected for installation and instrument errors. These errors are generally greatest at low speeds. At cruise speeds, calibrated airspeed and indicated airspeed are approximately the same.
407.	How does the vertical speed indicator (VSI) work?	The VSI is a sealed case with a calibrated leak and a diaphragm inside it. Slight difference in air pressure expands or contracts the diaphragm that is linked to the needles on the face of the instrument.
408.	Where do the VSI and altimeter get the information they base their readings on?	From the static air pressure provided by the static port.
409.	How does the altimeter work?	As the plane ascends or descends, the changing atmospheric pressure allows the aneroid wafers inside the altimeter to expand or contract. This expansion/contraction is mechanically geared to rotate the needles on the face of the instrument.
410.	How would the altimeter be affected if the pitot tube became blocked?	It would function normally. The altimeter does not use pitot pressure to display accurate altitude information.
411.	How would the altimeter be affected if the static port became clogged?	With static pressure trapped in the system, the altimeter would show a fixed altitude, regardless of whether the aircraft climbs or descends.

412.	How does the airspeed indicator work?	The airspeed indicator takes the difference between the ram air pressure from the pitot tube and the static pressure from the static vents and converts this pressure difference into indicated airspeed.
413.	What does the vacuum pump installed in your aircraft do?	The vacuum pump provides airflow to pneumatically powered gyroscopic instruments by drawing air through the pneumatic system.
414.	How do the gyroscopic instruments work?	Gyroscopic instruments work on the principle of rigidity in space. A vacuum pump or electrical power source spins a gyro in the instrument at a high rate of speed, thus keeping it rigid in space. If a force is applied, then precession happens 90° ahead of the force.
415.	Can you give me an example of a gyroscopic instrument?	The turn and bank indicator, the attitude indicator, and the heading indicator are all gyroscopic instruments.
416.	Why do some gyroscopic instruments run on electrical power while others are powered by the vacuum pump?	By using two different power systems, the aircraft benefits from a level of redundancy. That increases the margin of safety. If the electrical system fails, the vacuum-powered gyro instruments will still work. If the vacuum pump fails, the electrically powered instruments will continue to work.
417.	How does cabin heat work in your airplane?	In most general aviation training aircraft, either there is no cabin heat system or the cabin heat is provided by a muff surrounding the exhaust system. Heat radiated from the exhaust is routed into the cabin.
418.	What is the risk of using cabin heat?	Because the heater muff in most general aviation aircraft surrounds the exhaust system, there is a risk of carbon monoxide poisoning if the exhaust system has a leak. It is important to use a carbon monoxide detector in the cabin to warn of impending CO poisoning.
419.	What is the difference between deicing and anti-icing?	Deicing is designed to combat ice that has already formed. Anti-icing is designed to prevent icing from occurring.
420.	Does your aircraft have any deicing or anti-icing systems installed?	Most general aviation aircraft have carburetor heat, which is a deicing system.
421.	How does your carburetor heat work?	A control in the cockpit closes off the cold, fresh air source and routes hot air into the carburetor to melt ice that has formed in the intake.
422.	Does it have to be below freezing for carburetor ice to form?	No. Carburetor ice is possible in humid conditions when temperatures are as high as 70°.
423.	How do deice boots installed on wings work?	The boots can be switched on to expand and crack ice to a certain thickness as it forms, so that it is blown off the wing.

424.	If icing conditions are being reported and your airplane has no deice or anti-ice system installed, how much ice can you accumulate before you have to terminate your flight?	Flight into known icing conditions without appropriate deice or anti-icing systems is not permitted. With no way to prevent the formation of ice or rid the aircraft of ice once it begins forming, the airplane will gain weight and lose lift in icing conditions. If an airplane persists in flying through icing conditions with no means of combating it, the aircraft will eventually become unable to maintain level flight and may become uncontrollable.

Task H: Human Factors

425.	What is a good rule for flying if taking medication?	DO NOT fly if you are taking medication unless the medication is approved by the FAA or you are certain that the medicine will NOT impair your abilities.
426.	What if the medication is a common, over-the-counter drug?	The same rule applies. Pilots should not fly when taking medication unless the medication is approved by the FAA or they are absolutely certain that the medicine will not impair their judgment or abilities.
427.	How long must one wait after consuming alcohol before acting as a required crewmember on a civil airplane?	You must wait 8 hours after consuming alcohol before acting as a required crewmember on a civil airplane.
428.	What is hypoxia?	Hypoxia is an insufficient supply of oxygen in the blood.
429.	What are the signs of hypoxia?	Impairment of night vision, judgment, alertness, coordination, and the ability to make calculations. Headache, drowsiness, dizziness, and a possible sense of euphoria or belligerence may occur. Unconsciousness may be the end result of prolonged hypoxia.
430.	How can hypoxia be prevented or treated?	Hypoxia can be prevented or treated by flying at a lower altitude or by using supplemental oxygen.
431.	Once an individual becomes hypoxic, how long after beginning treatment will it take for him or her to regain his or her faculties?	Recovery from hypoxia is almost immediate. The person suffering from hypoxia will regain his or her faculties very quickly after sufficient oxygen is made available.
432.	What is hyperventilation?	Hyperventilation is a condition that describes insufficient carbon dioxide in the blood.
433.	What are some indications of hyperventilation?	Dizziness, rapid heart rate, tingling in the fingers and toes, and ultimately unconsciousness.
434.	How can hyperventilation be treated?	Hyperventilation can be treated by taking slow, deep breaths or by breathing into a bag.
435.	Why is it important that pilots not fly when they have a cold or allergic condition that causes congestion?	Pressure differences during climb or descent can cause severe pain and hearing loss due to ear blockage. Congestion can block the Eustachian tube and prevent the pressure equalization necessary to avoid this sort of aeromedical issue.

436.	Does the problem of pressure equalization only pertain to ear and hearing problems?	No, blocked passages in the sinuses can cause pain and possibly the discharge of bloody mucus from the nasal passages.
437.	If you were scheduled to fly but had a cold, would it be advisable to take an over-the-counter decongestant to avoid ear or sinus issues?	No. Pilots should not fly when taking medication unless the medication is approved by the FAA or they are absolutely certain that the medicine will not impair their judgment or abilities. Decongestants can have side effects that can significantly impair pilot performance.
438.	On what sense does your brain rely primarily when it receives conflicting information from the senses?	When given conflicting information, the brain tends to favor the information provided visually.
439.	What is spatial disorientation?	Spatial disorientation is a state of temporary spatial confusion that results from misleading information being sent to the brain from various sensory organs.
440.	Can you give me an example of how spatial disorientation might occur in flight?	When visibility is limited, the brain will rely on other input for orientation information. The ear may not be reliable because of fluid movement that does not correspond with the movement of the aircraft. This could cause the pilot to feel as if (s)he is in a steep turn when the aircraft is actually flying straight-and-level. It could also cause the pilot to feel as if (s)he is flying straight-and-level when (s)he is actually in a steep turn. That is why spatial disorientation can be a dangerous condition.
441.	What is the graveyard spiral?	If descending during a coordinated constant-rate turn that has ceased stimulating, the motion-sensing system can create the illusion of being in a descent with the wings level. A disoriented pilot will pull back on the controls, tightening the spiral and increasing the loss of altitude.
442.	How can you recover from spatial disorientation?	The best way to recover from spatial disorientation is to focus on the flight instruments and rely on their indications.
443.	Does motion sickness come on rapidly?	Not usually. Motion sickness is often an incremental progression of symptoms.
444.	How can you identify impending motion sickness in yourself or a passenger?	First, the subject loses his or her appetite. Heavy perspiration might follow with a tendency to salivate. Nausea, disorientation and headaches might also occur.
445.	How can you combat or prevent motion sickness?	By opening the air vents and getting air circulating in the cockpit. I would encourage passengers to loosen their clothing and avoid unnecessary head movements. I would also advise them to focus their eyes on a distant point near the horizon. While doing all this, I would be either returning to land at my home airport if it was close by, or diverting to a nearby airport to land.

446.	What is carbon monoxide poisoning?	Carbon monoxide poisoning occurs when carbon monoxide enters the blood, thereby causing hypoxia. Carbon monoxide poisoning is of particular concern to pilots because this colorless, odorless gas can cause incapacitation.
447.	What is the primary source of carbon monoxide in aircraft cockpits?	The most common source of carbon monoxide in aircraft cockpits is exhaust fumes leaking from a defective heater or other source.
448.	Why is the recognition of carbon monoxide poisoning so important to pilots?	Loss of consciousness and death are very real possibilities if the exposure to carbon monoxide continues.
449.	If you suspect carbon monoxide poisoning is occurring, what would be a reasonable course of action?	Ventilate the cabin to the extent possible and land at the first opportunity to seek first aid, if necessary. After dealing with the human element, I would make sure the aircraft was inspected and the leak found and repaired before it was flown again.
450.	What other aeromedical condition can carbon monoxide poisoning mimic?	The effects of carbon monoxide poisoning are very similar to the effects of hypoxia.
451.	Can carbon monoxide poisoning be treated with oxygen like hypoxia, resulting in a quick recovery?	No. Oxygen may be beneficial to the person suffering from carbon monoxide poisoning, but the carbon monoxide must be removed from the individual's bloodstream, which is a process that takes time. It cannot be remedied as rapidly as hypoxia.
452.	How can stress affect your flying?	Stress degrades decision-making ability and slows your reactions.
453.	When we talk about stress and flying, what kind of stress are we talking about?	Everyday stress that comes from personal interactions, job stress, family responsibilities, busy schedules in our lives. Stress can be subtle but cumulative, building to the point that it adversely affects the individual's ability to perform normal functions reliably.
454.	How can stress affect you as a pilot?	It can cause distraction that affects my decision-making abilities and may cause my judgment to erode to the point that I take unnecessary risks.
455.	What is acute fatigue?	Acute fatigue refers to the everyday tiredness felt after a long period of physical or mental activity that leaves the individual feeling drained.
456.	How can acute fatigue be remedied?	By getting sufficient rest, sleep, exercise, and nutrition.
457.	What is chronic fatigue?	Chronic fatigue occurs when there is insufficient recovery time between bouts of acute fatigue. Performance and judgment continue to degrade. Because it is a deeper form of fatigue, the recovery period requires a prolonged period of rest.

458.	What is dehydration?	Dehydration occurs when the body is deprived of fluids. Dehydration can occur on flights of long duration in which the pilot fails to drink adequate amounts of water, or it can be a pre-existing condition that started prior to the flight.
459.	How can dehydration affect you as a pilot?	Dehydration acts as a stressor and can degrade your decision-making ability.
460.	How does flying effect dehydration for pilots and passengers?	At altitude, the atmosphere is thinner and contains less moisture. This leads to more body fluids being lost.
461.	How can you combat dehydration?	Ensure an adequate intake of fluids before and, if necessary, during flight.
462.	What is hypothermia?	Hypothermia occurs when your body is unable to maintain its normal temperature. An internal temperature of 96°F or lower signals hypothermia.
463.	What are some signs that a person is suffering from hypothermia?	Extreme shivering; stiffness of the arms or legs; confusion or sleepiness; slow, slurred speech; and poor control over body movements all suggest the possibility of hypothermia.
464.	Does it have to be extremely cold for a pilot or passenger to succumb to hypothermia?	No. A drafty cockpit, and especially an open-cockpit aircraft, can cause a poorly prepared pilot or passenger to experience hypothermia in temperatures that might seem moderate when standing on the ground with no wind.
465.	How can hypothermia be prevented?	By dressing appropriately. Pilots and passengers should be aware that the temperature at altitude is usually lower than the temperature on the ground, and the wind blowing through the cockpit will cause our bodies more difficulty in maintaining a normal body temperature.
466.	What is the maximum allowable blood alcohol content while acting as a required crewmember on a civil airplane?	You may not act as a required crewmember on a civil aircraft while having .04% or more blood alcohol content by weight.
467.	How long should pilots and passengers wait to fly after scuba diving?	If a controlled ascent was required during the dive, wait 24 hr. before flying. If a controlled ascent was not required, wait 12 hr. before flying up to 8,000 ft. and 24 hr. for any altitude above 8,000 ft.
468.	Why is it important to wait before flying after scuba diving?	Just as the pressure decrease while ascending in the water can cause nitrogen gas trapped in the tissues to escape rapidly, a condition known as the bends, the same can occur when the ambient pressure decreases during an airplane's ascent. To avoid that possibility, individuals should wait before flying after scuba diving, to give the nitrogen gas time to leave the body.

AREA OF OPERATION II: PREFLIGHT PROCEDURES

Task A: Preflight Assessment

469.	When is it necessary to perform a preflight inspection?	Before any flight. Pilots should verify the condition and airworthiness of their aircraft before any flight, whether it is the first flight of the day or a subsequent flight made later in the day.
470.	Where would we find the documentation required for the aircraft to be airworthy?	The location varies, but the registration, airworthiness certificate, and radio license (if required) are typically found in a plastic-covered pocket on the sidewall of the cockpit area. The operating limitations are included in the POH/AFM, as well as in the form of placards in the cockpit, and the weight and balance information will be calculated by the pilot prior to each flight.
471.	Where is the pitot tube on your aircraft?	The location of the pitot tube can vary from aircraft to aircraft, but it is generally located midway along the leading edge of the wing. In some cases, especially in small, pusher configuration airplanes, it is located on or near the nose of the airplane.
472.	Where is the static port located on your aircraft?	The exact location of the static port varies from one aircraft to the next, but the static port is usually located on the rear of the pitot tube or along the side of the fuselage.
473.	How will we verify that we have sufficient fuel for our flight?	We will verify fuel levels before flight by visually inspecting the fuel tanks. We will monitor fuel use during our flight by estimating fuel burn using the performance charts found in the POH/AFM, and we will plan the duration of the flight accordingly.
474.	If you find water in a fuel sample, what would be the appropriate course of action?	I would continue sampling fuel from that tank until I found clear fuel samples that show no indication of water or other contaminants.
475.	Why is evidence of water in the fuel tank such a consideration during the preflight inspection?	Water is heavier than fuel and sinks to the bottom of the fuel tank, where the fuel is drawn from for use in the engine. Since water cannot support combustion, it can adversely affect performance. Small amounts of water can cause the engine to run rough. Larger amounts of water can cause engine failure and make it impossible to restart the engine without draining the contaminants in the tanks.
476.	What foreign matter would you be looking for in the air inlet to the engine compartment?	Birds often seek the warmth of a cooling engine and may attempt to build a nest on the engine or in the air inlet to the engine compartment. These as well as any other foreign materials should be completely removed before flight as they can limit airflow that is necessary to adequately cool the engine, and might even cause a fire if they come in close contact with the exhaust system.

477.	How would you check the oil level for your airplane?	Explain the location of the oil dipstick. Explain how to remove the dipstick, wipe it clean, reinsert the dipstick, and remove it again to check the level of the engine oil accurately. Only check the oil level when the engine is turned off and has had a few moments for the oil in the engine to settle into the sump.
478.	What are we looking for when we inspect the propeller during the preflight inspection?	We are doing a general condition inspection. Our inspection is verifying that there are no cracks in the prop, delaminations (wood or fiberglass props), bends, or obvious damage. We are also inspecting for nicks to the leading edge of the prop. If we find a large or deep nick, we should postpone our flight until we can consult with maintenance about the condition of the prop.
479.	Where can we find a checklist to follow when performing a preflight inspection on the airplane we will be flying today?	A preflight inspection checklist is included in the Pilot's Operating Handbook and/or Airplane Flight Manual appropriate to the specific type of aircraft. We will follow that checklist to assure ourselves that we have checked everything that needs to be checked in an organized, methodical manner.
480.	Where can we find information regarding the fuel capacity of the aircraft we are flying today?	Fuel capacity information can be found in the POH/AFM for the specific type of aircraft. We can look up the fuel capacity of the aircraft prior to our flight and visually inspect the tanks prior to flight to verify that we have a sufficient load of fuel before starting up the engine.
481.	What is meant when we talk about usable fuel as opposed to fuel capacity?	Fuel capacity refers to the amount of fuel the aircraft can carry. Not all of the fuel can be delivered to the engine, however. The small amount that remains in the tanks is referred to as unusable fuel and should not be included in endurance calculations.
482.	How do we know if we have the right amount of oil before starting the engine?	Oil capacity is listed in the POH/AFM. We can check the listed oil capacity for our aircraft based on that information and verify we have at least the minimum quantity during our preflight inspection.

Task B: Cockpit Management

483.	In the event of an emergency, what can you make use of to help you successfully and safely deal with the situation?	I can make use of every resource available to me, including ATC via the radio and you, my passenger, as an extra set of hands and eyes. If an emergency occurs, I will give you specific instructions regarding how you can be helpful. These may include finding an emergency checklist in the POH/AFM while I am flying the airplane, or configuring the cockpit (such as opening a door and blocking it open with a shoe or a book at the hinge point) in the event a forced landing becomes necessary.

484.	As a passenger, is there anything I can do to help you during a normal, uneventful flight?	Yes, I would appreciate it if you would point out any traffic that you feel may be a factor for us and hold onto some of the charts and manuals I will be using, for easier and quicker access. (Follow up by explaining how the examiner can be of help when (s)he is acting as a passenger. Be specific when asking for assistance to prevent misunderstandings.)
485.	Is there anything I should not touch during the flight?	Yes. I want you to be comfortable during our flight, but I will need you to keep your hands and feet clear of the controls. I will point out the controls and switches you need to be aware of when we get into the aircraft.
486.	At what point in the flight do you take on the role of PIC?	I will be acting as PIC well before we get to the airplane. As PIC, I will take responsibility for the safety of the flight and my passengers throughout the planning phase, during the preflight inspection, and throughout the entire flight, right up to the point that we shut down the engine after landing and depart the aircraft.
487.	Is there any information the pilot should share with his or her passenger prior to start-up?	Yes, the pilot should provide a basic safety briefing to be sure the passenger understands the proper use of safety belts and harnesses. The passenger should also be shown how to open the cockpit door and the location and use of the fire extinguisher.
488.	Why should the pilot brief the passenger before flight?	For safety reasons. It may be difficult to get the passenger's attention focused on a briefing after start-up, so we do it beforehand. In the event of a true emergency, the passenger can be helpful in dealing with some situations, so the pilot should provide this basic level of information before the flight gets underway.

Task C: Engine Starting

489.	In what position should the mixture control be during engine starting?	At or near sea level, the mixture should be kept in the "full rich" position to allow for a proper fuel/air mixture at the surface where the air is the most dense.
490.	If we are starting the engine at an airport that is not at or near sea level, what should we do with the mixture control?	At a high altitude airport, it may be necessary to lean the mixture somewhat to compensate for the less dense air at ground level.
491.	Where should the carburetor heat be positioned during engine starting?	The carburetor heat should be in the off position.

492.	After starting, what is the first instrument we should look at?	We should watch the oil pressure gauge to be sure that the pressure rises within a few seconds of the engine starting. Under cold conditions, it may take somewhat longer for oil pressure to reach the green range indicated on the gauge, but if the oil pressure does not register within 5 seconds of starting, it is wise to shut the engine down and investigate to verify that the engine has a sufficient oil supply and that there are no leaks in the system.
493.	What prevents the airplane from moving during engine start?	While engaging the starter, I will be holding the brakes with sufficient pressure to prevent the airplane from moving on the ramp.
494.	Our aircraft has only one engine, a fixed pitch propeller, and relatively simple systems. Can we start the engine using memory aids rather than a checklist?	No. Although our aircraft is simple to operate, it is important that we establish good safety practices at all times when operating an aircraft. We will use the engine start checklist taken from the POH/AFM for our airplane every time we start the engine, no matter how familiar we are with the process.
495.	Where will you keep your hands during engine start?	I will hold my hands on the controls during engine start. This is a safety precaution. In the event the aircraft's brakes fail, a pedestrian wanders in the direction of our propeller, or some other potential issue arises, I will be ready to shut the engine down quickly as a precaution.
496.	What specific precaution should we take immediately before starting the engine?	We should announce in a loud voice that we are about to start the engine by yelling, "Clear," or "Clear prop," while visually verifying that nobody is in the area of our propeller before we engage the starter.
497.	If you are ready to start the engine but notice another pilot is preparing to preflight the airplane tied down right next to yours, what should you do?	Safety is of paramount importance. I would let the other pilot know that I was preparing to start the aircraft and ask if (s)he could remain safely clear while I started the engine and prepared to leave the area. If (s)he were agreeable, I would start the aircraft and depart in an orderly manner. If (s)he were not agreeable, I would wait until (s)he finished the preflight and was no longer in any danger before continuing with my engine start procedure.
498.	If you find the aircraft you will be flying is parked in front of a hangar with the tail pointed toward the open door, what precaution would you take before starting?	I would reposition the aircraft if possible so the prop blast was not directed into the open hangar. If repositioning was not possible, I would ask to close the hangar door before I started the engine.
499.	How do we know that we are performing all the correct tasks in the correct order when starting the engine?	We use the engine start checklist included in the POH/AFM for the aircraft.

Task D: Taxiing

500.	How can you check the steering while taxiing?	Ground steering is controlled by the rudder pedals. I will verify that I have sufficient control authority as I begin my taxi. (NOTE: Some aircraft feature rudder and nosewheel controls that are interconnected, while others utilize only rudder control for ground steering. Be aware which system your aircraft uses and be prepared to explain the advantages or limitations to your examiner if asked.)
501.	Assuming our aircraft has interconnected rudder and nosewheel steering controls, how does that affect your control on the ground?	Aircraft that interconnect the rudder and nosewheel controls have much greater ground steering capability, especially at low speeds and low throttle settings.
502.	Assuming our aircraft is steered on the ground by rudder alone, how does that affect your control on the ground?	Aircraft that do not have nosewheel steering tend to have less ground control authority when taxiing, especially at low speeds and low throttle settings. I can compensate for that limitation by using differential braking. However, it is important that I use differential braking sparingly to avoid overheating the brakes.
503.	Immediately after releasing the brakes and adding throttle to get the aircraft to taxi, what safety precaution do we take?	We apply the brakes to verify that they have enough power to bring the aircraft to a stop. We do this as a safety precaution before the aircraft has built up any appreciable speed.
504.	Why is it important to check the brakes immediately?	If the brakes are spongy or weak, it is best to find out when the aircraft is just barely moving rather than when it is rolling down the taxiway with traffic ahead.
505.	If the brakes seem weak, what would you do?	I would shut down the aircraft and report the potential problem to maintenance. If a mechanic clears the airplane for service, I can continue. If the mechanic suggests that maintenance is required, I will either fly another aircraft or cancel our flight.
506.	How does a pilot apply brakes when making a brake check?	The aircraft will either have toe brakes, which allow differential braking, or a single brake handle that applies both brakes simultaneously (usually located between the seats). The important thing is to apply the brakes with sufficient force to be sure the aircraft can be stopped and to apply differential brakes evenly to stop the aircraft without causing it to swerve in one direction.
507.	If you were to encounter a quartering headwind from the right while taxiing, what control inputs would you use, if any?	I would turn the ailerons into the wind (raising the right aileron) and apply back pressure on the elevator to spoil any lift that might be generated.
508.	Is there a memory aid you use as a reminder of how to position the controls for the winds when taxiing?	Yes, I remember to "climb into the wind and dive away from it." I position the flight controls when taxiing so the elevator is up for headwinds (to spoil lift) and down for tailwinds (to prevent the wind from getting under the tail). The same principle is true for the aileron positions.

509.	What is a safe taxiing speed?	A good rule of thumb is to maintain no more than a brisk walking speed when taxiing.
510.	Why is it necessary to maintain a low taxi speed, even if no other traffic is in view?	Aircraft are generally bulky, gawky machines on the ground. Their center of gravity is often higher than other ground vehicles, with a significant amount of that weight held in fuel tanks that are outboard of the center line of the aircraft. This tends to make aircraft prone to ground accidents if they are taxied too quickly or if heavy braking is employed in a turn.
511.	Where would you stop before transitioning from the taxiway to the runway?	I would stop at the hold short lines, which are indicated by two solid yellow lines followed by two dashed yellow lines on the taxiway. I would hold on the side with the solid lines to verify that the runway is clear (Class G airport) or to await clearance to take the runway (Class B, C, or D airport).
512.	If the controller tells us we are cleared to taxi and hold when we are at the hold short line prior to entering the runway, what is (s)he clearing us to do?	We are allowed to taxi out to the center line of the runway and hold there until (s)he clears us to take off.
513.	If, while holding short of the runway, we get a call from the controller asking us if we can expedite our takeoff, what does (s)he mean?	The controller is asking if we can take off immediately if (s)he clears us to take off. We may hear this call when there is an incoming aircraft on long final.
514.	If the controller instructs us that we are cleared to take off and instructs us to expedite, do we have to accept the clearance?	No. The controller is trying to help us get out without having to wait a long time while holding. But, if we are not ready to go, or if we feel rushed, we are entitled to respond that we are unable to expedite and wait at the hold short line for our next opportunity to take off at the controller's convenience.
515.	If you are number two behind another aircraft that is holding for longer than you think is necessary on the taxiway ahead of you, is it permissible to pass them in order to expedite your takeoff?	The aircraft in the lead has the right-of-way because it is difficult for the pilot of that aircraft to see behind him or her. On an airport without an operating control tower, we can call them on the radio and ask for permission to pass them (provided there is ample room to do so without the risk of a collision), but if we are unable to contact them directly, we should operate as if they have the right-of-way. We will wait for them to move rather than try to slip around them on the taxiway.
516.	If you are taxiing on a wide ramp and find yourself converging head-on with another aircraft taxiing in the opposite direction, which way should you deviate your course in order to pass safely?	When aircraft are approaching head-on, both aircraft should alter course to the right in order to safely pass each other.

517.	If, while on the ramp or taxiway, you encounter an aircraft that is acting erratically (or in some way that prevents you from anticipating what they might be planning to do), what would you do?	I might stop and wait for them to get clear, depending on the circumstances. If it is an airport with an operating control tower, I should be able to hear ground controller instructions to them, which should give me an idea of their intentions. At an airport without an operating control tower, I could call on the radio to the other aircraft and ask their intentions. If I could not raise them, I would be inclined to wait for them to clear the area, rather than potentially cause an incident or accident.
518.	Why would an airport's rotating beacon be operating during daylight hours?	If an airport's rotating beacon is on during daylight hours, it usually indicates that the prevailing weather is below basic VFR minimums, i.e., visibility of less than 3 SM and/or a ceiling of less than 1,000 ft.
519.	What is a displaced threshold?	A displaced threshold can only be used for taxi, takeoff, and the landing rollout. Displaced thresholds are indicated by white arrows that point to the runway threshold, which is a thick white line perpendicular across the runway.
520.	How is a displaced threshold indicated?	Displaced thresholds are indicated by white arrows that point to the runway threshold, which is a thick white line perpendicular across the runway.
521.	What are hold short lines?	Hold short lines indicate the active runway environment. If you are at a tower-controlled field, you cannot cross hold short lines until you are cleared to do so. At a non-towered field, you should visually scan the area for traffic, then announce your intentions before crossing hold short lines.
522.	How is a hold short position indicated?	Hold short lines are depicted by four yellow lines, two broken and two solid. The two solid lines are always on the side where the aircraft is to hold.
523.	What color are mandatory instruction signs?	Mandatory instruction signs have white letters on a red background.
524.	What color are taxiway location signs?	Taxiway location signs have yellow letters on a black background.
525.	What color are direction signs?	Direction signs have black letters on a yellow background.
526.	What color are taxiway markings and lighting?	Taxiway markings consist of a yellow centerline and yellow shoulder markings. If lights are installed on the taxiway centerline, they will be steady green. Taxiway edge lights are steady blue.

527.	What color are runway markings and lighting?	Runway markings consist of a white centerline and white shoulder markings. Runway centerline lights are all white. The last 3,000-ft. section of runway may be identified by alternating red and white centerline lights. The final 1,000-ft. section of runway may show only red centerline lights. Runway edge lighting is white, except on instrument approach runways. Yellow edge lighting replaces white on the last 2,000 ft. or half of the runway, whichever is less, to form a caution zone for landing.
528.	What is a non-movement area?	A non-movement area is a designated area where aircraft can taxi without being in contact with the tower. For example, the ramp at an FBO is often a non-movement area.
529.	What color is a civilian land airport beacon?	Civilian land airport beacons are alternating white and green flashes.
530.	What color is a military airport beacon?	A military airport beacon flashes two whites and a green.
531.	What color are runway lights?	Runway lights are white.
532.	What color are taxiway lights?	Taxiway lights are blue.
533.	What do red lights across the runway indicate?	A row of red runway end identifier lights (REIL) may be installed across the end of the runway.
534.	If you see a row of red REILs, what color light is on the opposite side of those lights?	On the opposite side of the red runway end identifier lights is a series of green lights that mark the approach end of the runway.
535.	What does a red sign with white numbers on it signify?	That is a runway sign. The numbers are the identifiers for the runway that the sign indicates.
536.	What does a yellow sign with black numbers and arrows signify?	That is a direction sign that points the way to each indicated runway.
537.	What would a black sign with a yellow letter indicate?	That would be a taxiway sign. The letter is the identifier for the taxiway it is posted on.

Task F: Before Takeoff Check

538.	What constitutes a "runway incursion"?	The FAA defines runway incursion as any occurrence at an aerodrome involving the incorrect presence of an aircraft, vehicle, or person on the protected area of a surface designated for the landing and takeoff of aircraft.
539.	What elements of taxiing make it more demanding than when flying the airplane?	Taxiways, unlike the sky, are one lane roads. Proper planning and compliance with ATC instructions are very important to ensure that a collision hazard is not created with other aircraft or vehicles on the ground or with aircraft that are taking off or landing at the airport. Because aircraft and vehicles can come from many different directions, you must maintain increased vigilance when operating on the ground.

540.	How can you identify areas at an airport where runway incursions may be more likely to occur?	Airport diagrams describe hot spots for runway incursions. These hot spots are usually the intersection of runways or runways and taxiways. They are areas where an increased chance of runway incursions may exist.
541.	Explain how you can identify areas on the airport where you need to hold short.	Hold short markings are painted on the taxiway and feature two solid lines and two dotted lines. The solid lines indicate that you should stop when taxiing toward them. Hold short signs feature the same illustration as the painted markings. Red runway boundary signs are located next to the hold short markings and further indicate that you should stop and either clear the area (at a non-towered airport) or wait for ATC clearance (at a tower-controlled airport).
542.	Assume that ATC and/or a passenger is communicating with you while you are taxiing at an unfamiliar airport. What steps will you take to ensure you avoid a runway incursion?	My first priority is to ensure safety during the taxi. I must control and eliminate distractions to do that effectively. I would politely ask the passenger to wait for a better time to converse with me. I would ask ATC to standby or ask for taxi instructions to an airport holding area where I could stop the airplane and complete the necessary conversation with ATC.
543.	Some pilots expect certain instructions from ATC when operating out of a familiar airport. How will you avoid this pilot error and ensure you comply with the instructions you actually receive?	All instructions and clearances from ATC should be written down to ensure that I get the correct message. Doing so will also help me when I read back my instructions or clearance to ATC.
544.	How will you maintain situational awareness during taxi operations?	I will use proper scanning techniques, minimize head-down time, control and eliminate distractions in the cockpit, and use a taxi diagram to ensure I am taxiing safely and toward my intended destination.
545.	What special procedures will you employ at night to avoid runway incursions?	Taxiing at night requires some additional concentration because it is more difficult to spot airplanes and vehicles as well as their direction of travel. I will maintain positive situational awareness regardless of day or night operations, but I will pay special attention to airport and airplane lighting systems to determine where I am in relation to taxiways and runways as well as other traffic.
546.	What airport lighting aids exist to help you avoid a runway incursion when operating at night?	Primarily, taxiway lights are blue and runway lights will either be white or use a color-coding system. Regardless, I can easily identify what is a taxiway and what is a runway. Airport sign illumination will also help me find my way and avoid crossing onto an active runway. Other more advanced runway status lighting systems also exist, and I can easily identify what systems will be available at the airports I intend to use and research any unfamiliar systems in the AIM.

547.	What airplane lighting aids exist to help you avoid a runway incursion when operating at night?	My airplane is equipped with position lights that will help other aircraft identify my direction of travel. Likewise, I will use the position lights of other aircraft to determine their direction of travel. Anticollision lights are also effective in helping pilots identify other aircraft at night. I can use my landing/taxi light(s) to help me see the area in front of me or signal to other aircraft, if necessary and appropriate.
548.	How can we tell on the ground if our aircraft is rigged properly?	When we turn the yoke to the right (or move the stick to the right), the right aileron should move upward, while the opposite aileron should move downward. Similarly, depressing the right rudder pedal should make the rudder deflect to the right. Depressing the left rudder pedal should make the rudder deflect left. Pulling back on the yoke (stick) should cause the elevator to move upward, and pushing it forward should make it move downward. If we see any other results, we should cancel the flight and report the issue to maintenance for repair before the aircraft flies again.
549.	When switching the ignition switch from the "Both" position to the "Left" or "Right" position, what should we expect to happen?	We should expect to see a slight drop in RPM, but not so much that power output is significantly compromised.
550.	What engine accessory are we testing when we move the ignition switch from "Both" to the "Right" or "Left" position?	We are testing the magnetos to verify that they are supplying the ignition system with an appropriate amount of electrical energy to produce a good spark at the spark plugs.
551.	Why does the RPM drop slightly when we move the ignition switch from the "Both" position to either the "Right" or "Left" position?	The RPM drops because the engine uses a redundant ignition system that makes use of two magnetos to feed two separate sets of spark plugs. When we switch from "Both" to either "Right" or "Left," we are removing one magneto or the other from the system, and using only one set of spark plugs instead of both sets. This deprives the engine of some of its potential, which results in a slight drop in RPM.
552.	What is the risk if we take off with a cold engine?	The oil may not be warm enough to circulate freely through the engine, causing damage or possible engine failure when we increase power for takeoff and climb out.
553.	Oil pressure gauges often have two red lines. Why is that?	There is one red line at the low end of the scale that indicates insufficient oil pressure is being developed, which could lead to engine damage or failure. The second red line is at the upper end of the scale and indicates that too much pressure is being developed, which can also lead to engine damage or failure.
554.	Does it matter in which direction we position the aircraft for the before-takeoff check?	If possible, we will position the aircraft into the wind to help cool the engine. This is especially important for an engine that is entirely air-cooled, rather than liquid-cooled.

555.	Are there any other positioning considerations when preparing to do a run-up before takeoff?	We want to be sure the aircraft is positioned in such a way that it is not likely to pick up excessive dirt, pebbles, or other foreign matter that could damage the propeller or airframe or blow into other aircraft or hangars and cause damage.
556.	Is there any special consideration for the position of the nosewheel?	We want to be sure the nosewheel is straight. If the brakes were inadvertently released with the nosewheel turned to one side, the potential stress could cause damage to the nosewheel assembly.
557.	Will we do the before-takeoff check on the taxiway?	Some airports have a before-takeoff check, or run-up, area that allows us to perform the check without blocking the taxiway. If that option is available, we will position the aircraft there. If there is no designated area, we will use the taxiway for our before-takeoff check.
558.	Where will you be focusing your attention during the before-takeoff check?	I will be careful to divide my attention between the aircraft's instruments and controls and the environment outside the aircraft. I will be looking for the appropriate indications on the aircraft's instrumentation to be sure that the aircraft is ready to fly. But I will also be monitoring the outside environment for aircraft, vehicles, and personnel that may be moving into our area during the before-takeoff check.
559.	How can we be sure the engine is warmed up properly before takeoff?	The oil temperature gauge is our best indication of the engine's operating temperatures. EGT and CHT should both be monitored to be sure they are in the operational range, too. When the oil temperature has risen into the green arc, we can be sure the engine is warmed up sufficiently.
560.	If we see a low oil pressure indication that does not come up into the green arc or a high oil pressure indication that stays consistently above the green arc, what should we do?	While we are on the ground, we would return the aircraft to maintenance and bring the issue to the attention of a mechanic. It would be unsafe and unwise to take off in an airplane that is indicating a potentially serious engine problem during the before-takeoff check.
561.	If the aircraft begins to move during the ignition check when you have the power at a high RPM setting, what would you do?	I would immediately retard the throttle to prevent the aircraft from lurching forward. Controlling the aircraft is my first priority. I would then resume the ignition check, paying special attention to hold the brakes firmly. If the aircraft begins to move again, I would return the aircraft to maintenance to check the brakes. If I am able to hold the brakes firmly and the aircraft does not move, I will continue with the before-takeoff check (including the ignition check) to verify that the aircraft is ready to fly.
562.	Where would we stop on the taxiway prior to takeoff?	On the hold short side of the hold short line.
563.	Which side of the hold short line is the hold short side?	The side with the two solid lines is the hold short side. The side with the dashed lines is beyond the point where we should be stopped and waiting for our turn on the runway for takeoff.

AREA OF OPERATION III: AIRPORT OPERATIONS

Task A: Communications and Light Gun Signals

564.	What does CTAF mean?	CTAF stands for Common Traffic Advisory Frequency. It is the frequency that pilots use to self-announce their position and their intentions at an airport without an operating control tower.
565.	What is one aspect of using a CTAF to self-announce that could cause confusion?	More than one airport within the range of our radio receiver may use the same frequency as a CTAF. To prevent confusion, we will announce the airport we are flying from at the start and conclusion of our radio calls.
566.	If we were approaching to land at an airport without an operating control tower, when would we typically make our first radio call on the CTAF?	We would announce our position and our intentions when we were approximately 10 miles from the airport.
567.	After we make that first call, what other calls would we make?	We would make a call on the CTAF to announce we are entering the traffic pattern, another call to announce we are established on the downwind, a call to announce that we are turning to the base leg, and a call to announce that we are established on the final leg of the pattern.
568.	Are we required to make radio calls at an airport without an operating control tower?	No, radio contact is not required at airports without an operating control tower. But for safety and the expedient flow of traffic, the FAA and common sense encourage us to make CTAF calls if we have the equipment to do so.
569.	If we intend to land at an airport with an operating control tower, when should we contact ATC to announce our intentions?	We should contact the tower to announce our intentions and our position when we are approximately 10 miles out from the airport.
570.	Is there anything we need to know before we make that initial call?	We should tune to the airport's ATIS frequency and become familiar with the information being broadcast before making our initial call to the tower.
571.	After that initial call to report our position and intentions, when would we make our next call to the tower?	The tower controller will tell us when (s)he wants us to make our next call. (S)he will respond to our first call with information like, "Report right downwind for Runway 2." That tells us to enter the traffic pattern on a right downwind for Runway 2. We will call to report our position again when we are entering or established on that right downwind.
572.	If we were departing an airport with an operating control tower, who would we make our first radio call to after starting the aircraft?	We would call ground control to advise them where we are on the airport and what our intentions are (taxi to the active runway for takeoff).
573.	At that same airport with an operating control tower, when would we make our first call to the tower?	We would call the tower only when ground control advises us to contact them.

574.	If we were flying in to an airport without an operating control tower, how could we find the CTAF for that particular airport?	The CTAF is printed on sectional charts and is available in the Chart Supplement.
575.	What is the frequency for emergency voice communication?	ATC continuously monitors 121.5 MHz for emergency calls.
576.	After being cleared to taxi by the ground controller, how would we know which frequency we should use to contact the tower?	The ground controller will assign us a frequency to use when contacting the tower. The tower frequency is also available in the Chart Supplement and on the sectional chart.
577.	What is the procedure if you have lost communication with the tower at a tower-controlled field?	If you have lost your ability to communicate with the control tower, you should observe the flow of traffic, enter the pattern, and look for light gun signals. When you receive a signal, acknowledge it by rocking your wings.
578.	What code should you set your transponder to following a radio failure?	The transponder code that indicates radio failure is 7600.
579.	Can you give me an example of a CTAF radio call when departing Runway 18 at Flying Ten Airport?	"Flying Ten traffic, Cessna 123 Alpha-Bravo departing Runway one-eight, Flying Ten traffic."
580.	How do we let the tower controller know we are familiar with the information being broadcast on the ATIS frequency?	During the initial call we will say, "Cessna 123 Alpha-Bravo, with Information X-Ray (or whatever the current ATIS broadcast identifier is)," then report our position and intentions to the tower controller.
581.	Where would we find the CTAF frequency for an airport without an operating control tower?	The sectional chart will list the CTAF, as will the Chart Supplement.
582.	Which light gun signal indicates that you are cleared to land?	A steady green light gun signal indicates that you are cleared to land.
583.	Which light gun signal indicates that you are cleared for takeoff?	A steady green light gun signal indicates that you are cleared for takeoff.
584.	What does a steady red light gun signal indicate on the ground?	A steady red light gun signal on the ground means to stop.
585.	What does a steady red light gun signal indicate when you are in the air?	In the air, steady red means to give way to other aircraft and continue circling.

Task B: Traffic Patterns

586.	If we fly to an unfamiliar airport, how would we know whether the runway we use makes left-hand traffic or right-hand traffic?	If the airport has an operating control tower, they will assign us an entry to the pattern. If the airport does not have an operating control tower, we will observe other traffic to determine the pattern in use. If there is no other traffic, we will use visual indicators at the airport and wind sock information to select a runway and determine the traffic pattern to use.

587.	As we prepare to enter the traffic pattern, what is our biggest concern?	Collision avoidance is key. We will keep our radio tuned to the appropriate frequency and monitor the radio for calls from other aircraft that would give us an indication of where they are and what their intentions might be. We will also keep a good visual look-out, and I will encourage my passenger to look for traffic and point it out to me, as well.
588.	How will you enter the traffic pattern at an airport with an operating control tower?	I will enter in any way the controller advises. The controller has the authority to give me a straight-in approach, to enter in the base leg, or to fly either left or right patterns. Unless there is a compelling safety issue involved, I will fly the pattern I am assigned.
589.	How will you enter the traffic pattern at an airport without an operating control tower?	After identifying which runway is in use and whether they are using standard (left-hand turns) or a nonstandard (right-hand turns) pattern, I will enter on a 45° angle to the downwind leg at midfield.
590.	If another airplane is on short final to the runway you intend to use for takeoff, are you allowed to taxi into position and take off ahead of that aircraft's landing?	At an airport with an operating control tower, I will not taxi past the hold short line until I am instructed to do so by the tower controller. At an uncontrolled field, I will have to make the decision about when to taxi onto the active runway myself. In the interest of safety, I would prefer to taxi and take off when no traffic is on final. If the airport is particularly busy, I will only take the runway if I am confident that I can perform my takeoff and be clear of the runway well before the airplane on final is over the fence at the approach end of the field.
591.	How could you let the airplane on final know what your intentions were?	I would be making calls on the CTAF with my position and my intentions before taxiing onto the runway, regardless of whether I see any other traffic in the pattern.
592.	After lift-off, what would be a navigational concern?	I want to maintain a line straight out from the runway. If I stray from that line, it could affect my ability to fly a rectangular pattern effectively. I will apply enough right rudder to counteract the airplane's left turning tendency, and monitor my ground track visually for indications of drift caused by a crosswind.
593.	If you notice you are drifting due to a crosswind, how would you deal with that?	I would crab into the wind for my climbout, correcting as necessary as I gained altitude. I would also keep that wind in mind through the various legs of the pattern, since the wind would have an effect on the aircraft for each leg of the pattern.

AREA OF OPERATION IV: TAKEOFFS, LANDINGS, AND GO-AROUNDS

Task A: Normal Takeoff and Climb

594.	What are two speeds that we need to be aware of during a normal or crosswind takeoff?	V_R, which is the speed at which we rotate the aircraft, and V_Y, which is the best rate of climb speed. (NOTE: Be familiar with these two speeds for your aircraft and be prepared to share them with the examiner upon request.)
595.	What does "best rate of climb" mean?	V_Y is the best rate of climb speed. When performing a normal or crosswind takeoff, V_Y is the appropriate speed for climbout. By establishing V_Y as we climb out following takeoff, we will gain the most altitude over a period of time.
596.	What does V_R, or rotation speed, indicate?	When the aircraft accelerates to V_R during takeoff, I will raise the nose slightly to increase the aircraft's angle of attack. The resulting increase in lift will allow us to leave the runway and climb out.
597.	How do you know what the appropriate V_R and V_Y are for your aircraft?	Both V_R and V_Y are listed in the Normal Takeoff Checklist in the POH/AFM for the aircraft.
598.	After leaving the runway, what will you be focused on as the pilot in command?	I will be dividing my attention between several concerns. I will pitch and trim for V_Y (best rate of climb speed), scan the area for traffic, adjust my ground track to compensate for the effects of the wind and maintain the center line of the runway on climbout, make radio calls as appropriate, and monitor my engine and systems to be sure everything is operating as expected.
599.	How will you ensure collision avoidance after takeoff and during your climb?	Aircraft tend to congregate at the airport. There is likely to be other traffic in the traffic pattern and in the surrounding area. At a controlled airport, I should not assume the tower controller has assumed full responsibility for collision avoidance. As PIC (pilot in command), I have the ultimate responsibility for maintaining the safety of the flight. At an airport without an operating control tower, there may be traffic in the pattern, or entering the pattern, that is not in radio contact with the field or the pilots flying there. In either case, I have to keep an eye out for potential conflicts and be aware of where other aircraft are in my vicinity.
600.	If you were taking off from a field with an operating control tower, would you clear the area even if the tower has cleared you to take off?	Yes. I would proceed with my takeoff as instructed by the tower. I would still visually scan for traffic in the area and, if necessary, bring traffic that may be an issue to the attention of the controller and ask for confirmation that I was cleared to take off. (NOTE: At an airport with an operating control tower, it is rarely necessary to query the controller about potentially conflicting traffic. Nevertheless, the PIC should never begin a takeoff if (s)he believes that complying with the clearance will result in a conflict with another aircraft or vehicle.)

| 601. | Assuming a crosswind from the left, how would you position the flight controls during your takeoff roll? | I would have my ailerons positioned into the wind, with the left aileron up as the roll begins. With the left aileron up, I can prevent the wind from getting under the wing and lifting it prematurely. As our speed builds, I will gradually neutralize the ailerons to prevent a sudden roll to the left as the ailerons gain control authority. By the time we lift off, the ailerons will be neutralized, and I will shift to a crab that is sufficient to maintain a straight ground track as we climb out. |

Task B: Normal Approach and Landing

602.	What is the approach speed based on?	Approach speed is typically 1.3 times V_{SO}. However, it is reasonable to add a few knots to the approach speed to accommodate wind gusts in order to minimize the risk of an unintentional stall.
603.	Where would you find the appropriate approach speed for a normal or crosswind landing?	The approach speed is listed in the POH/AFM for the aircraft type.
604.	How close should the touchdown point be to the intended point of landing?	The ACS specifies that the aircraft should touch down within 400 feet of the intended point of landing.
605.	Would it be advisable to touch down slightly before the intended point of landing?	No, touching down before the intended point would risk hitting runway end identifier lights, the lip of the runway, or the airport fence. It is always our intention to touch down on or after the intended point of landing, while staying within the 400-foot tolerance established by the ACS.
606.	If you are cleared to land on a 5,000-foot runway but find the airplane that landed ahead of you has not yet cleared the runway when you are on short final, what should you do?	If an aircraft or a vehicle were on the active runway when I was on short final, I would perform a go-around rather than potentially have a conflict during the touchdown or the landing rollout.
607.	What issue would you have when landing in a crosswind that you would not have when landing without a crosswind?	The crosswind is going to tend to push me off the centerline of the runway. To maintain a straight line, I will have to either crab the aircraft or slip with the upwind wing held slightly down.
608.	Why is it important to hold the upwind wing down?	When landing with a crosswind, I do not want the wind to get under the upwind wing and lift it unexpectedly. So whenever I slip to a landing, I will be sure to hold the upwind wing slightly low and maintain my ground track with rudder inputs.
609.	If you crab into the crosswind on approach, can you carry the crab all the way to touchdown?	No, it is risky to touch down in a crab. The side loads could damage or collapse the landing gear, and the aircraft is likely to have control issues because it is not pointed straight down the runway when it touches down. Rather than touch down in a crab, I would transition from the crab to a slip just before touchdown, holding the upwind wing slightly low and maintaining my ground track with rudder inputs.

610.	If the crosswind is strong and the runway is wide, how close to the centerline should we be at touchdown?	We should always land on the centerline, regardless of the strength of the crosswind or the width of the runway.
611.	During a strong crosswind landing, after touchdown, what control inputs might be required that would not be required after touching down from a normal landing?	After touchdown, the aircraft is still in motion, so air is moving over the lifting surfaces of the aircraft and may have an effect. I will have to remain aware of the wind direction and strength, and position the controls so the upwind aileron is raised to prevent the wind from lifting it. I will also position the ailerons and elevator as I taxi clear of the runway to prevent the wind from causing control problems or damaging the aircraft.
612.	How far from the centerline of a runway should you adjust in a strong crosswind scenario?	We should always land on the centerline, regardless of the strength of the crosswind or the width of the runway. If the crosswind is excessively strong, it might be worth considering landing at another airport that is nearby, assuming that they have a runway more closely aligned with the prevailing wind.
613.	After landing without a radio at a controlled field, what must you do after clearing the runway?	After landing without a radio at a tower-controlled airport, you are required to stop after clearing the runway and wait for another light gun signal before you are allowed to taxi. The signal clearing you to taxi will be a flashing green light.

Task C: Soft-Field Takeoff and Climb

614.	When taxiing to take off on a soft field, what concern do we have that we would not have when taking off from a hard surface?	We do not want to come to a complete stop or let the power bleed off to the point that the aircraft bogs down in the soft ground. Therefore, keep the aircraft moving, but in a safe manner.
615.	What is our power setting when taxiing on a soft field?	It may take very near full power to get the aircraft to begin rolling. From that point, we will adjust power as needed to keep the aircraft moving at a speed that is safe, but we will not allow the aircraft's wheels to bog down in the soft ground.
616.	Does that mean that you would not have to clear the area, as you would before a normal takeoff?	No, we always clear the area before departing the runway (especially when departing a field without an operating control tower). But when performing a soft field takeoff, we will clear the area without stopping.
617.	Assuming a tricycle-gear aircraft, as we advance the power to takeoff power, what is different about the soft-field takeoff roll?	I will be holding the yoke (stick) back to get the nosewheel off the ground as soon as possible. This reduces friction and drag caused by the wheel rolling along the ground, lowers the chances of damaging the nosewheel as the aircraft accelerates, and increases lift due to the higher angle of attack.
618.	In a tricycle-gear aircraft, what is the technique to advance the power to takeoff power and what are you trying to accomplish?	During the soft-field takeoff, we want to get the aircraft off the ground and into ground effect as soon as possible. We will level off and allow the aircraft to accelerate to V_Y in ground effect, then we will pitch up to climb out normally.

619.	What would be the biggest risk when performing a soft-field takeoff?	It is important to remain in ground effect until the speed builds up sufficiently to support a climb out of ground effect. If we were to try to climb out of ground effect as soon as we came off the ground, our airspeed would be too low and we would risk an inadvertent power-on stall very close to the ground.
620.	Is the aircraft configured the same for a soft-field takeoff as it is for a normal takeoff?	The proper configuration for the aircraft is described in the Soft-Field Takeoff Checklist found in the POH/AFM for the aircraft type. (NOTE: If equipped, it is common for aircraft manufacturers to specify the use of a specific flap setting for soft-field takeoffs. Be familiar with the specific configuration that is described for your aircraft.)

Task D: Soft-Field Approach and Landing

621.	How does the soft-field landing approach differ from the normal landing approach?	The approach is virtually identical, although airspeed control is arguably more important during the soft-field landing approach since we may need to plan our touchdown and rollout more carefully.
622.	Why would we potentially want to plan our touchdown and rollout more carefully for a soft-field landing?	Our goal is to minimize the distance we need to taxi on the soft field to prevent unnecessary wear or damage to the aircraft. So we will plan our touchdown point to put us closer to our destination, allowing us to taxi a relatively short distance after touchdown.
623.	After touchdown, will you handle the controls any differently when performing a soft-field landing than you would when rolling out during a normal landing?	(Tricycle-gear aircraft only) I will hold the elevator control in the full aft position during rollout and taxi to minimize the amount of weight being supported by the nosewheel, and I will avoid using the brakes unless it is absolutely necessary.
624.	What are the special considerations when braking on a soft field?	Typically, we try to avoid using brakes on a soft field. Braking increases the weight and wear transferred to the nosewheel, and it increases the risk of bogging down in the soft surface. The additional rolling resistance presented by a soft field is usually sufficient to allow us to stop by just reducing the power to idle.

Task E: Short-Field Takeoff and Maximum Performance Climb

625.	How would you position the aircraft before beginning your takeoff roll when performing a short-field takeoff?	I would be sure the aircraft was positioned to use the entire runway. To do that, I would begin my takeoff roll at the very beginning of the runway. Ideally, the tail would be hanging out over the grass with the wheels on the first foot of pavement.
626.	How would you configure the aircraft for a short-field takeoff?	The correct configuration is included in the short-field takeoff checklist in the POH/AFM for the aircraft. (NOTE: Be prepared to discuss the specific flap position, if installed, and configuration considerations for your type of aircraft.

627.	Will you begin your takeoff roll any differently when performing a short-field takeoff than you would for a normal takeoff?	Yes, I will hold the brakes while I advance the throttle to full power. That will allow me to be sure we have full power before I begin using runway for my takeoff roll.
628.	What speeds are we primarily interested in when performing a short-field takeoff?	We are going to rotate at V_R, then we will climb at V_X until we reach a safe altitude. When we are clear of obstacles, we can transition to V_Y to continue our climb to cruise altitude. (NOTE: Be prepared to identify the specific speeds that equate to V_R, V_X, and V_Y for your type of aircraft.)
629.	Can you define V_X?	V_X is the best angle of climb speed. It is the speed that will allow us to gain the most altitude over a given distance. When taking off from a short-field that may have obstacles at the departure end of the runway, we would use V_X to clear the obstacles, then transition to V_Y (best rate of climb) for our climb to altitude.
630.	Assuming there are no obstacles at the airport we are operating out of, how high will we hold V_X before transitioning to V_Y during our short-field takeoff?	The ACS specifies that we maintain V_X until we clear the obstacle or reach 50 feet above the surface. With no actual obstacles to clear, we will maintain V_X until we reach 50 feet above the surface, then we will transition to V_Y.
631.	If there are obstacles on our route of flight, can we transition to V_Y at 50 feet above the surface during the practical test?	The practical test is like any other flight. Safety is our first priority. If there are obstacles on our route of flight, we will maintain V_X until we clear them, then we will transition to V_Y to continue our climb.

Task F: Short-Field Approach and Landing

632.	Can you list some of the considerations you would have when making a short-field approach and landing?	The assumption is that the field is short and potentially has obstructions on the approach end of the field. With that in mind, I would be selecting the most advantageous touchdown point based on the wind and terrain while I was still in the pattern. I would evaluate and account for any obstructions in selecting that touchdown point. I want to make my approach with minimal power and with flaps (if the aircraft is equipped with flaps) set to the position indicated by the short-field landing checklist in the POH/AFM for the aircraft. I would clear the obstacles on final and touch down within 200 feet of the touchdown point I selected at the minimum controllable airspeed so that I would be able to stop the aircraft without overrunning the end of the runway.
633.	How would you go about stopping the aircraft?	I would hold the nose high to make the most of aerodynamic braking (drag). As soon as the nose settled, I would apply full brakes. My goal is to stop the aircraft as quickly as possible without compromising safety.

634.	If you touch down at minimal controllable airspeed, does that mean that you will make a hard landing?	The short-field landing may be firm so that the aircraft does not float down the runway and provide an opportunity for better braking, but it should still be smooth. There should not be a bone-jarring impact when we touch down.
635.	How close to your point of intended touchdown will you land when making a short-field approach and landing?	The ACS stipulates that I must land within 200 feet of the point of intended touchdown.

Task M: Forward Slip to a Landing

636.	Describe the control inputs you would use to slip to a landing.	The controls are crossed, with the ailerons deflected one way and the rudder deflected the other. The more extreme the control deflection, the more pronounced the sink rate of the approach.
637.	Why would you use a forward slip to a landing?	It is a method of increasing the sink rate of the aircraft without increasing the forward speed. The slip to a landing is especially useful for aircraft that do not have flaps.
638.	What is the risk when doing a forward slip to a landing?	Airspeed control is critical because the controls are crossed. A stall with crossed controls could be disastrous, so we will be sure to maintain an airspeed at or slightly above the usual approach speed while slipping.
639.	Would a crosswind affect our decision to use a slip to a landing?	Yes, it would. We can still slip to a landing in a crosswind, but we would need to be sure that the upwind wing is held low throughout the approach. This would keep the wind from getting under it and rolling the aircraft unexpectedly.
640.	Are there any manufacturers limitations to doing a forward slip to a landing?	Yes, some aircraft may have an issue with the flaps affecting airflow over the tail, or aileron control may be limited allowing only a certain amount of bank, or the placement of fuel tanks may limit the duration that a slip is allowed before fuel flow is interrupted. There are a variety of reasons why slips may not be permitted under certain conditions, or for longer than a brief period of time.
641.	When slipping to a landing, how close to your touchdown point will you land?	I will set down within 400 feet of the point of intended touchdown, as the ACS requires.
642.	Will you touch down while still in the slip?	It depends on the winds. If there is no wind, the slip is just a means of losing altitude in a short distance without having to increase speed. In that case, I would be inclined to transition from the slip to coordinated flight for the touchdown. However, if there is a crosswind, I could maintain the slip right up to the point of touchdown in order to maintain a straight ground track and keep the upwind wing low so the wind cannot get under it and raise it unexpectedly.

Task N: Go-Around/Rejected Landing

643.	Can you give me an example of a situation where you might consider a go-around?	There are many good reasons to perform a go-around rather than force a landing. If there is traffic or some other obstruction (including animals) on the runway, I would be inclined to perform a go-around. If I had not configured the airplane correctly or if I did not feel I had sufficiently stabilized my approach, I might go around. I might go around, rather than closely follow, a larger airplane that may generate wingtip vortices.
644.	In your opinion, is the go-around an emergency maneuver?	No. The go-around is a normal operation that can be performed as a preventive measure rather than forcing yourself into a situation that you may not be ready for, or set up correctly for, or that you are just uncomfortable with.
645.	Do we need to communicate anything to the tower or our fellow pilots if we choose to go around?	Yes. We would announce that we were going around so that the tower controller and any other traffic in the area would be aware that we have not committed to a landing, and that we will be climbing up and reentering the traffic pattern again.
646.	After a go-around, is it necessary to leave the traffic pattern and then reenter, or can you continue in the pattern without departing?	The go-around is a normal procedure, so it is perfectly acceptable to remain in the traffic pattern. At an airport with an operating control tower, the controller will advise us as to what he wants to do. At an airport without an operating control tower, we should make radio calls on the CTAF as appropriate to each leg of the pattern we fly, and make our intentions clear so other traffic in the pattern knows what to expect from us.
647.	When considering a go-around, when is the best time to initiate the maneuver?	As soon as it becomes clear that a go-around may be advisable, it is reasonable to then announce that you are going around and begin the process. The lower you carry the approach, the more complicated the go-around can become. It is better to decide and start the process early than to wait until you are on short final, at low altitude, and potentially slower than you would like to be for initiating a climb to begin the go-around.

AREA OF OPERATION V: PERFORMANCE MANEUVERS

Task A: Steep Turns

648.	What are the parameters you will be concentrating on while performing a steep turn?	I want to be sure I roll into the maneuver and maintain a 45° bank angle throughout a full 360° turn. My goal is to maintain my altitude plus or minus 100 feet, and roll-out of the maneuver within 10° of the heading I rolled into it on.
649.	Besides watching your heading indicator, what can help you anticipate your rollout point?	Because I will be performing this maneuver in VFR conditions, I should pick out a prominent landmark when I roll into the bank to help me maintain my orientation as I near the rollout point of the maneuver.
650.	What do we need to do prior to entering a steep turn?	Before performing any maneuver, we need to clear the area to verify no air traffic in the vicinity, including above, below, or around us, that might inhibit our ability to complete the maneuver safely and successfully.
651.	How can you clear the area before performing a maneuver?	To get a clear 360° view of the sky, we can either make two 90° turns in opposite directions, or a single 180° turn, scanning the sky above, below, and around us throughout the process.
652.	If you are in the middle of a steep turn and see oncoming traffic that you had not noticed during your clearing turns, what should you do?	If there is any possibility of a conflict, I should terminate the maneuver, steer clear of the oncoming traffic, and wait for them to clear the practice area. Then, I should clear the area and begin the maneuver again. Safety comes first, always.
653.	How would you correct for a loss of altitude during a steep turn?	I would reduce the bank slightly, increase back pressure on the elevator control, and increase power slightly until I reached my target altitude. Then, I would increase bank angle to my target bank angle, ease off the back pressure on the elevator, and evaluate whether I should maintain the higher power setting or retard it slightly.
654.	How would you correct for a gain in altitude while performing a steep turn?	I would increase the bank angle if possible, reduce some of the back pressure on the elevator, and perhaps reduce power slightly if that was warranted.

Task B: Ground Reference Maneuvers

Rectangular Course

655.	What normal aspect of flying does the rectangular course approximate?	The rectangular course is very similar to the airport traffic pattern.
656.	What is a pilot's greatest challenge when flying a rectangular pattern?	Because we fly four sides of a box, the wind is a factor that the pilot has to contend with and compensate for. Just like in the airport traffic pattern, the downwind leg will have a higher ground speed than the upwind leg. The crosswind and base legs require a crab into the wind to maintain a straight course line.

657.	When is the steeper bank angle required, during the downwind to base turn or during the upwind to crosswind turn?	The groundspeed is higher during the downwind to base turn, so the bank angle has to be steeper in order to compensate for the amount of ground being covered with the higher groundspeed.
658.	How can you maintain orientation when flying a rectangular course?	By using a landmark like a road, a river, or a tree line, it is possible to maintain a consistent ground track during the maneuver.
659.	What is the lowest safe altitude we can perform the rectangular pattern at?	We should be at 700 ft. AGL or above throughout the maneuver.
660.	How will you enter the rectangular pattern?	I will enter on a 45° angle to the downwind, just as if I were entering an airport traffic pattern.
661.	Is it necessary to clear the area before doing a low altitude maneuver, such as the rectangular pattern?	In the interest of safety, it is always necessary to clear the area before doing any maneuver.

S-Turns

662.	Describe the S-turn from entry to exit.	I will enter the maneuver on the downwind at 700 ft. AGL or above. Next, I will roll into a bank upon crossing the established reference line, and will perform a 180° turn to either the right or left, rolling wings level as I pass over the reference line a second time. Immediately after, I will roll into another 180° turn in the opposite direction, with wings level as I pass again over the reference line.
663.	Where will you use the shallowest bank angle?	When I roll into the second turn, I will be headed upwind and I will have the lowest ground speed. That is the point where I will need the shallowest bank angle to maintain a turn that follows a similar ground track to the one I flew during the first half the maneuver.
664.	Where will the bank angle be steepest in this maneuver?	Since we enter on the downwind, our ground speed will be highest, and our bank angle will be steepest, right as we enter the maneuver.
665.	Is there any relationship between the first half of the S-turn and the second half?	Yes, the ground track should be the same, even though the ground speed and bank angle change throughout the maneuver. If viewed from above, each half of the S-turn should look like one half of a circle.
666.	Is there anything we have to do before performing the S-turn?	In the interest of safety, we must first clear the area by using either two 90° turns in opposite directions or a single 180° turn.

Turns around a Point

667.	When performing a turn around a point, is the bank angle constant, or does it vary?	The bank angle is constant if there is no wind. But if there is any wind at all, the bank angle has the vary throughout the maneuver to compensate for the changing ground speed of the aircraft.

668.	Where is the steepest bank angle when performing a turn around a point?	When the aircraft is traveling downwind, it has the highest ground speed and needs the steepest angle of bank to compensate for that speed and fly a circular ground track.
669.	Imagine that we perform a turn around a point with a reference point a half-mile away. Then we perform the same maneuver with the reference point only a quarter-mile away. Will we use a steeper or shallower bank to perform the maneuver?	We will use a steeper bank. The closer the reference point, the steeper the bank angle required to fly the turn around a point.
670.	How will you enter the maneuver?	The steepest bank will be required when the airplane is headed downwind. So, I will enter on the downwind and establish a bank of less than 45°. By entering on the downwind, I can establish the maneuver and be sure I will not need to increase the bank beyond 45° during the remainder of the maneuver.
671.	Does the bank angle shallow out throughout the entire maneuver?	My steepest bank angles will be at the entry and just prior to rollout at the completion of the maneuver. I will shallow out the bank angle for the first 180° of the turn, which will put the aircraft on an upwind heading. From the 180° point to completion, the bank angle will increase until just before I roll out, when it will be the same bank angle that I rolled into the maneuver on.
672.	Why is it important that the bank angle does not go beyond 45°?	We need to maintain a bank angle of 45° or less because the stall speed of the aircraft begins to rise dramatically above 45° of bank. Even with that limitation, I will need to add some throttle as I roll into the maneuver to maintain speed and ensure safety throughout the maneuver.
673.	Why is it necessary to bump up the throttle when entering a maneuver with a steep bank angle?	As the bank angle increases, more of the vertical component of lift is redirected to a horizontal component of lift. To replace enough of the lost vertical component and maintain altitude, I need to increase the angle of attack by increasing back pressure on the yoke (stick). That will increase drag, which will tend to slow the aircraft down if I don't compensate by adding additional power.
674.	In an area with flat terrain and no obstacles on the ground, is it permissible to fly a turn around a point at 500 ft. AGL in Class G airspace?	It might be legal, but it would not allow for a reasonable safety margin. We should enter and fly the maneuver at 700 ft. AGL or higher.

AREA OF OPERATION VI: NAVIGATION

Task A: Pilotage and Dead Reckoning

675.	Can you give me a definition for the term "pilotage?"	Pilotage is a method of navigation that uses landmarks, checkpoints, and visual references.
676.	What makes a good landmark or reference point?	The bigger and more obvious a landmark is, the better. A highway, a lake, a river, railroad tracks, or a ridge line are all good landmarks.
677.	What makes for a bad landmark or reference point?	Landmarks and reference points should be unique to be most useful. A mountain is a good landmark if it stands alone, but it loses its value if it is surrounded by other mountains. Similarly, a lake is a good landmark if it is the only large body of water in a wide area. If, however, there are several other lakes in the same general region, it is a less valuable landmark since a pilot could potentially mistake one lake for another, and find himself or herself lost.
678.	What is dead reckoning?	Dead reckoning is another method of navigation that involves using sectional charts to select a course, and then establishing a heading to maintain that course based on current weather information.
679.	Is it necessary to use only one method of navigation?	No, it is actually preferable to use pilotage and dead reckoning together when flying cross-country. The two methods complement each other.
680.	Can you give me an example of how the two methods are complementary?	By plotting a course and figuring in the current weather reports, I can have a very accurate indication of what heading I should fly as I start out on a cross-country flight. But as I fly along my route, the checkpoints and landmarks I selected to use can give me a good indication if the wind is affecting my course more or less than I anticipated. By using the two methods together I can fly a more accurate route and be more confident while flying cross country.
681.	How would you use the airplane's magnetic compass to make turns in flight?	The magnetic compass can be used to set the heading indicator's rotating card or as a back-up heading instrument should the heading indicator fail. Because the magnetic compass is susceptible to various magnetic errors, such as variation (the angular difference between true and magnetic north), deviation (caused by magnetic disturbance in the airplane), and magnetic dip (the tendency of the compass to point down as well as to the magnetic pole), I will use timing to make turns and then correct myself based on the compass indication. For example, if I want to turn from north to east, I know that is a 90° turn. Using a standard-rate turn, I know it will take 30 seconds to complete that heading change. Once I roll out, I will use the compass to verify my heading.

682.	If I choose to fly a cross-country flight from a field with an elevation of 120 ft. AGL, on a course of 270° and a cruising altitude of 3,500 ft. MSL, have I made a good decision?	No, to fly a westerly course above 3,000 ft. AGL, you should be at an altitude of even thousands plus 500 ft. (in this case, either 4,500 ft. MSL or 6,500 ft. MSL). The odd-thousand-plus-500-foot altitudes are used by flights headed in an easterly direction. (NOTE: Use the memory aid, "East is odd and west is EVEN odder.")

Task B: Navigation Systems and Radar Services

683.	How can you use ATC to your advantage when flying cross-country?	Flight following (also known as VFR radar traffic advisory service) is available to VFR pilots on a workload-permitting basis. This allows the VFR pilot to maintain communications with ATC throughout much of a cross-country flight.
684.	To participate in flight following, what must you do?	I must have the ability to communicate with ATC, be in a radar coverage area, and be radar identified by ATC.
685.	What can we expect when we request flight following from ATC?	We can expect to be assigned a squawk code to put into the transponder, and we will often be asked to press "Ident," which will allow the controller to identify us on his or her radar screen.

Task C: Diversion

686.	When flying a cross-country flight, what might cause me to divert from my destination to an alternate airport?	There are several good reasons to divert. Some reasons you might divert include unforecast weather conditions with heavy rain, turbulence, or conditions that do not allow for continued VFR flight; a sick passenger; fuel capacity concerns due to higher than forecast headwinds; maintenance issues such as falling oil pressure or rising oil temperature; or the closing of your destination airport for any number of reasons. All would be good reasons to divert to an alternate airport.
687.	Once the decision is made to divert, what is the first thing you should do?	I should immediately turn in the general direction of my alternate airport, make radio calls as necessary, change my flight plan, and work out an exact heading based on my location after that first turn.
688.	What information would you need to gather after making the decision to divert?	After making the turn in the general direction of my new destination, I would want to pick a landmark to keep me oriented in the right general direction while I worked out a specific course. I would also locate the destination on my sectional chart to get field elevation, CTAF or tower frequencies, and the ATIS frequency if one is available.
689.	What limitations might you consider when picking an alternate to divert to?	My alternate airport should be one that is close enough that my remaining fuel will get me there with endurance to spare and should have a runway that is sufficiently long to handle my arrival. The weather conditions en route and at the new destination should be VFR and within the capabilities of both myself and my aircraft.

Task D: Lost Procedures

690.	If you begin to suspect you are lost, what is the first thing you would do?	I would climb. Weather permitting, I will be able to see farther from a higher altitude, and my radio will have a more extensive range.
691.	Once you have climbed to a higher altitude, what would you do?	Remain calm, fly the aircraft first, and begin to gather information visually that would help me identify my location. I would look for large, unique landmarks that would help suggest where I am, including major highways, population centers, lakes, rivers, or coastlines.
692.	What do you imagine your major consideration would be if you were lost?	I would have two major considerations high on my priority list. One would be fuel quantity. If I know I have 3 hours of fuel remaining, I can reasonably expect to find a solution to my predicament before fuel becomes a serious issue. My second major consideration would be weather conditions. If the weather along my proposed route is degrading but the weather behind me remains clear, I would be inclined to either head back in the direction I came from to retrace my route to more familiar territory and regain my bearings to continue my flight or abandon my cross-country plans and return home.
693.	If you cannot find any landmarks to help orient you, what might you do?	I would use the radio to communicate with resources on the ground. If necessary I would call 121.5 and set my transponder to 7600 to help ATC identify my location.
694.	What if the aircraft you are flying is not equipped with a radio or a transponder?	If I could identify landmarks behind me that I had passed on my route and was confident I could use them to find my way home or to a familiar airport I had passed en route, I would turn back, retrace my route, and land at the first available airport.
695.	If your aircraft is equipped with a GPS unit, what might you do to help locate your position?	If the GPS unit has power and I am confident it is working correctly, I could use the "Nearest" function to find the closest airport, turn toward it, and obtain the radio frequency for the tower or to self-announce my intentions. Once on the ground, I would take my time and find where I went wrong. This would allow me to determine my next course of action based on weather and other variables while relaxed on the ground rather than while under pressure in the air.
696.	If you were able to use the GPS to reorient yourself, would it be reasonable to continue your flight?	Yes, it would. If using the GPS allows me to find my way back to my planned route of flight and all other factors remain unchanged, it would be reasonable to use the GPS as a backup to pilotage and dead reckoning in order to continue to my destination with confidence.

AREA OF OPERATION VII: SLOW FLIGHT AND STALLS

Task A: *Maneuvering during Slow Flight*

697.	What would be a good altitude to initiate slow flight?	I would be at 1,000 ft. AGL or higher before initiating slow flight. Preferably, I would be at 1,500 ft. AGL, an altitude that provides plenty of room for obstacle clearance and a safe altitude for stall recovery if that became necessary.
698.	Is it necessary to clear the area before entering slow flight?	Yes, because the aircraft will be moving at a much slower rate of speed than is typical, for our own safety as well as the safety of transitional aircraft we may encounter, we clear the area before entering slow flight.
699.	How would you define slow flight?	Slow flight is a maneuver where the aircraft is flown at a very low airspeed, using pitch to control airspeed and power to maintain altitude. I will be attempting to fly the aircraft at a slow enough speed that any increase in angle of attack or power reduction would result in a stall.
700.	Can you turn while in slow flight?	Yes, but very slowly, with rudder inputs, not using ailerons. An increase in load factor from a bank could result in a stall, so turns are done with the rudder alone, very slowly.
701.	How would you recover from slow flight?	I would add power smoothly and let the nose drop as airspeed speed increases to maintain altitude. When we are back at cruising speed, I can bring the power back and trim for level flight.

Task B: *Power-Off Stalls*

702.	What does a power-off stall simulate?	It mimics the situation on final when power is very low or off entirely. On final approach if the nose comes up too high, and the airspeed is allowed to bleed off excessively, a power-off stall can result.
703.	What is the first indication that a stall is approaching?	The controls will tend to feel mushy and sluggish. We may feel a bit of a buffet just before the stall. And the stall warning system (a buzzer or a light in most aircraft) should provide a warning just before the airplane breaks as the stall occurs.
704.	If one wing falls during the stall, will the ailerons be able to pick the wing back up again?	We would use rudder to control our heading. We want to keep the ailerons centered during a stall because they have very little control authority during the stall and because we want to avoid inadvertently crossing the controls and turning a simple stall recovery into a stall/spin recovery.
705.	If the nose falls off to the left or the right during the stall, how do we correct for that?	With rudder inputs. Since the wing is stalled, the ailerons are of minimal effectiveness to control our heading during a stall.

706.	What will break the stall?	The stall can be broken by lowering the nose to reduce the angle of attack. An increase in power will allow me to raise the nose and resume level flight without slowing down further and risking a secondary stall.
707.	How much power should be added during the recovery?	I have been trained to add full power for the recovery. Once the recovery is complete, I will reduce power to a cruise setting.
708.	Would it be acceptable to raise the nose briskly immediately after the stall to prevent any loss of altitude?	After lowering the nose to break the stall, I would raise the nose smoothly as I increased the power. If I were to yank the nose upward to prevent a loss of altitude, we would enter a secondary, and possibly deeper, stall that would almost certainly cause us to lose altitude – the exact thing we want to prevent when recovering from a stall.
709.	Is it necessary to clear the area before doing a power-off stall?	I will clear the area before every maneuver, in the interest of safety.
710.	Where could I find a procedure for how to recover from a power-off stall in the airplane we will be flying today?	The POH/AFM include a procedure for the proper power-off stall recovery to use in the airplane we will be flying today.

Task C: Power-On Stalls

711.	What does a power-on stall simulate?	Power-on stalls are a good simulation of what would happen if the pilot raised the nose too high and let the airspeed bleed off during a takeoff.
712.	If you were to perform a power-on stall, what would you be using as a power setting?	I will use a power setting of 65% or higher. It is possible to use full power on some aircraft, but on others, full power requires a pitch up of 30° or more. For the sake of safety, I prefer to simulate the takeoff condition without pitching the nose high.
713.	How is the recovery from a power-on stall performed?	Lower the nose to break the stall, smoothly bring in full power, then raise the nose smoothly to level flight and regain any altitude that was lost during the maneuver.
714.	Would it be best to raise the nose into a climb immediately to recover any lost altitude?	No, it is important to raise the nose to level flight after applying full power. The aircraft needs a few seconds for the speed to increase enough to allow us to raise the nose into a gradual climb.
715.	What is the risk of raising the nose too high too quickly during the recovery?	If the nose is raised too high too quickly, it is possible to enter a secondary stall that might be deeper than the first stall was.
716.	Where could I find a procedure for how to recover from a power-on stall in the airplane we will be flying today?	The POH/AFM include a procedure for the proper power-on stall recovery to use in the airplane we will be flying today.

Task D: Spin Awareness

717.	What has to happen first in order to spin the airplane?	The airplane has to be stalled to spin. If you can avoid stalling the airplane, you will avoid spinning the airplane.
718.	If an airplane can only be spun after it stalls, why don't all stalls result in spins?	The airplane has to be stalled and have a yawing motion for a spin to occur. By keeping the ailerons centered and using the rudder to maintain directional control during a stall, it is possible to avoid entering a spin.
719.	Which is more likely to get into a spin, an airplane with a forward CG or an airplane with an aft CG?	An airplane with an aft CG is more likely to spin than an airplane with a forward CG.
720.	Would the location of the CG have any effect on the recovery from a spin?	An airplane with an aft CG is harder to recover from a spin and may take longer to recover from the spin than an airplane with a forward CG.
721.	What should I avoid to prevent a spin from occurring?	Keep the airplane coordinated at all times, avoid crossed controls, and avoid trying to steer the airplane with ailerons in a stall. If you're coordinated when turning the airplane and use the rudder for directional control during stall recoveries, the airplane should not enter a spin.
722.	How can I avoid entering a spin?	By not stalling the airplane.
723.	How can I avoid entering a spin if I do stall the airplane, even if I stall it accidentally?	If you use the proper stall recovery technique, the airplane will not enter a spin after stalling.
724.	What is the spin recovery procedure for the airplane we will be flying today?	Power to idle, neutralize the ailerons, full rudder opposite the direction of spin rotation, and yoke (stick) forward briskly to break the stall. When the rotation stops, center the rudder, raise the nose smoothly, and apply power as necessary. NOTE: This is a generic procedure. The procedure published in the POH/AFM for your aircraft is the procedure you should memorize and use for spin recovery in that aircraft.

AREA OF OPERATION VIII: BASIC INSTRUMENT MANEUVERS

Task A: Straight-and-Level Flight

725.	Which instruments can give you an immediate indication of your pitch when flying by instruments?	The attitude indicator (AI), altimeter (ALT), and airspeed indicator (ASI) can give me an almost immediate indication of a change in pitch. The vertical speed indicator can also provide an indication, although there is a lag of several seconds that prevents its use as a primary instrument for pitch change.
726.	If your airspeed indicator shows an increase, and your altimeter shows a decrease, what does that indicate?	An increase in airspeed and a decrease in altitude indicates that the nose has dropped. I would increase back pressure on the elevator slightly, and trim the nose upward slightly.
727.	If the airspeed indicator is stable, and the altimeter is stable, but the vertical speed indicator shows a 200-foot-per-minute descent, what would that suggest?	That condition suggests that we are flying at a constant altitude. The airspeed and altimeter holding solid is what we are trying to achieve. The vertical speed indicator is not a primary instrument, so we would not implement a control input based on information from that one instrument when the other instrumentation suggests we are flying level.

Task B: Constant Airspeed Climbs

728.	What is the primary pitch instrument when establishing a constant airspeed climb?	The airspeed indicator. Assuming we climb at full power, as we usually do, the airspeed indicator will become our primary pitch instrument. It will allow us to maintain pitch and airspeed to establish and maintain the climb.
729.	Do we have to climb at full power?	No, it is not necessary to climb at full power. However, in light general aviation airplanes it is often most expedient to climb at full power if the altitude gain desired is more than a simple altitude adjustment. If leaving one altitude for a higher one, full power is generally preferred to the longer, slower climb that would result from a lower power setting.
730.	What instrument would indicate a turn when in a constant airspeed climb?	The heading indicator would indicate a turn, whether it was coordinated or not.
731.	Why wouldn't the attitude indicator be the primary instrument for indicating a turn in a constant-speed climb?	The attitude indicator would indicate a bank, but a bank is not necessarily a turn. It could be the result of crossed controls in the climb where a slight bank is offset by opposite rudder to obtain straight but uncoordinated flight.
732.	Is there a key to maintaining a constant airspeed when in a climb?	There are a lot of very small control inputs required to maintain a constant airspeed. Large control inputs result in large airspeed changes. Small control inputs result in small airspeed changes.

Task C: Constant Airspeed Descents

733.	What are the three methods of establishing a descent?	To descend you can reduce power, increase drag, or lower the nose of the aircraft.
734.	When establishing a constant airspeed descent, what concerns do we have with the configuration of the aircraft?	If we are descending by increasing drag, we need to be sure that the airspeed is below V_{FE} (when deploying flaps) or V_{LO} (when lowering landing gear) to avoid causing structural damage to the aircraft.
735.	What is a good rule of thumb method for establishing a constant airspeed descent below cruise speed?	Reduce power to a predetermined power setting, maintain level flight while speed dissipates, then lower the nose to maintain a constant airspeed throughout the descent.
736.	What is your primary power instrument during the constant airspeed descent?	The tachometer or MAP. They will tell me if I have an appropriate power setting that will allow for a descent at the speed I am shooting for.
737.	What is the primary pitch indicator during the constant airspeed descent?	The airspeed indicator will dictate pitch. I will pitch up slightly to lower my speed and pitch down to increase airspeed.
738.	What is your primary bank indicator in a constant airspeed descent?	Even a slight turn will cause my heading to wander.

Task D: Turns to Headings

739.	What bank angle is recommended during turns to headings when flying by instruments?	Standard-rate turns are recommended when making turns to headings when flying by instruments. The bank angle will change with the speed of the airplane, but the rate of change will remain constant at 3° per second, regardless of how fast or slow we are cruising.
740.	How can we tell if we are established in a standard-rate turn?	When the wingtip of the airplane in the turn coordinator lines up with the reference mark, we are in a standard-rate turn. If the airplane has a turn-and-slip indicator, the pointer will line up with the doghouse marker to indicate a standard-rate turn has been established.
741.	What is a common error when flying by reference to instruments alone?	Fixation is common. It is when a pilot stops scanning the instruments and begins to focus on just one instrument to the exclusion of all others.
742.	What is the primary pitch instrument when making a turn in using only instruments as a reference?	The primary pitch instrument is the altimeter. Changes in altitude will show up immediately, indicating a need to increase or decrease elevator pressures to compensate for the change.
743.	How far ahead of your desired heading should you begin your rollout from a turn when navigating by instruments alone?	Generally I would begin my rollout approximately 10° before I reached my desired heading. Although if the bank angle was very shallow, as it would be in a turn that only transitions through a few degrees of the compass, the rollout might begin later.

744.	What constitutes a good instrument scan?	Checking and cross-checking instruments in a methodical fashion that continues throughout the flight. It is important that the pilot check all the flight instruments on a continual basis, not fixating on any one instrument, and not omitting any instruments from the scan.

Task E: Recovery from Unusual Flight Attitudes

745.	What cautions do you have to adhere to when recovering from unusual attitudes?	I need to keep the airspeed in a safe operating range, and I need to be cautious not to overstress the aircraft during the recovery process.
746.	If you saw your airspeed was well into the yellow arc and increasing, your altitude was decreasing, and your aircraft was in a 50-degree left bank, what would you do to recover the airplane?	First I would reduce power to stop the airspeed from climbing. I would level the wings to prevent overloading the aircraft in the recovery, then I would smoothly increase elevator pressures until the aircraft was level. Then I would increase power as necessary to maintain level flight.
747.	If you saw your airspeed was near the bottom of the green arc, your altitude was slowly climbing, and your aircraft was in a 45-degree right bank, how would you recover?	I would increase power to prevent a stall. Then I would level the wings as I simultaneously pushed the nose over to establish level flight. I would let the speed build before reducing power to establish a normal cruise.
748.	When you realize you are in an unusual attitude when flying by reference to instruments, what is your primary concern?	As a general rule, any time there is an instrument rate of movement or indication other than those associated with basic instrument flight maneuvers, assume an unusual attitude and increase the speed of cross-check to confirm the attitude, instrument error, or instrument malfunction. When a critical attitude is noted on the flight instruments, the immediate priority is to recognize what your airplane is doing and decide how to return it to straight-and-level flight as quickly as possible.

Task F: Radio Communications, Navigation Systems/Facilities, and Radar Services -- See Tasks III.A and VI.B.

AREA OF OPERATION IX: EMERGENCY OPERATIONS

Task A: Emergency Descents

749.	What in-flight situations may require an emergency descent?	This maneuver is a procedure for establishing the fastest practical rate of descent during emergency conditions that may arise as the result of an uncontrollable fire, a sudden loss of cabin pressurization, smoke in the cockpit, or any other situation demanding an immediate and rapid descent.
750.	Where would you find the prescribed emergency descent procedure for your airplane?	Because the emergency descent is an emergency procedure, it would be found in Section 3 of the airplane's POH/AFM.
751.	How should you correctly perform an emergency descent?	I would first refer to the airplane POH/AFM under Section 3, Emergency Procedures, to determine if a specific procedure is outlined for the airplane I am flying. If not, I will use the following technique: 1) Reduce the power to idle. 2) Move the propeller control to the high RPM position (if equipped with a constant-speed propeller). This will allow the propeller to act as an aerodynamic brake to help prevent excessive airspeed during the descent. 3) As quickly as practicable, extend the landing gear (if retractable) and full flaps to provide maximum drag so that a descent can be made as rapidly as possible without excessive airspeed. 4) To maintain positive load factors and for the purpose of clearing the area below, a 30° to 45° bank should be established for at least a 90° heading change while initiating the descent. 5) Do not exceed V_{NE}, V_{LE}, or V_{FE}, depending on the airplane's configuration.
752.	Describe the appropriate airspeed and configuration for an emergency descent.	The airplane should be in its highest drag configuration – gear and flaps extended, propeller control at high RPM setting (if equipped with a constant-speed propeller). The throttle should be in the idle position, and the airspeed must be kept within the operating range appropriate to its configuration. For example, operating above V_{FE} with the flaps fully extended could damage the flaps and/or the wings, which only creates another problem for me as the pilot.

Task B: Emergency Approach and Landing (Simulated)

753.	Given an engine failure, what is the first thing you would do?	I would pitch and trim for best glide speed immediately. After that, I would attempt a restart while picking out a suitable emergency landing spot.

754.	What would suggest a good field for an emergency landing?	I would be looking for someplace that is relatively flat and has enough length to allow me to put the aircraft down and roll out without hitting any solid obstacles, like trees or rocks. I want to be aware of any wires on the approach end, as well as fencing or other obstacles that would make a safe landing difficult or impossible.
755.	Once you have established best glide speed and begun your search for a suitable landing spot, what will you do?	Assuming an engine failure, I will analyze the cause of the failure and, if the altitude permits, I will attempt a restart. I will be using the emergency checklist included in the POH/AFM for the aircraft to be sure that I do not miss any steps in that process.
756.	During that process of establishing the best glide speed, selecting a field to land in, getting out your emergency checklist, and possibly attempting a restart, what will you be focusing your attention on primarily?	My first priority is to fly the airplane. I will be doing a number of things during an emergency, but flying the airplane remains my primary focus. It is critical to the safe outcome of the flight that I do not allow myself to become distracted from that task.
757.	When performing an emergency landing, what is your primary responsibility?	The safety of the flight and my passengers, the same as at any other point in any other flight.
758.	Is there any circumstance that would allow us to turn around and land on a runway we had just taken off from?	Yes, if we have sufficient altitude, we can potentially make the turn and get back safely. But in order to line up on the runway, the turn will be more than 180° (180° plus an intercept angle). If there is a wind, it will work in our favor since it will be helping us to reach the runway. But it will also give us a longer rollout because of our higher groundspeed when landing downwind. Unless we are above 500 feet, I would not attempt a return to the runway. Above that altitude the chances of making a successful emergency landing improve. Below 500 feet the likelihood of getting the aircraft turned around and lined up on the runway without running out of altitude is not good.
759.	Would a parking lot be a good choice for an emergency landing field?	It depends on the parking lot. If it is large and wide open with few cars and plenty of room to roll out, then it might be a good choice. If it is a crowded parking lot with light poles and other obstacles, it would be a less desirable option.
760.	Would a road be a good choice?	A wide road with light traffic and minimal trees, electrical wires, and other obstacles may be a valid option. But a busy road or a narrow road bordered by trees and light poles would be a poor choice for an emergency landing spot.
761.	What might be a weather consideration when picking out that landing spot?	The wind is going to be my biggest weather concern. I will make my decision on where to land partly based on the direction and intensity of the wind. With no power, my glide upwind will be shorter than a downwind glide, and I will have to make a choice of where to land accordingly.

762.	If the engine were to fail on takeoff, and we had reached an altitude of approximately 300 feet, could we just turn back and land on the runway we just took off from?	Not from 300 feet, we couldn't. That altitude does not allow for a successful 180-degree turn without power. At that altitude, we would have to select and commit to the best possible landing spot that lies in front of us.
763.	If you are able to get the aircraft on the ground successfully, but you do not have sufficient space to stop before reaching a tree line, what would you do?	I would use aerodynamic braking and whatever means available to me to slow the aircraft down before reaching the trees. If it became unavoidable that I was going to hit the trees, I would steer the aircraft to allow the fuselage to miss the trees and allow the wings to absorb the impact.
764.	Why would you steer to allow the wings to take the brunt of the crash and cause a significant amount of damage to the aircraft?	My responsibility is to the safety of the flight and my passenger. As much as I would hate to damage the aircraft in an emergency landing, it is more important that I prevent damage to my passenger, as well as people on the ground.
765.	Would it make sense to perform an emergency landing if you lost partial power but the engine continued to operate?	I would have to make that decision based on the specifics of the situation. It is difficult to answer in absolute terms. The best course of action would depend on the circumstances. If I was in an area that offered me good, safe options for an emergency or a precautionary landing, but the route ahead did not, then it might be a reasonable option to land rather than press on and get into a situation that is significantly less likely to have a safe outcome. On the other hand, if I am over water or inhospitable terrain but still have enough power to maintain altitude, or I am losing altitude slowly, it might make more sense to work on the problem while attempting to get to a place where an emergency landing would be less dangerous.

Task C: Systems and Equipment Malfunction

766.	If a system failure occurs in the air, what is your primary responsibility?	My primary responsibility is to fly the airplane regardless of whether I have a system failure or not.
767.	If you suspect a system failure, how would you verify the failure and determine which system is involved?	I can perform basic troubleshooting tasks to determine which system has failed, confirm whether it is a partial failure or a complete failure, and make a determination on how that failure might affect my flight.
768.	Are there system failures that would not have a detrimental effect on your flight?	Yes. An electrical failure would be inconvenient, but when flying VFR in daylight in Class G airspace, when my destination is in Class G airspace, an electrical failure would probably not qualify as an emergency that would adversely affect my ability to complete my flight.
769.	Can some system failures be remedied in flight?	Yes. A radio failure may be the result of a popped circuit breaker or a switch that was inadvertently turned off. A fuel system issue may be remedied by switching to another tank or employing an electric fuel pump to increase fuel pressure and quantity.

770.	What is the necessary action if you lose a magneto in flight?	If you suspect that you have lost a magneto in flight, you can identify the bad magneto by switching from both to either left or right. The bad magneto will be evident when the engine will not run on that particular magneto. After you identify the bad magneto, be aware that the engine should continue to run on the good one. There is often no harm done by continuing to leave the switch in the "Both" position, even if one magneto has failed. Land and make repairs before continuing your flight.
771.	What is the procedure if you have an engine failure in flight?	As soon as you realize an engine failure has occurred, establish and trim for the best glide speed for your airplane. Select an emergency landing site. Then, if time permits, go through the restart checklist in an attempt to regain power. If that fails and you have no choice but to make a forced landing, be sure to leave time to make use of the forced landing checklist in a calm and organized manner.
772.	What are some common causes of a rough-running engine in flight?	There are numerous factors that can cause an engine to run rough. The most common causes are carburetor ice, a problematic magneto, or fouled spark plugs.
773.	What would you do if your engine began running rough in flight?	Carburetor ice is one of the few issues for which I have direct access to a remedy, so I would apply the carburetor heat for a few minutes to hopefully melt the ice, then turn it off to find out if the engine would return to running normally.
774.	Is there any other possibility that you can directly affect?	Yes, I could change fuel tanks. It is possible that contaminated fuel would make the engine run rough. Switching tanks could allow the contaminated fuel to clear the system and be replaced by good fuel that will return the engine to normal operation.
775.	If the engine continued running rough, what would your next course of action be?	I would turn toward the nearest airport while checking the oil temperature and pressure gauges. As long as they were in the green I would continue on to make a precautionary landing at a nearby airport. It would be appropriate to have a maintenance technician investigate the problem before I carried on with the flight.
776.	Is it necessary to make a precautionary landing when the engine is running rough?	No, but if the safety of the flight is in question, it is always better to make a precautionary landing rather than push on and create a potentially more serious problem.
777.	What indication would you expect if carburetor or induction icing is impeding the air passages to the engine?	The engine may run rough, and the RPM may drop as power is reduced.
778.	How could you prevent or correct for carburetor or induction icing?	Applying carburetor heat or opening an alternate air source may prevent or correct carburetor or induction icing.

779.	What would you expect to see after applying carburetor heat?	The engine would run rougher, and the RPMs may drop due to the less-dense heated air entering the induction system.
780.	If you suspect icing, what would you expect to see after opening an alternate air source?	The RPMs would rise to their previous level as a result of airflow being restored to the induction system.
781.	What should you do if you notice that you are losing oil pressure?	A loss of oil pressure should be viewed as an emergency situation. The engine will tend to overheat and may not continue to run with low oil pressure. If you are in the pattern, return for a full stop landing. If you are flying outside the pattern, turn toward the nearest airport and land as soon as possible. If you are a significant distance from an airport, be prepared for a possible forced landing and choose your route of flight accordingly.
782.	Why is fuel exhaustion an issue of concern for pilots?	Because it is often preventable by taking on sufficient fuel before departure, accurately estimating fuel use, and planning flights to allow for a reasonable surplus of fuel that allows us to reach our destination and fly on to an alternate if necessary.
783.	Is fuel exhaustion common?	It is not common, but it is a leading cause of aircraft accidents. Careful monitoring of fuel is one of the simplest ways for a pilot to prepare for a safe flight.
784.	Is running out of fuel the only cause of fuel starvation?	No, carburetor or induction icing can cause fuel starvation even when fuel is on board. If the ice chokes out the airflow to the induction system, the fuel/air mixture cannot reach the engine, even if there is plenty of fuel on board.
785.	In the event of fuel starvation in flight, do you have any options?	If icing is the cause, I may be able to restore the fuel/air mixture by using carburetor heat or the alternate air source. If the aircraft has more than one fuel tank and a selector valve, I could switch to the other tank. If there is fuel in that tank, I may be able to prevent the engine from failing, or I may be able to restart the engine if it has shut down.
786.	Is fuel starvation an emergency situation?	Yes. In the event of a real fuel starvation situation, if another fuel source and a restart is not possible, it will be necessary to make an emergency landing.
787.	What does a low voltage light indicate when it is illuminated?	A low voltage light indicates that the alternator or generator is not working and the electrical equipment is running from the battery.
788.	How would you deal with a low voltage indication in flight?	Turn off all non-essential electrical equipment to limit the drain on the battery and land as soon as practical.
789.	What is the procedure if a circuit breaker pops?	If a circuit breaker pops and it is resettable, push it back in once. If it pops out again, leave it out and determine the next course of action. Pushing the breaker in more than once may lead to an electrical fire.

790.	What would happen if the vacuum pump failed in your airplane?	A failed vacuum pump will result in the loss of the attitude indicator and the heading indicator.
791.	How is a vacuum pump failure in flight different from most equipment failures?	A vacuum pump failure is not considered an emergency situation in VFR conditions because the instruments powered by the vacuum pump are not necessary for safe flight.
792.	What would happen to the altimeter if the pitot-static system were obstructed?	If the pitot-static system were blocked, the altimeter would indicate the altitude where the system became blocked.
793.	What would happen to the VSI if the pitot-static system were obstructed?	With the pressure in the system remaining stable due to the blockage, the VSI would show no indication in a climb or descent.
794.	What would happen to the airspeed indicator?	Without the ability to compare pitot, or ram air pressure, to static pressure, the airspeed indicator would read zero.
795.	What error does the altimeter indicate if you are using an alternate static source?	Because alternate static sources are usually located inside the cockpit where the pressure is lower than it is outside the airplane, the altimeter is likely to indicate a higher altitude than normal.
796.	What is the most serious flap malfunction that could occur?	Asymmetric flap deployment is a serious problem. This is when one flap extends and the other does not, or when one flap extends farther than its counterpart. This causes asymmetric lift, an imbalance that can be powerful enough to render the aircraft uncontrollable.
797.	If asymmetric flap deployment occurs, what can you do?	Retract the flaps immediately. This is not a problem that can be remedied in the air. The aircraft should be flown without flaps for the remainder of the flight. After landing, the airplane should go to maintenance for repair.
798.	If you cannot deploy flaps, is that a flap malfunction?	Yes, if a system does not work, that is by definition a malfunction.
799.	Is it a serious problem if the flaps cannot be deployed?	It is inconvenient, but it is not a serious problem. If the aircraft is on the ground, it should go to maintenance for repair before flight. If the aircraft is in the air, the pilot should operate normally, albeit without flaps, through the landing phase of the flight. After landing, the aircraft should go to maintenance for repair before it is flown again.
800.	What can cause the trim system to be inoperative?	It depends on how the trim system works. It can be the result of an electrical failure or a stuck switch. It may also be the result of a kinked cable, a loose fastener, or a broken cable or fastener.

801.	Is an inoperative trim system a serious problem?	It can be, depending on the type of failure. A runway trim system is the result of a stuck switch on an electrical system that causes the trim to run fully to the stop in one direction. In some cases this can cause control pressures extreme enough to make control of the aircraft impossible.
802.	If your trim system is manual but cannot be adjusted – is that a serious problem?	No, it is not serious, but it is a reason for concern. Increased control pressures will cause pilot fatigue to occur much more rapidly than on a normal flight. While this is not an emergency situation, it does warrant a precautionary landing at the first opportunity to repair the system.
803.	What is the risk to the safety of flight with an inadvertent door or window opening?	The biggest risk is that the pilot will become so distracted by the noise and draft that (s)he stops flying the aircraft. The consequences of that distraction can be dire.
804.	What is the best course of action if a door or window opens in flight?	If the door or window cannot be closed easily, make a precautionary landing at the earliest convenience to close and secure the door or window on the ground.
805.	Will the airplane fly with the door or window open?	A door or window that pops open will rarely affect flight performance so negatively that the aircraft becomes uncontrollable. It may degrade performance to the point that it is not possible to maintain altitude, or it may have almost no effect at all. It is best to remain calm, fly the airplane, and find a place to land and deal with the situation on the ground, if necessary.
806.	If you were flying and noticed ice building up on your airplane, what would your best course of action be?	Since most light general aviation aircraft have no anti-ice or deice equipment aside from carburetor heat, my first choice would be to land at the first available airport. If possible, I would get below the freezing level, while still maintaining adequate altitude above the surface, to hopefully prevent further ice buildup and possibly melt off at least some of the existing ice while en route.
807.	What causes structural ice to form?	Visible moisture and an ambient temperature below the freezing level.
808.	Can structural ice be avoided?	Yes, it can be avoided in many cases. By avoiding flight above the freezing level when moisture is present in the form of clouds, drizzle, or rain, structural ice can largely be avoided.
809.	Is it legal to fly when icing is reported?	It is legal if the airplane you are flying is equipped to deal with icing. If the airplane is not equipped for flight into known icing conditions, it is neither legal nor wise to continue flight into known icing conditions.
810.	How serious is a fire in the cabin?	Very serious. That would more than likely meet the standards for declaring an emergency. I would look for a place to land immediately, shut off the master switch to prevent an electrical fire from worsening, and follow the emergency checklist in the POH/AFM for a cabin fire.

811.	If shutting the master switch off stops the fire, would you continue with the flight?	That depends on the situation. If there were no safe landing sites available, I would continue, leaving the electrical system turned off. (NOTE: Become familiar with the appropriate emergency checklist in the POH/AFM for your aircraft and be prepared to discuss it with your examiner.)
812.	How could you troubleshoot an electrical fire in flight?	With the master switch turned off, I would turn off each device individually until all the electrical items on board were shut down. Then I would turn the master switch back on. One by one, I would turn on only the device or devices I need to conduct the flight. If the fire started up again, I would shut off the device that caused the fire but continue to use the other devices until landing if there were no indication that a fire would result.
813.	How would you deal with an engine compartment fire?	It depends on whether the fire occurs on the ground or in the air. On the ground, if the fire starts during engine start, it may be best to shut off the fuel supply while continuing to turn the engine over to suck the fire inside the engine. In the air, an immediate emergency landing might be in order. (NOTE: Become familiar with the specific emergency checklist in your POH/AFM and be prepared to discuss it with your examiner.)
814.	If the elevator fails in flight, what would you do?	I would control the airplane with power and elevator trim and return for landing.
815.	Would that qualify as an emergency?	Yes, it probably would, especially if there is heavy traffic in the area. I would declare an emergency to make it clear that I have limited control and ensure that I have a clear path to the runway without conflicting traffic.
816.	Could you still control the airplane if the rudder failed?	Yes, although my control would be limited. I could make shallow banked, slipping turns back to the airport for a landing.
817.	If the ailerons failed, could you control the airplane in flight?	Yes, I could control the aircraft with rudder and elevator and return to the airport for a landing.
818.	Would you be tempted to make an emergency landing off airport due to a flight control malfunction?	No, probably not. The aircraft would be less maneuverable than usual, but it would be controllable. I would be better off landing back at the airport, or at another airport, where emergency equipment might be available and the runway would provide me with a wide, long landing area.
819.	Why are ballistic parachute systems installed in aircraft?	A ballistic parachute system offers an extra measure of safety to airplane operations. When deployed, the parachute allows the airframe to descend slowly to the ground, under control.
820.	How does a ballistic parachute system operate?	The pilot pulls a handle/level that ignites a rocket motor. The rocket deploys the parachute, and the airflow opens the parachute.

| 821. | What precautions must be taken when operating an aircraft equipped with a ballistic parachute system? | Pilots must be careful not to hold/pull the handle/level to avoid inadvertent deployment. Most systems employ safety pins that must be removed prior to flight. Refer to the emergency procedures checklist regarding how to operate the system before you find yourself in an emergency situation. |

Task D: Emergency Equipment and Survival Gear

822.	If you were planning a cross-country flight that crossed mountainous terrain, what emergency equipment might you carry?	Because the risk in mountainous terrain includes cold, I would carry blankets for myself and my passenger. I would also carry flashlights, food, water, and flares to help rescuers locate us.
823.	If you were planning to fly over a large body of water, what emergency gear would you carry?	I would be sure to have life vests for myself and my passenger, as well as a raft that would allow us to get out of the water in the event of a ditching.
824.	Is there any electronic gear you would consider carrying?	Yes, I would consider carrying a portable ELT that would send out a signal to help rescuers locate myself and my passenger on the water.
825.	If your route of flight takes you over the desert, would you carry any particular emergency equipment?	Water is the most important emergency item to have when in the desert. So I would carry drinking water, blankets, flares, and flashlights when flying over the desert, in case an emergency landing is necessary.
826.	What additional equipment might you carry if flying through an area where extreme temperature changes might occur?	If extreme heat was a possibility, I would be sure to carry drinking water and appropriate light clothing. If extreme cold was possible, I would carry blankets, a winter coat, extra socks, boots, a hat, and mittens or gloves. Exposure can be very dangerous, so carrying the appropriate emergency equipment to deal with the situation is important.

AREA OF OPERATION XI: NIGHT OPERATIONS

Task A: Night Preparation

827.	How long does it take your vision to fully adjust to darkness?	It takes approximately 30 minutes for a pilot's eyes to fully adjust to darkness after leaving a lighted area.
828.	Can you give me an example of what might impair a pilot's vision?	Good vision depends on the pilot being in good physical condition. If the pilot is sick, has a vitamin deficiency, is overly tired, smokes, or is taking medication – all of these variables can have an adverse effect on vision.
829.	What is a false horizon?	The false horizon is an illusion that can cause the pilot to become disoriented by mistaking a false horizon for the actual horizon. It is most common when a featureless sky merges with an unlit surface, which can cause the actual horizon to be difficult to distinguish from a false horizon.
830.	What is autokinesis and how can it adversely affect pilots?	Autokinesis is the illusion that a stationary object is moving. It is most commonly experienced when staring at a star or a fixed light in the distance. The illusion of movement can cause a pilot to become disoriented, which may result in unnecessary or erratic control inputs.
831.	How can ground lighting adversely affect pilots at night?	Bright lights viewed on a clear night can appear closer than they actually are. This can cause pilots on approach to misjudge their altitude above the surface, encouraging them to flair for landing prematurely.
832.	What color is a civilian airport beacon light?	Civilian airport beacons display an alternately flashing green and white light.
833.	If you're in flight and see a flash of green light followed by two flashes of white light, what does that indicate?	A green flash of light followed by two quick flashes of white light indicates a military airport.
834.	Is there an illusion or a limitation to VASI or PAPI lights that pilots need to be aware of?	Yes. When below the glide path, there may be an erroneous indication that the pilot is above the glide path. It is important that the pilot monitor the glide path throughout the approach and not be confused by appearing to suddenly go from being too low on the approach to too high, without an indication that the flight was on the glide path in between.
835.	What is the basic principle of VASI and PAPI lighting systems?	The lights show red, green, or amber colors to indicate whether the pilot is below, on, or above the glide slope on approach to landing.
836.	What color are taxiway lights?	Taxiway lights are blue.
837.	What color are runway lights?	Runway lights are white.
838.	How are obstructions lighted on the airport grounds?	They may be lighted by solid or flashing red lights or by solid or flashing white lights. In the case of white lights, the intensity is typically reduced for nighttime operations.

839.	At an airport with pilot-controlled lighting, how would you turn the lights on to locate the runway?	I would click the microphone three, five, or seven times in quick succession to turn on the lights and select the intensity of lighting that I needed in order to locate the runway and make an approach for landing.
840.	Where would you find a description of the pilot-controlled lighting available at a given airport?	The Chart Supplement lists information about pilot-controlled lighting at airports, including the frequency needed to operate them.
841.	What color light is on the right wingtip of an airplane with standard navigation lights?	The nav light on the right wingtip is green.
842.	What color light is on the left wingtip of an airplane with standard navigation lights?	The nav light on the left wingtip is red.
843.	If you see a green and a white light in the sky when flying at night, what does that indicate?	It suggests that an airplane is passing in front of me from left to right. I am looking at the green nav light on the right wing and the white light on the tail.
844.	If you see a red and a green light in the sky when flying at night, what does that indicate?	It suggests that I am looking at the front of an airplane headed in my general direction. The red and green nav lights can only be seen from in front of or to the side of an aircraft. By seeing both colored nav lights I can be sure the aircraft is headed my way, and I should alter course, altitude, or both accordingly to pass safely by as the other aircraft approaches.
845.	What is an anticollision light?	Anticollision lights can be a simple rotating beacon located on the fuselage of the aircraft or a strobe system that includes the wingtips as well. The system is designed to attract the eye and make aircraft easier to see and avoid at night.
846.	Is a landing light required on an airplane flying at night?	Only if the airplane is operated for compensation or hire. However, for enhanced collision avoidance and better visibility when landing or taking off, landing lights are strongly encouraged even in airplanes that are not operated for compensation or hire.
847.	Is there any particular equipment you would take on a night flight that would be unnecessary on a VFR flight during the day?	I would take at least one flashlight on a night flight and would probably take a second as a backup.
848.	What is the advantage of using a red lens on a flashlight when operating at night?	The red light does not have the adverse effect on night vision that white light does. Many pilots prefer red light when operating at night.
849.	What is the disadvantage of using a red lens on a flashlight when operating at night?	The red light washes out any red features or notes included on sectional charts, making them impossible to see. It is also more difficult to focus the eye on a chart illuminated by red light.

850.	How could you be sure your flashlight, or flashlights, would work as expected during your flight?	I would turn them on to be sure they were operating properly before departure, and I would carry an additional set of each type of battery required as a safety issue in case the existing batteries failed in flight.
851.	How is cockpit organization more important during a night flight than it is during a daytime flight?	Because my vision of the cockpit area is reduced, it would be very difficult to find anything that I dropped during the flight. Consequently, it is even more important to maintain an orderly cockpit during a night flight, keeping all charts, pens, pencils, calculators, or other tools in established places where they are easy to retrieve without causing items to fall around the cockpit in the process.
852.	How would forecast cloud layers affect your planning for night flights?	I would plan to cruise below the forecast or reported cloud layers. It is difficult to see clouds at the same altitude when cruising at night, so I would fly below that level to avoid inadvertently flying into the clouds and creating a problem for myself.
853.	Would you plot your course differently, or work with charts differently, when planning a night flight?	I would be careful not to make any notes or draw my course line in red ink. Red lighting that would preserve my night vision would render those notes invisible to me.
854.	How would your checkpoints differ when planning a night flight?	I would have to select checkpoints that are well lighted. Lakes, mountains, rivers, railroad tracks, and many roads are not visible at night, although they make great landmarks during the day.
855.	What would you use as a primary navigation method during a night flight?	If possible I would use GPS, but VOR or ADF would be helpful, too. I would avoid flying at night by reference to the ground alone, because the terrain and landmarks would look very different in the dark, which may make navigation difficult if no electronic or radio navigation aids were used.
856.	In an emergency, how would you locate an alternate airport when on a night flight?	Because it can be difficult to locate alternate airports in the dark, I would be sure to record radio frequencies and important details of airports near my route of flight before I departed on the flight. If I had a GPS unit available to me, I would use the "Nearest" function to help in any necessary diversions during my flight.
857.	How would you adjust the panel lighting when making a night flight?	I would adjust the panel lighting to be as low as possible to preserve my night vision while turning it up enough that I could read the instruments clearly.
858.	Is night flying any different from flying during the day?	I would prepare differently for a night flight, although the actual flying is very similar. My additional preparations would be to accommodate that fact that I could not see emergency landing fields or recognize landmarks as easily at night.

859.	How would the actual flying skills necessary to be safe be different at night than they are in the daylight hours?	A night flight may require a much greater reliance on instruments for orientation and navigation than a daytime flight might. That is especially true on a moonless night, when there is very little visible information outside the cockpit that would help pilots orient themselves or navigate from one point on the map to another.
860.	If you were to suffer an engine failure at night, what is your primary responsibility?	Like during the daytime, my primary responsibility is to control the airplane. I would try to restart just as I would during the day, but I would be limited in my choice of emergency landing spots because an empty field is not easy to differentiate from a forest at night. The important factor is to fight the impulse to panic and to fly the airplane throughout the descent while I attempt to restart the engine.
861.	Are private pilots allowed to fly at night?	Yes, provided they have the mandatory training, and their pilot certificate does not carry a restriction that disallows them from flying at night.
862.	What is the definition of night?	Night means the time between the end of evening civil twilight and the beginning of morning civil twilight, as published in the American Air Almanac, converted to local time.
863.	Are the currency requirements for carrying passengers at night the same as the currency requirements for carrying passengers during daylight hours?	Not quite. To carry passengers during daylight hours, a pilot is required to log three landings within 90 days in the same category and class of aircraft the passenger will be carried in. But to carry passengers at night, a pilot is required to make three night landings to a complete stop within 90 days in the same category and class of aircraft.

AREA OF OPERATION XII: POSTFLIGHT PROCEDURES

Task A: After Landing, Parking, and Securing

864.	Where would we clear the runway at an airport without an operating control tower?	We would clear the runway at the first available taxiway after slowing the aircraft to a safe speed that would allow for the turn.
865.	Where would we clear the runway at an airport with an operating control tower?	We would turn off the runway onto the taxiway assigned by the tower controller. When we are clear of the runway, we will call ground control and request permission to taxi to our destination.
866.	When is it appropriate to start cleaning up the aircraft by retracting the flaps, turning off the carburetor heat, and so on?	For safety reasons, we only start to clean up the aircraft after we have cleared the runway and have the opportunity to stop and perform tasks in an orderly fashion without distractions.
867.	After clearing the runway at an airport without an operating control tower, when can we taxi to our destination?	We can taxi to our destination when the aircraft is cleaned up, our after-landing checklist is completed, and we have verified that the taxiway is clear for us to continue.
868.	If you are at a large, unfamiliar airport with an operating control tower, how can you navigate the taxiways to your destination?	If I am unfamiliar with the airport layout, I can request a progressive taxi from the ground controller, who will then provide me with directions that will help me taxi to my destination.
869.	What safety consideration do you have when taxiing into the ramp area at any airport?	There are several safety considerations that are all important. The ramp area contains aircraft that are tied down, aircraft that are arriving and departing, fuel trucks and other support vehicles, and pilots and passengers walking between the terminal and their aircraft. I have to be sure to carefully identify any risks so that I can evaluate and avoid conflicts with them as I taxi onto the ramp area.
870.	What concerns might you have about tie-downs on the ramp?	I will be careful not to taxi over tie-down ropes or chains while taxiing on the ramp area. I will only taxi in the designated areas in such a way that I can pull directly into the tie-down spot without putting the propeller in close proximity to any ropes or chains. If that is not possible, I will shut the aircraft down and move it into the tie-down spot manually.
871.	Once you are in the tie-down space, how will you shut the engine down and secure the aircraft?	I will be using the checklists available in the POH/AFM appropriate to the aircraft to shut the engine down and verify that the aircraft is configured and secured properly.
872.	When will your passenger be exiting the aircraft?	My passenger will be exiting the aircraft only after I have shut the engine down and verified that the aircraft is secured from rolling or being blown in a way that could cause an injury.
873.	Is your passenger allowed to help you secure the aircraft?	Yes. If the wind comes up to the point that it might cause the aircraft to move while it is being tied down, I can ask my passenger to help secure the aircraft and direct him or her specifically on what to do.

APPENDIX A
SOURCES

The sources we used for the questions and answers in this book include the below. These publications can be obtained from the FAA, the Government Publishing Office, and aviation bookstores.

AAH	*Advanced Avionics Handbook*
AC	Advisory Circular
ACL	Aeronautical Chart Legend
AFH	*Airplane Flying Handbook*
AIM	Aeronautical Information Manual
AvW	Aviation Weather
AWBH	Aircraft Weight and Balance Handbook
AWS	Aviation Weather Services
CS	Chart Supplement
FAR	Federal Aviation Regulations
FI Comp	Flight Computer
IFH	*Instrument Flying Handbook*
NTSB	National Transportation Safety Board Regulations
PHAK	*Pilot's Handbook of Aeronautical Knowledge*

APPENDIX B
ABBREVIATIONS AND ACRONYMS USED BY PRIVATE PILOTS

14 CFR	Title 14 of the Code of Federal Regulations
A&P	certified mechanic
AATD	advanced aviation training device
AC	advisory circular or convective outlook bulletin
ACS	Airman Certification Standards
AD	airworthiness directive
ADC	air data computer
ADIZ	Air Defense Identification Zone
ADM	aeronautical decision making
AFM	Airplane Flight Manual
AGL	above ground level
AHRS	attitude and heading reference system
AI	attitude indicator
AIM	Aeronautical Information Manual
AIRMET	Airmen's Meteorological Information
ALT	altimeter
AME	aviation medical examiner
AOA	angle of attack
ASEL	airplane single-engine land
ASI	airspeed indicator
ASOS	automated surface observing system
ATC	air traffic control
ATD	aviation training device
ATIS	Automatic Terminal Information System
AWC	aviation weather center
AWOS	automated weather observing system
AWSS	automated weather sensor system
AWW	severe weather forecast alert
BATD	Basic Aviation Training Devices
BECMG	becoming
CAS	calibrated airspeed
CAT	clear air turbulence
CDI	course deviation indicator
CFI	certificated flight instructor
CFIT	controlled flight into terrain
CG	center of gravity
CRM	crew resource management
CTAF	Common Traffic Advisory Frequency
CWA	center weather advisory
DF	direction finding
DH	decision height
DME	distance measuring equipment
DOD	department of defense
DP	departure procedure
DUATS	Direct User Access Terminal System
EFD	electronic flight display
EFIS	electronic flight information system
ELSA	experimental light-sport aircraft
ELT	emergency locator transmitter
ETA	estimated time of arrival
ETE	estimated time en route
FA	area forecast
FAA	Federal Aviation Administration
FADEC	full authority digital engine control
FAR	Federal Aviation Regulations
FB	winds and temperatures aloft forecast
FBO	fixed-base operator
FFS	full flight simulator
FIP	forecast icing potential
FL	flight level
FMS	flight management system
fpm	feet per minute
FRZ	flight restricted zone
FSDO	Flight Standards District Office
FSS	flight service station
FSTD	flight simulation training device
FTD	flight training device
GA	general aviation
GAJSC	general aviation joint steering committee
GMT	Greenwich Mean Time
GPH	gallons per hour
GPS	global positioning system
GPWS	Ground Proximity Warning System
HI	heading indicator
HIWAS	hazardous inflight weather advisory service
HSI	horizontal situation indicator
IA	inspection authorization
IAP	instrument approach procedure
IAS	indicated airspeed
ICAO	International Civil Aviation Organization
IFR	instrument flight rules
ILS	instrument landing system
IMC	instrument meteorological conditions
KOEL	kinds of operation equipment list
L/D$_{MAX}$	best lift/drag
LAA	local airport advisory
LAHSO	land and hold short operations
LLWAS	low-level wind shear alert system
LOC	ILS localizer
LRU	line replaceable unit
MC	magnetic course
MDA	minimum descent altitude
MEF	maximum elevation figure
MEL	minimum equipment list
METAR	aviation routine weather report
MFD	multi-function display
MH	magnetic heading
MOA	military operations areas
MP	manifold pressure
MSA	minimum safe altitude
MSL	mean seal level
MTR	military training routes
MVFR	marginal VFR
NAS	National Airspace System
NAVAID	navigational aid
NEXRAD	next generation radar
NM	nautical miles
NOTAM	notice to airmen
NSA	national security areas
NTSB	National Transportation Safety Board
NWS	National Weather Service
OAT	outside air temperature
OBS	omnibearing selector
PAPI	precision approach path indicator
PFD	primary flight display
PIC	pilot in command
PIM	Pilot's Information Manual
PIREP	pilot weather report
POH	Pilot's Operating Handbook
PROG	short-range surface prognostic
PSK	personal survival kit
RAIM	receiver autonomous integrity monitoring
RNAV	area navigation
ROT	rate of turn
RVR	runway visual range
S.B.	service bulletin

SFRA	special flight rule areas
SIGMET	Significant Meteorological Information
SIGWX	significant weather
SM	statute miles
SODA	statement of demonstrated ability
SRM	single-pilot resource management
SSR	secondary surveillance radar
STC	supplemental type certificate
STOL	short takeoff and landing
SUA	special use airspace
T&SI	turn-and-slip indicator
TAC	terminal area chart
TACAN	tactical air navigation
TAF	terminal aerodrome forecast
TAS	true airspeed
TAWS	Terrain Awareness and Warning System
TC	turn coordinator or true course
TCAS	traffic alert and collision avoidance system
TDWR	terminal doppler weather radar
TFR	temporary flight restriction
TIS	traffic information system
TRSA	terminal radar service areas
TSA	Transportation Security Administration
TSOC	transportation security operations center
UTC	universal coordinated time
V_A	design maneuvering speed
VASI	visual approach slope indicator
$V_{Best Glide}$	best glide speed
VDP	visual descent point
V_{FE}	maximum flap extended speed
VFR	visual flight rules
VHF	very high frequency
VHF/DF	VHF direction finder
V_{LE}	maximum landing gear extended speed
V_{LO}	maximum landing gear operating speed
VMC	visual meteorological conditions
V_{ME}	maximum endurance speed
V_{NE}	never-exceed speed
V_{NO}	maximum structural cruising speed
VNR	VFR flight not recommended
VOR	VHF omnidirectional range
VOR/LOC	VOR/localizer
VORTAC	co-located VOR and TACAN
V_R	rotation speed
V_{S1}	stalling speed in a specified configuration
VSI	vertical speed indicator
V_{SO}	stalling speed in the landing configuration
VV	vertical visibility
V_X	best angle of climb speed
V_Y	best rate of climb speed
WA	AIRMET
WAAS	Wide Area Augmentation System
WCA	wind correction angle
WS	SIGMET
WSP	weather system processor
WST	convective SIGMET

INDEX